Cultural History

ROGER CHARTIER

CULTURAL HISTORY
Between Practices and Representations

Translated by
Lydia G. Cochrane

Cornell University Press
Ithaca, New York

First published 1988 by Cornell University Press.

Printed in Great Britain

Library of Congress Cataloging-in-Publication Data
Chartier, Roger, 1945–
  Cultural history.
  Translated from the French.
  Bibliography: p.
  Includes index.
  1. History—Methodology.   I. Cochrane, Lydia G.
II. Title.
D16.C438   1968   901'.8   88–3823
ISBN 0-8014-2223-X

CONTENTS

ACKNOWLEDGEMENTS

Chapter 1 has appeared as Roger Chartier, 'Intellectual History or Sociocultural History? The French Trajectories', in *Modern European Intellectual History: Reappraisals and New Perspectives*, edited by Dominick LaCapra and Steven L. Kaplan, pp. 13–46. Copyright © 1982 by Cornell University Press. Used by permission of the publisher. Published in French as 'Histoire intellectuelle et histoire des mentalités. Trajectoires et questions', *Revue de Synthèse* ser. 3, nos 111–12, 1983. Copyright © Editions Albin Michel, 1983.

Chapter 2 is translated from 'L'histoire ou le récit véridique' in *Philosophie et Histoire*, Centre Georges Pompidou, 1987. © Editions du Centre Pompidou, 1987.

Chapter 3 is translated from the preface to the new edition of *La société de cour*, Librairie Ernest Flammarion, 1985. Copyright © Librairie Ernest Flammarion, 1985.

Chapter 4 is reprinted from the *Journal of Modern History*, 57:4, 1985, University of Chicago Press, by kind permission. Copyright © University of Chicago, 1985.

Chapter 5 is translated from *L'Arc*, 65, 1976. Copyright © *L'Arc*, 1976.

Chapter 6 is translated from *Annales ESC*, 37:1, 1982, by kind permission. Copyright © Armand Colin, 1982.

Chapter 7 is translated from *Dix-Huitième Siècle*, 18, 1986, by kind permission of the Société Française d'Etude du Dix-Huitième Siècle. Copyright © Editions Garnier Frères, 1986.

Chapter 8 is reprinted from 'The Two Frances: the history of a geographical idea', in *Social Science Information*, vol. 17, 1978. Used by permission of Sage Publications Ltd, London. Copyright © 1978 by Sage Publications and ISSC. Published in French in *Cahiers d'Histoire*, 1978. Copyright © *Cahiers d'Histoire*, 1978.

INTRODUCTION

Two routes led to writing the eight essays published between 1976 and 1986 that make up this book. First, I encountered documents and accepted solicitations that led to a series of case-studies. This route was not hemmed in by traditional chronological divisions but straddled, for instance, the canonical boundary between the *ancien régime* and the nineteenth century and permitted a rare amount of vagabondage among seemingly unrelated topics: depictions of the world turned upside-down, the frustrations of *declassé* intellectuals in the seventeenth century, peasant reading habits in the Age of the Enlightenment and geographical divisions of the French territory between 1750 and 1840. On a second route paralleling these studies and centred on the analysis of a particular body of texts or pictorial materials, I set out to examine critically the ways of thinking about and practising cultural history in the historiographical tradition that has been mine and that it is convenient, though not totally accurate, to identify with the *Annales*. People I happened to meet and my writing obligations played a role in this enterprise as well and have led to unexpected confrontations, for example, with history's use of symbolic anthropology and with philosophical discourse on history. They have also led to closer readings (in this instance, of the work of Norbert Elias) that bolstered a certain number of hypotheses, formulated in chapter 1. It occurs to me, with hindsight, that even though these two routes have led to very different results – on the one hand, studies of specific topics; on the other, historiographical or epistemological discussions – they share operating principles and ideas which, while in no way new, were by and large foreign to French cultural history. It is with these underlying ideas that these introductory remarks are concerned.

First, let me state that this new approach developed gradually in response to a dissatisfaction with French cultural history of the 1960s and 1970s, both as the history of *mentalités* and as 'serial', quantitative history. The new approach can only be understood in its relation to the state of the discipline of history in France during those decades. Briefly, it is fair to say that at the time history was institutionally powerful and threatened intellectually.[1] It was assured a dominant position in the universities by the sheer weight of its numbers: in letters and the humanities in 1967 history was second only to French literature and well ahead of linguistics, psychology, or sociology. The experience and preparation of its professors assured it a solid 'educational capital': nine out of ten university teachers of history held their *agrégation*, and two out of ten were graduates of the Ecoles Normales Supérieures. Measured by standards of institutional legitimacy, then, history belonged among the leading disciplines, even though in this respect it was surpassed by French language and literature, classical studies and philosophy, and it differed in important ways from the newer disciplines, which were less available and taught by teachers (the younger ones in particular, *assistants* rather than *professeurs*) who lacked the more prestigious academic titles.

This dominant position, based on the primacy of the study of economic and demographic conjunctures and of social structures, was precisely what the more recently institutionalized social sciences attempted to shake during the 1960s. The social sciences could count on a strong growth rate (varying from 200 to 300 per cent between 1963 and 1967 for linguistics, sociology and psychology) and on the recruitment of new teachers, many of whom, although their diplomas were less impressive than in the canonical disciplines, had the advantage of an important 'social capital'. Their challenge to history came in a variety of forms, structuralist and other, all, however, focusing on history's objects of study (either by shifting attention from social hierarchies to social relations or from objective positions to intellectual representations) or on history's methodological axioms (judged to be questionably founded by the standards of the new theoretical demands). By applying to fields hitherto outside the interests of socio-economic history scientific standards and working models often imitated from the exact sciences (such as formalization and the use of models, the statement of explicit hypotheses and techniques of group research), the social sciences moved ahead to undermine the dominant position of history in both the academic realm and the intellectual scene in general. Furthermore, by importing into the domain of letters new principles of legitimacy that rejected history as an empirical discipline, they attempted to convert their institutional fragility into an intellectual hegemony.

Historians responded in two ways. First, they attempted to tap into the source of the social sciences' success by moving into areas that the latter had opened up. New objects of study appeared on history's *questionnaire* – attitudes towards life or death, beliefs and religious behaviour patterns, kinship systems and family relations, rituals, forms of social intercourse, the operation of the educational system and so forth – all of which were new territories for history, won by annexation from other disciplines. This also meant returning to one of the basic interests of the first *Annales* of the 1930s, the study of *outillages mentaux* (intellectual tools), which history's predominantly social orientation had relegated to a secondary level. A new field of study arose – *l'histoire des mentalités*, or *psychologie historique* – distinct from both the older intellectual and literary history and from the reigning economic and social history. Approaches borrowed from neighbouring disciplines could be tried in connection with these new or newly revived objects of study: the techniques of linguistic and semantic analysis, for example, or the statistical instruments of sociology or of certain models borrowed from anthropology.

This strategy of taking over fields of study, techniques, or standards of scientific objectivity could only succeed on the condition that historians did not abandon any of what had been responsible for the original success of the discipline, supported by the bold innovations of time-series analyses of massive data sources (for example, price-lists and parish registers, port of entry archives and notarial acts). In its more widespread forms, then, the *histoire des mentalités* was built by applying to new objects of study the principles of analysis prevalent in the disciplines of economic and social history. This explains its preference for the largest data sets, and hence for the investigation of 'popular' culture, its confidence in figures and in quantification, its taste for the *longue durée* and its endeavour to distribute cultural differences in strict accordance with the scale of social hierarchies. Defined in this way, the particular characteristics of cultural history – in which new fields of research branch out from the respected axioms of social history – are exactly analogous to the strategy of the discipline itself, which strove to acquire new scientific legitimacy through a reliance on the intellectual achievements that had bolstered its institutional predominance.

By assigning the characteristics of the history of *mentalités* to the scientific world where they were forged, I intend to emphasize that any study of the shifts or conflicts within a discipline necessarily supposes identification of its position in the academic realm and of the internalized legacies and shared postures that define it as a field. For too long historians have written the history of their own discipline using categories of thought that they would have challenged for the analysis of any other topic. For too long the history of history as a discipline has been haunted by the 'concepts engendered by disincarnated minds' that Lucien Febvre denounced as the old history of ideas at its worst. [2] In this book I hope to give evidence (discreetly, however, since the central subject of the book lies elsewhere) of a different way of conceiving of intellectual evolutions and intellectual debates. I hope to do so, first, in the two initial chapters, by sketching the specific, objectively determined characteristics, expressed in the habitus of the several disciplines, that governed the relation of French cultural history to other closely related but often neglected branches of knowledge: literary history, the epistemology of the sciences and philosophy. Secondly, I hope to do so in the last chapter by identifying the successive and often contradictory political and ideological stakes invested in the 'scientific' discourses that attempted to explain regional disparities in France between the mid-eighteenth and the mid-nineteenth centuries.

An approach of this sort, borrowed from the sociology of knowledge, also allows a closer understanding of the rifts that are described in this book: the break, for example, between sociology as practised by Norbert Elias and the historical traditions that were his target, or the cleavage between historiographical use of American symbolical anthropology, as proposed by Robert Darnton, and French socio-cultural history. These debates, formulated in terms of conceptual and methodological differences (which is what they really are), are embodied in struggles for predominance, both between and inside the disciplines and in the intellectual sphere in general, which are not the same in German universities of the 1930s and the intellectual world of the 1980s. Only the specific configurations in these debates and the particular strategies that they engender can fully account for the positions they arrived at and the routes they followed. To say this is not to reduce intellectual debates to mere sham power struggles (between schools, between disciplines, between national traditions). Nor is it to hold that analysis can permit the investigator to ignore the underlying rules of his or her own position. The problem lies elsewhere: in the need to consider the divergences that have arisen in our academic world or the evolution of academic disciplines by situating them in their intellectual space.

The principal aim of this book, composed through the years, study by study, is to note how, in different times and places, a specific social reality was constructed, how people conceived of it and how they interpreted it to others. A task of this sort falls into several parts. The first concerns the classifications, divisions and groupings that serve as the basis for our apprehension of the social world as fundamental categories of the perception and evaluation of reality. These categories vary with social classes or intellectual milieux and are produced by stable, widely shared dispositions within the group. It is these internalized intellectual schemata that produce the configurations through which the present can take on meaning, other human beings can become intelligible and space can be deciphered. An over-production of university graduates, rustic reading habits, or the two Frances are thus so many motifs to illustrate the will to understand and to impose order, hence to domesticate an incomprehensible history, a baffling 'otherness', or an illegible geography.

Even if they claim the universality of a judgement founded on reason, the representations of the social world that are constructed in this fashion are always a product of the interests of the group that forged them. This means that for each motif, what is said must be related to the social position of whoever says it. In the cases under consideration here, those who produced representations all belonged to the sphere of the professionals of culture, people endowed with knowledge and often with power. The task at hand is thus not to explore so-called popular culture yet again but to analyse how various elite groups – state administrative personnel, enlightened notables, specialists in the social sciences – have understood and presented a fragment of the reality in which they lived.

State perceptions of social phenomena are never neutral. They engender social, educational, or political strategies and practices that tend to impose one authority at the expense of others that are discredited, to lend legitimacy to a project for reform, or to justify an individual's choices and behaviour. A study of representations thus sees them as always captive within a context of rivalries and competition, the stakes of which are couched in terms of power and domination. Rival representations are just as important as economic struggles for understanding the mechanisms by means of which a group imposes (or attempts to impose) its conception of the social world, its values and its dominion. The historian examining classifications and groupings is not, as a short-sighted history has long thought, straying from the social realm. Quite the opposite: he or she is identifying trouble-spots that are all the more conclusive for being less immediately material.[3]

One might hope that this approach closes the false debates over the separation, given as irreparable, between the objectivity of structures (which are taken to be the proper terrain for the surest history, the history that uses massive amounts of quantifiable documentary data to reconstruct societies as they really were) and the subjectivity of representations (in this view the subject-matter of a sort of history devoted to the illusions of discourse and far removed from reality). A cleavage of this sort has profoundly divided not only history but other social sciences such as sociology or ethnology. Structuralist and phenomenological approaches have stood opposed, the first working on a grand scale on the positions and relations of different groups (often identified with social classes) and the second preferring the study of the values and behaviour patterns of communities of more restricted scope (often taken as homogeneous). Recent debate between the champions of *microstoria*, or case-studies, and those of serial socio-cultural history – the direct heir of social history – are a good illustration of this polarization over what constitutes the essence of the social sciences. An attempt to overcome this polarization demands first that we accept the schemata found in each group or milieu (and which generate classifications and perceptions) as true social institutions incorporating, in the form of mental categories and collective representations, the divisions set up in social organization itself: 'The first logical categories were social categories; the first classes of things were classes of men, into which these things were integrated.'[4] These representations thus form the matrix for a variety of distinct sorts of discourse and practices ('Even the highest collective representations have existence and are truly what they are only to the extent that they command acts')[5] which permit the construction of the social world and, by that token, the contradictory definition of one's own identity and that of others.

To go back to Marcel Mauss and Emile Durkheim may, paradoxically, promote reflection on what the conceptual tools of the *histoire des mentalités* lacked. The notion of 'collective representation', in Mauss's definition of the term, permits us to articulate clear mental images (what Lucien Febvre called *matériaux d'idées*) with the internalized schemata and categories that engendered them and gave them structure. It also obliges us to trace the fashioning of those schemata and those categories not to psychological processes, individual or shared, but to the very divisions of the social world. This implies that this notion supports a cultural history of the social realm that has as its goal the comprehension of configurations and motifs – of representations of the social sphere – that give unconscious expression to the positions and the interests of social agents as they interact, and that serve to describe society as those social agents thought it was or wished it to be.

Identifying those motifs opens a first debate: are we to take as symbols and hold to be 'symbolic' all signs, acts, or objects, all intellectual figures or collective representations by means of which groups give conceptual organization to the social or the natural worlds and thus construct the reality they perceive and communicate? Reference to Ernst Cassirer claimed by American symbolic anthropology (after Erwin Panofsky) might lead us to this conclusion, since Cassirer defines the symbolic function (which he calls 'the various representative – symbolic operations') as a mediating function that shapes the various modes of apprehension of reality, whether it operates by linguistic signs, the images of myth and religion, or the concepts of scientific knowledge.[6] The tradition of critical idealism thus designates as 'symbolic forms' all the categories and processes that construct 'the world as representation' as Schopenhaver writes .[7] The next step is to assign all 'productions' like representations or figurations to a universal function of the mind, the corollary to which is maximal extension of the concept of 'symbol' to subsume all forms and all signs by which consciousness constitutes 'reality'.

The essays grouped in this book use the concept of 'representation' in a more specific sense and with a more historically determined meaning. The term is pertinent to the topics treated here for two reasons. First, it is clear that not only was the notion known to *ancien régime* societies but it held a central place in them. Several remarks follow from this. The older definitions of the term (for example, in Furetière's dictionary) show a tension between two interrelated groups of meanings. On the one hand, 'representation' permits envisaging something that is absent, which supposes a radical distinction between what is doing the representing and what is being represented. On the other hand, 'representation' exhibits a presence; it is like a public presentation of something or someone. In the first sense, representation is the instrument of a mediated knowledge that makes an absent entity visible by substituting for it an 'image' capable of recalling it to mind and picturing it as it is. Certain 'images' of this sort are material and offer a likeness. One illustration of this is the wax, wooden, or leather effigies (which were in fact called *représentations*) that were placed over the royal coffin during the funeral ceremonies for French and English sovereigns to give a visual sign of a now-invisible entity, the immortal dignity perpetuated in the mortal person of the monarch.[8] Other representations, however, operate on the level of the symbolic relation that, for Furetière, consists in the 'representation of some moral thing by the images or the properties of natural things. . . .The lion is the symbol of valour; the ball that of inconstancy; the pelican that of paternal love.'[9] A comprehensible relationship (which of course does not necessarily mean a stable or univocal relationship) is thus postulated between the visible sign and the referent it signifies.

The relation of representation, understood as the establishment of a relation between a present image and an absent object in which the one is a valid equivalent of the other because it is in conformity with it, underlies the entire 'theory of the sign' that shaped classical French thought and was elaborated most fully by the logicians of Port-Royal. On the one hand, varying the applications of this relation permits the discrimination of the different categories of signs (certain or probable, natural or learned, inherent in or apart from what is represented and so forth) and allows us to identify the symbol (in the strict sense of the term) as distinct from other signs. [10] On the other hand, by identifying the two conditions necessary to render such a relation intelligible – knowledge of the sign as a sign and as distinct from the thing signified, and the existence of shared conventions regulating the relation of the sign to the thing[11] – the *Logique* of Port-Royal set out the terms of the fundamental historical question of variability and plurality in the comprehension (or incomprehension) of the representations of the social and natural world offered in texts and images.

It should be noted, finally, that it was precisely the fundamental distinction between representation and the represented, between the sign and the signified, that are distorted by the theatricality of social life in *ancien régime* society. All forms of dramatization aimed at assuring that being would be inferred from appearance, identity from representation and the thing would have no other existence save in the sign that exhibited it. Furetière gives as an example: '*Ce Seigneur a bien l'air et la représentation de ce qu'il est*' ['That lord has indeed the air and representation of what he is']. When Pascal speaks of imagination, he strips bare the mechanism of 'show' that lends credence to appearance as a valid substitute for reality:

> Our magistrates know this secret. Their red robes, the ermine in which they wrap themselves like furry cats, the courts where they sit, the *fleur-de-lis* – they needed all that solemn paraphernalia, and physicians without their cassocks and mules, and lawyers without their square caps and gowns four times too big, would never have taken in the world, which cannot resist so convincing a display. Did the former possess the justice, and physicians the true art of healing, they would not need their caps; the majesty of the sciences would be reverend enough by itself. But as their science is merely imaginary, they have to employ these childish gauds which strike the imagination they turn to account, and thereby in fact inspire respect. [12]

The relation of representation is thus muddled by imagination, 'man's ruling faculty, queen of lies and error',[13] which makes one take the decoy for true and visible signs for the proofs of a non-existent reality. Redirected in this manner, the representation is transformed into a mechanism for the fabrication of respect and submission; it is an instrument to produce internal constraint, useful where immediate recourse to violence is impossible. As Pascal says, 'Soldiers alone do not dress up like that, because the part they play is more substantial; they establish themselves by force, not by make-believe.'[14]

My reflections on court society, which find their immediate source in a reading of Norbert Elias's classic work, follow Pascal's definition of the problem in two ways. Pascal defines the 'objective' position of each individual in traditional French society as dependent on the credit accorded to that individual's own representation of himself by those to whom he turns for recognition. He understands the forms of symbolic domination by means of one's *appareil* or *attirail* (pomp, display), as La Bruyère was to put it,[15] as corollary to the absence or the weakening of brute force. It is within the long-term process of the eradication and monopolization of violence that we must set the increasing urgency of struggles between competing representations. What was at issue was imposing order, hence defining hierarchy, in the very structure of society. When it studies groups' representations of themselves or of others – hence when it moves away from too strict a dependence on the traditional view of social history – cultural history is able to reflect usefully on social questions, since it focuses its attention on the strategies that determine positions and relations and that assign to each class, group, or milieu a perceived being which constitutes its identity.

The notion of representation can thus be constructed on the basis of its traditional definitions. It is, in fact, one of the foremost concepts manipulated by writers of the *ancien régime* when they set out to comprehend the functioning of their society or to define the intellectual operations that enabled them to apprehend the physical or social world. This is a first and an excellent reason to make it the corner-stone of a cultural approach to history. There is another reason, however. Better than the concept of *mentalité*, the idea of representation permits the description of three modes of relations vis-à-vis the social world. These are, first, the operation of classification and delineation that produces the multiple intellectual configurations by which reality is constructed in contradictory ways by various groups. Next, the practices that aim at providing for the recognition of a social identity, at exhibiting a specific way of being in the world, at signifying a status or a rank symbolically. Finally, the institutionalized objective forms by means of which 'represen-

tants' (collectively or individually) mark in visible and perpetuated
fashion the existence of the group, the class, or the community.[16] As
a rule, the case-studies that compose this book make use only of the
first of these definitions and attempt to comprehend the invention
and the circulation of a particular intellectual motif by relating it to
the gaps and divisions that they create. In their fashion, the upside-
down world or a split France are indeed elementary forms of classification. But we must guard against losing sight of the other side of the
coin: the practices, great or small, generated by these divisions, that
constitute the visible indices of a proclaimed, desired, or demanded
identity.

I have chosen to consider homogeneous discourse series that have
enough coherence to permit the analysis of significant variations.
More often than not this has not required the use of statistics, but, as
the example of the depictions of the world turned upside-down
attests, it has not excluded them either, since figures are a useful tool
for tracing essential thematic shifts within a given body of materials.
Three questions underlie each study, questions that are necessary to
any historical treatment of a series of discourses: the place (or the
milieu) in which statements were made and the conditions that made
them possible; the schemata that lent them order and the principles
of regularity that governed them; and the specific forms dictating the
separation of the true from the false or, to put it differently, the
criteria that enabled a proposition to be accepted as true or condemned it to being rejected as false.

Michel Foucault stated that 'Discourse must be treated as a dis-
continuous activity,'[17] and I have attempted to heed his injunction
on both its levels, first by taking discourses as practices – that is, not
reading them only in order to ascertain the overall ideology that they
contain but taking into account their mechanisms, their rhetorical
apparatuses and their demonstrative strategies. Often my analysis
could have and should have been carried further, but its incomplete-
ness stands as evidence that the arrangements of discourse –
classification systems, criteria for distinctions, modes of representation, for example – can by no means be reduced to the theories
that produce them and that they are supposed to verify. They have
their own logic – as do administrative, judicial, medical, or
educational practices, with which they maintain a double relation of
veracity – on the one hand, by furnishing those other practices with
a justification and a reason for being, and on the other, of prescrip-
tion, by stating and programming what such practices should be.
Foucault's second lesson is to treat the procedures of discourse in
their discontinuity and their specificity. This points to the study of

circumscribed and unconnected bodies of material with no pretence to global history. For a long time it seemed possible to characterize a particular *mentalité* through the thematic analysis of a certain number of texts. This task appears less simple today, as it requires the patient, fragmented treatment of discordant series of data before one can consider their interrelations. Cultural history has lost its ambition to be all-embracing, to be sure, but it has perhaps gained an unprecedented attention to the texts, henceforth freed from the reduction to ideology that had destroyed them as discursive practices.

Consideration of the interrelated problems pertaining to the 'world as representation' (a world fashioned by means of the series of discourses that apprehend and structure experience) necessarily leads to reflections on the way in which any such figuration can be appropriated by the readers or viewers of the texts and pictures that interpret or depict reality. Hence the interest, in this work and in others more specifically devoted to reading practices,[18] in the process by which a meaning is produced historically and differences in sense arise. An approach of this sort obviously coincides with that of hermeneutics when it attempts to understand how a text can 'be applied' to the situation of the reader and, consequently, how a narrative configuration can carry a refiguration of experience. A theory of reading capable of comprehending the appropriation of discourse – that is, of grasping how discourses affect the reader and lead to a new form of comprehension of oneself and of the world – necessarily stands at the juncture between the world of the text and the world of the subject. Paul Ricoeur has attempted to elaborate such a theory of reading on the basis of a phenomenology of the act of reading, on the one hand, and an aesthetics of reception, on the other.[19] He aims both at grasping how the effectuation of the text as it is read serves as the condition for the realization of its semantic possibilities and the task of refiguring experience, on the one hand, and at understanding the reader's appropriation of the text as a mediation necessary to the constitution and the comprehension of self, on the other.[20] Any study that purports to investigate how the configurations inscribed in a series of texts have constructed representations (accepted or imposed) of the social sphere must necessarily subscribe to Ricoeur's aims and go on to pose the all-important question of what are the modalities of the reception of such representations.

It is in the answer to this question that the hermeneutic perspective proves inadequate. To grasp how, through history, people have appropriated the configurations in texts requires a break with the concept of the universal and abstract subject found in phenomenology and, despite appearances, in the aesthetics of reception. Both phenomenology and aesthetics construct the subject either on the basis of an invariable individual who transcends history and is considered to remain unchanged throughout time, or by the projection to the universal level of the singularity of an 'I' or a 'we' of our own time. This is quite obviously where phenomenology and aesthetics of reception part company with another way of thinking, following Norbert Elias, that posits the basic discontinuity of social and cultural formations, hence the discontinuity of philosophical categories, psychic economies and forms of experience. Modalities of action and suffering (as Paul Ricoeur writes) must always be seen in their relation to the ties of interdependence that govern relationships between individuals and which are shaped – differently in different situations – by power structures. Following this way of conceiving individuality in its historical variations involves not only a break with the concept of the subject as universal; it also places mutations in personality structure within a long-term process characterized by the transformation of both the state and interpersonal relations. By this means the intuition shared by Lucien Febvre and the *histoire des mentalités* concerning the disparity of intellectual equipment (*outillage mental*) in different times and places can be rooted in the long time-span of the history of European societies.

When this view is applied to the theory and the history of reading, we can see the inadequacy of the approaches that consider reading as a transparent relationship between the 'text' (given as an abstraction and reduced to its semantic content, as if it existed outside the written objects that present it for decoding) and the 'reader' (also an abstraction, as if the practices through which the reader appropriates the text were historically and socially invariable). Texts are not deposited in objects – manuscripts or printed books – that contain them like receptacles, and they are not inscribed in readers as in soft wax. To consider reading to be a concrete act requires holding any process of the construction of meaning (hence, of interpretation) as situated at the crossroads between readers endowed with specific competences, identified by their positions and their dispositions and characterized by their practice of reading, and texts whose meaning is always dependent on their particular discursive and formal mechanisms – in the case of printed texts we might call them 'typographical' (in a broad sense of the adjective). Awareness of this enables us to describe a working space, sketched out in the essays grouped in this volume and treated more in depth elsewhere, that identifies the production of meaning – the 'application' of the text to the reader – as a mobile and differentiated relation dependent on variations (simultaneous or separate) in the text itself, on the varying ways that the printed text is presented and on how it is read (silently or aloud, as sacralized or secularized, in community or singly, in public or in private, with difficulty or with ease and sensitivity, on the popular level or the highly literate level and so forth). [21]

At this point we can reformulate the notion of appropriation and place it at the centre of a cultural historical approach that focuses on differentiated practices and contrasted uses. This reformulation, which accentuates plural uses and diverse readings which are not aimed at or inscribed in the text, diverges from the meaning that Michel Foucault gave appropriation when he held 'the social appropriation of discourse' to be one of the primary procedures for gaining control of discourse, subjecting it, and putting it beyond the reach of those who through limited competence or inferior position were denied access to it. [22] It also parts company with the meaning that hermeneutics gives to appropriation, understood as the moment at which, on the basis of particular textual configurations, the task of the refiguration of phenomenological experience (postulated as universal) takes place. [23] In my own perspective, appropriation really concerns a social history of the various interpretations, brought back to their fundamental determinants (which are social, institutional and cultural), and lodged in the specific practices that produce them. To concentrate on the conditions and the processes that quite concretely bear the operations of the construction of meaning (in the reading relation but in many other relations as well) is to recognize, unlike traditional intellectual history, that minds are not disincarnated and, unlike universalist lines of thought, that the categories that seem the most unvarying must be constructed in the discontinuity of ongoing history.

Representation, practice, appropriation: this book is built on these three notions, although reflection on them did not precede the case-studies assembled in it. Case-studies and reflection have progressed together in a constant dialogue between direct confrontation with the documents and the demands of methodological elucidation. At the (provisory) end of this journey, the questions posed in the first chapter in this volume can perhaps now be, if not resolved, at least formulated with greater rigour. The definition of cultural history may be found to have shifted. On the one hand, it must be conceived as the analysis of the process of representation – that is, of the production of classifications and exclusions that constitute the social and conceptual configurations proper to one time or one place.

Structures of the social world are not an objective given, any more than intellectual and psychological categories. They are all produced historically by the interconnected practices – political, social and discursive – that construct their figures. It is such differentiations and the schemata that fashion them that are the objects of a cultural history that has come to rethink completely the relation traditionally postulated between the social realm (identified with a very real sort of reality, existent in itself) and the representations that are supposed to reflect it or distort it.

This history must also be understood as the study of the processes by which meaning is constructed. Breaking with the old idea that endowed texts and works with an intrinsic, absolute and unique meaning which it was the critic's task to identify, history is turning to practices that give meaning to the world in plural and even contradictory ways. This is the basis for characterizing discursive practices as productive of ordered disposition, distancing and delineation and for the recognition of practices of cultural appropriation as differentiated forms of interpretation. Both sorts of practices are determined socially, but their determination cannot be limited to the oversimplified sociography that the history of societies has long dictated to the history of cultures. Comprehending these deeply rooted origins demands taking into account the specific nature of the field of cultural practices, which is not immediately congruent with that of hierarchies and social divisions.

In its critical fidelity to the cultural history of the *Annales*, often called *histoire des mentalités*, this volume hopes to throw light on an intellectual journey that had two goals. My first objective has been to examine the internalized legacies and the unquestioned postulates of a highly respected historiographical tradition claimed by myself and many other historians. The other goal is to make use of several major sociological and philosophical works to propose opening up a working-space between texts and readings so as to grasp the complex, multiple and highly differentiated practices that construct the world as representation.

NOTES

1   Data on the morphological transformations in the various academic
    disciplines, on which this argument is based, are gathered in Pierre
    Bourdieu, Luc Boltanski and Pascale Maldidier, 'La Défense du
    corps', *Information sur les sciences sociales*, 10, 4 (1971), pp. 45–86. These

data also furnish the statistical base for Pierre Bourdieu, *Homo Academicus* (Editions de Minuit, Paris, 1984 [tr. Peter Collier, Polity, Cambridge, 1988]).

2 Lucien Febvre, 'Leur Histoire et la nôtre', *Annales d'histoire économique et sociale*, 8 (1938), reprinted in his *Combats pour l'histoire* (A. Colin, Paris, 1953), pp. 276–83.

3 My discussion of methodological choices is largely indebted to the work of Pierre Bourdieu, in particular, *La Distinction: Critique sociale du jugement* (Editions de Minuit, Paris, 1979) [*Distinction: A Social Critique of the Judgement of Taste*, tr. Richard Nice (Harvard University Press, Cambridge, MA., 1984)].

4 Emile Durkheim and Marcel Mauss, 'De quelques formes primitives de classification. Contribution à l'étude des représentations collectives', *Année sociologique*, 6 (1903), reprinted in Marcel Mauss, *Oeuvres* (3 vols, Editions de Minuit, Paris, 1969), vol. 2: *Représentations collectives et diversité des civilisations*, pp. 13–89; quotation p. 83 [*Primitive Classification*, tr. and ed. Rodney Needham (University of Chicago Press, Chicago, 1963), vol. 2, p. 82].

5 Marcel Mauss, 'Divisions et proportions de la sociologie', *Année sociologique*, n.s. 2 (1927), reprinted in his *Oeuvres*, vol. 3: *Cohésion sociale et divisions de la sociologie*, pp. 178–245; quotation p. 210.

6 Ernst Cassirer, *La Philosophie des formes symboliques* (3 vols, Editions de Minuit, Paris, 1972), in particular his 'Introduction et exposition du problème', in vol. 1: *Le Langage*, pp. 13–58 [*The Philosophy of Symbolic Forms*, tr. Ralph Manheim, pref. and intro. Charles W. Hendel (3 vols, Yale University Press, New Haven), 1953–7; 'Introduction and Presentation of the Problem', vol. 1, pp. 73–114].

7 Cassirer, *La Philosophie*, vol. 3: *La Phénoménologie de la connaissance*, p. 310 [*Philosophy of Symbolic Forms*, vol. 3, p. 276].

8 Ernst H. Kantorowicz, *The King's Two Bodies: A Study in Medieval Political Theology* (Princeton University Press, Princeton, NJ., 1957), pp. 419–37.

9 Antoine Furetière, *Dictionnaire universel* (The Hague and Rotterdam, 1690), articles 'Représentation' and 'Symbole'.

10 Antoine Arnauld and Pierre Nicole, *La Logique ou l'art de penser*, critical edn by Pierre Clair and François Girbal (Presses Universitaires de France, Paris, 1965), bk 1, ch. 4, pp. 52–4.

11 Ibid., bk 2, ch. 14, pp. 156–60.

12 Blaise Pascal, *Pensées*, 104, in his *Oeuvres complètes*, ed. Jacques Chevalier (Bibliothèque de la Pléiade, Paris, 1954), p. 1118 [quoted from *Pascal's Pensées*, tr. H. F. Stewart (Routledge and Kegan Paul, London, 1950), p. 43].

13 Ibid., p. 1116 (Stewart tr., p. 39).

14 Ibid., p. 1118 (Stewart tr., p. 43).

15 La Bruyère, *Les Caractères* (Garnier/Flammarion, Paris, 1965), 'Du Mérite personnel', 27, pp. 107–8.

16 See the treatment of the notion of representation in Luc Boltanski, *Les*

Cadres: La formation d'un groupe social (Editions de Minuit, Paris, 1982), pp. 57–8.

17 Michel Foucault, *L'Ordre du discours* (Gallimard, Paris, 1971), p. 54 [quoted from 'The Discourse on Language', tr. Rupert Swyer, in *The Archaeology of Knowledge*, tr. A. M. Sheridan Smith (Pantheon Books, New York, 1972), p. 229].

18 Roger Chartier, *The Cultural Uses of Print in Early Modern France*, tr. Lydia G. Cochrane (Princeton University Press, Princeton, NJ., 1987).

19 Paul Ricoeur, *Temps et récit* (Editions du Seuil, Paris, 1985), vol. 3: *Le Temps raconté*, pp. 243–59.

20 Paul Ricoeur, 'La Fonction herméneutique de la distanciation', in his *Du Texte à l'action. Essais d'herméneutique* (Editions du Seuil, Paris, 1986), vol. 2, pp. 101–17.

21 Roger Chartier, ed., *Les Usages de l'imprimé (XVe–XIXe siècle)* (Fayard, Paris, 1986). [For English tr. see *The Culture of Print*, tr. Lydia G. Cochrane, Polity, Cambridge, forthcoming.]

22 Foucault, *L'Ordre du discours*, pp. 45–7 (Swyer tr., p. 227).

23 Ricoeur, *Temps et récit*, vol. 3, p. 229.

Part I

DEBATE AND INTERPRETATIONS

1

INTELLECTUAL HISTORY AND THE HISTORY OF *MENTALITÉS*

A Dual Re-evaluation

Formulating problems of intellectual history is surely one of the most difficult things in the world to do. The first reason for this lies in its vocabulary. In no other branch of history is the terminology in use so specific to each nation or so difficult to acclimatize elsewhere, indeed, simply to translate into another language or transfer to a different intellectual context.[1] American historiography includes two sorts, the relation between which is ill-defined and has always been problematic: intellectual history, which appeared with the 'new history' at the beginning of the century and was constituted as a particular field of research with Perry Miller, and the history of ideas, developed by A. O. Lovejoy to define a discipline that already had its own object, programme and research procedures and its own institutional locus, the *Journal of the History of Ideas*, which Lovejoy founded in 1940. In the various European countries, neither of these designations had much success. In Germany *Geistesgeschichte* remained dominant; in Italy the term *storia intellettuale* does not appear, even in the work of Delio Cantimori. In France, *histoire des idées* hardly existed, either as a notion or as a discipline (in fact, it was historians of literature such as Jean Ehrard who laid claim to the term, albeit cautiously and with reservations). The term *histoire intellectuelle* seems to have arrived too late to take the place of the traditional terms (*histoire de la philosophie, histoire littéraire, histoire de l'art* and the like), and it has been powerless to resist a new vocabulary forged essentially by the *Annales* historians that includes *histoire des mentalités, psychologie historique, histoire sociale des idées* and *histoire socio-culturelle*. These barriers operated both ways, however, and the term *histoire des mentalités* has proved difficult to export, seems awkward in languages other than French and remains a source of considerable confusion. We are forced to leave the expression untranslated, recognizing the inevitable specificity of each nation's way of considering historical questions.

Thus, unlike the lexical certainties of the other kinds of history (economic, social, political), the vocabulary that describes intellectual history is doubly uncertain. Each national historiography has its own conceptualization, and in each one poorly differentiated ideas compete.

But do similar realities lie behind these different words? Is the object that they designate so diversely unique and homogeneous? Nothing seems more unsure. Consider, for example, two attempts at taxonomy. For Jean Ehrard, the 'history of ideas' includes three kinds of history: 'individualistic history of the great world systems, history of the collective and widespread reality that is opinion, and structural history of forms of thought and sensibility.'[2] For Robert Darnton intellectual history includes

> the history of ideas (the study of systematic thought, usually in philosophical treatises), intellectual history proper (the study of informal thought, climates of opinion and literary movements), the social history of ideas (the study of ideologies and idea diffusion), and cultural history (the study of culture in the anthropological sense, including world views and collective *mentalités*).[3]

These definitions actually use their different vocabularies to say the same thing: that the branch of history known as intellectual history in fact covers all forms of thought, and that its object is no more precisely defined, a priori, than that of social or economic history.

More important than classifications and definitions are the way or ways in which historians, at any given moment, divide this immense and vague territory and treat the units of observation thus constituted. Caught between both intellectual and institutional oppositions, each of these diverse ways of dividing reality determines its own object of study, its conceptual tools and its methodology. Nonetheless, explicitly or not, each one embodies a representation of the totality of the field of history and delimits both the place it claims to occupy and the places it leaves or denies to others. The uncertainty and compartmentalization of the vocabulary of designation quite certainly relate to intra- or interdisciplinary struggles, the forms of which are peculiar to each intellectual field and the stakes in which are hegemony – above all, lexical hegemony.

I intend to examine here some of the oppositions that have reshaped and reapportioned French intellectual history. I am fully conscious of two limitations. First, owing to insufficient research on these topics, it is impossible to reconstruct fully the institutional or political stakes involved in methodological confrontations; and second, my own personal experience leads me to stress certain debates, in particular the ones that centred on the *Annales* from 1930 to the present, thus perhaps distorting the general picture.

THE FIRST *ANNALES* GENERATION AND INTELLECTUAL HISTORY

In the twentieth century, the rising trajectory of intellectual history in France, both in the sense of thematic and methodological changes and in its shifting positions within the discipline of history, was controlled externally by the changing discourse of historians who were working to formulate a new way of writing history between the First World War and the Second. This is where we must begin – to try to understand how the historians of the *Annales*, Lucien Febvre and Marc Bloch in particular, thought intellectual history ought to be constituted. This is important not for some kind of retrospective celebration of these 'founding fathers' but because their approach to the history of ideas has gradually become dominant among historians, to the exact degree that the group designated – perhaps inaccurately – as the *Annales* school came to dominate the scene, first intellectually in the 1930s and after 1945 institutionally. [4]

Febvre conceived of intellectual history primarily as a reaction to the history written in one's own time. From this point of view, there is a high degree of consistency between the first reviews he published before 1914 in Henri Berr's *Revue de synthèse historique* and those he contributed to the *Annales* during and after the Second World War. This is clear, for example, in two long review articles Febvre published in Berr's journal, the first concerning Louis Delaruelle's book on Budé (1907) and the second Edouard Droz's study of Proudhon (1909). Two questions formulated in these reviews provided the groundwork for Febvre's great works on Luther (1929) and Rabelais (1942). The first was whether it is possible to fit the thoughts of a man or a milieu – which are occasionally contradictory and often composite, and at any event ever-changing – into the traditional categories used by the history of ideas (Renaissance, humanism, Reformation and the like). Such retrospective and classifying terms lead to contradictions and betray the signs of an outdated psychological and intellectual life experience.

> Thus, for example, by giving the name 'reformation' to those efforts of religious renewal and Christian renaissance undertaken by Lefèvre and his disciples at the beginning of the sixteenth century, are we not, by interpreting it, falsifying the psychological reality of that epoch? [5]

The task of the 'historians of the intellectual movement' (as Febvre wrote) was above all to rediscover the originality – which eludes a priori definition – of each system of thought in all its complexity and its vicissitudes by ridding history of labels which, while claiming to identify former ways of thinking, in fact disguise them.

The second preoccupation formulated by Febvre even before 1914 concerned an effort to examine the relation between ideas (or ideologies) and social reality using categories other than influence or determinism. As he states in 1909 regarding Proudhonism:

> There are no 'creative' theories, properly speaking, because as soon as an idea, fragmentary though it may be, has been realized, however imperfectly, in the domain of facts, it is no longer the idea that counts and acts, it is the institution situated in its [own] place and time, incorporating within itself a complicated and mobile network of social facts, producing and undergoing a thousand diverse actions and a thousand reactions.[6]

Even if the procedures for the 'incarnation' of ideas are more complex than Febvre would have us believe in this passage, it is nonetheless true that he clearly affirms his intention to break with an entire tradition of intellectual history (the inverted image of a simplified Marxism), which deduced all the processes of social transformation from a restricted number of voluntarist thoughts. For him, social phenomena could never be dissolved into the ideologies that aimed at shaping them. Febvre thus established two sorts of divergence in these youthful texts. He noted the gap, first between older ways of thinking and the notions, for the most part meagre, by which historians claimed to catalogue them, and second, between those old ways of thinking and the social terrain in which they were set. In doing so, Febvre opened the way to a historical analysis that took as its model the descriptions of *faits de mentalité* as then construed by sociologists of the Durkheim school or ethnologists following the lead of Lucien Lévy-Bruhl.

Forty years later, Febvre's tone was more critical and biting as he protested a history of ideas that he perceived as petrified into abstractions. He chastised the historians of philosophy in 1938 thus:

> Of all the workers who cling to the generic title of historian, with or without a qualifying adjective, there are none who fail to justify some part of it in our eyes save, all too often, those who, applying themselves to rethinking for their own purposes systems that are sometimes several centuries old, with not the slightest effort to show their connections with other manifestations of the epoch which saw their rise, end up doing precisely the opposite of what historical

method demands. Then, faced with these concepts engendered by disincarnated minds – which take on a life of their own outside time and space – they forge strange chains the links of which are both unreal and closed.[7]

Febvre's criticism of the intellectual history of the time was thus twofold. Because it isolated ideas or thought-systems from the conditions that authorized their production, but also because it separated them radically from the various forms of social life, this disincarnated history instituted a universe of abstractions in which thought seemed limitless since it depended on nothing. Reviewing (admiringly) Etienne Gilson's *La Philosophie au Moyen Age*, Febvre returned in 1946 to this central idea:

> We must not underestimate the role of ideas in history. Even less should we subordinate them to the action of interests. We need to show that a Gothic cathedral, the market hall of Ypres, and a great cathedral of ideas of the sort that Etienne Gilson describes for us in his book are daughters of a single epoch, sisters reared in the same household.[8]

Without making it explicit or mapping it out theoretically, Febvre here suggests a reading that postulates the existence, in a given epoch, of 'structures of thought' (the term is not his) determined by the socio-economic evolutions that organize intellectual constructions and artistic productions, collective practices and philosophical thoughts.

Architecture and scholasticism: Febvre's words prompt a comparison between his remarks and Erwin Panofsky's contemporary *Gothic Architecture and Scholasticism* (a series of lectures given in 1948 and published in 1951).[9] Both men, in parallel fashion and quite probably without reciprocal influence, were attempting in the same period to equip themselves with the intellectual means to conceptualize this 'spirit of the times', this *Zeitgeist* which, among other things, underlay Burckhardt's entire approach but which, for both Panofsky and Febvre, was what must be explained rather than what explains. In so doing, each in his own way marked his distance from principles that up to that point lay implicitly behind all works of intellectual history. These were:

1 the postulate of a conscious and transparent relation between the intentions of those who produced intellectual works and their products;
2 the ascription of intellectual or aesthetic creation uniquely to individual inventiveness or freedom – an idea that led to the notion of the precursor, cherished by a certain kind of history of ideas;

3 the explanation of agreements noted among the different intellectual (or artistic) productions of a time by borrowings or influences
(other key words in intellectual history), or by reference to a
composite 'spirit of the times' made up of philosophical, psychological and aesthetic characteristics.

A different conceptualization of these various relations (between
the work and its creator, between the work and its time, between
different works of a given period) required the forging of new
concepts. In Panofsky, these were the concepts of mental habits
(habitus) and of a habit-forming force; in Febvre, that of mental
equipment (*outillage mental*). Both used these new notions to take a
position that diverged from the standard procedures of intellectual
history. As a result, the very object of historical inquiry shifted.

In his study of Rabelais, published in 1942, Febvre does not
define mental equipment, but he does describe it:

> Every civilization has its own mental tools. Even more, every era of
> the same civilization, every advance in technology of science that
> gives it its character, has a revised set of tools, a little more refined for
> certain purposes, a little less so for others. A civilization or an era has
> no assurance that it will be able to transmit these mental tools in their
> entirety to succeeding civilizations and eras. The tools may undergo
> significant deterioration, regression, and distortion; or, on the
> contrary, more improvement, enrichment, and complexity. They are
> valuable for the civilization that succeeds in forging them, and they
> are valuable for the era that uses them; they are not valuable for all
> eternity, or for all humanity, nor even for the whole narrow course of
> development within one civilization.[10]

This has three implications: first, following Lucien Lévy-Bruhl (*La
Mentalité primitive*, 1922), categories of thought are not universal and
therefore cannot be reduced to the categories used by the twentieth
century; and second, ways of thinking depend above all on material
instruments (the techniques) or conceptual instruments (the sciences)
that make them possible. Finally and in disagreement with a naïve
evolutionism, there is no continual and necessary progress (defined
as passage from the simple to the complex) in the succession of the
various sets of mental tools.

Two other texts are helpful to an understanding of what Febvre
means by the very notion of mental tools or mental equipment: the
first volume of the *Encyclopédie française*, published in 1937 under the
title, *L'Outillage mental. Pensée, langage, mathématique*, and part 2,
book 2 of his *The Religion of Rebelais*. What defines mental equipment
in these pages is the state of language in its lexicon and its syntax,

the tools and the scientific languages available and also the 'sensitive support of thought' represented by the system of perceptions, the variable economy of which determines the structure of affectivity: 'Rabelais's contemporaries, so seemingly close to us, are quite far removed from us in every aspect of their intellectual equipment. Its very structure was not the same as ours.'[11] In any given epoch, the criss-crossing of these various lines of support (linguistic, conceptual, affective) determines certain 'modes of thought' that shape specific intellectual configurations (for example, the limits between the possible and the impossible or the boundaries between the natural and the supernatural).

The first task of the historian, as of the ethnologist, is thus to reconstruct these earlier representations in their irreducible specificity, without either shrouding them within anachronistic categories or measuring them against the standards of the twentieth century's mental equipment, given implicitly as the necessary result of continual progress. Once again, Febvre joins Lévy-Bruhl in warning against an erroneous reading of the old ways of thinking. For proof we need only note the similarity between the opening pages of Lévy-Bruhl's *The Primitive Mentality* and Febvre's *Amour sacré, amour profane. Autour de l'Heptaméron* (1944). Lévy-Bruhl tells us:

> Instead of imagining the primitives whom we are studying to be like ourselves and making them think as we should do in their places – a proceeding which can only lead to hypotheses, at most merely probable, and nearly always false – let us on the contrary endeavour to guard against our own mental habits, and try to discover, by analysing their collective representations and the connections between these, what the primitives' way of thinking would be.[12]

And Febvre says:

> In all innocence to attribute to these forebears factual knowledge – hence idea materials – which we all possess, but which the wisest among them would have found it impossible to procure; to imitate all those good missionaries who used to return from 'the islands' all agog because the savages they had encountered believed in God (another tiny step and they would be true Christians); to endow, with boundless generosity, the contemporaries of Pope Leo with conceptions of the universe and of life that our knowledge has forged for us, none of the elements of which (or hardly any) ever inhabited the mind of a man of the Renaissance – one can unfortunately count the historians, the prestigious ones, I mean, who recoil before such a distortion of the past, such a mutilation of humanity in its evolution. And all this, most likely, for lack of having asked the question we asked earlier, the question of intelligibility. Indeed, a man of the sixteenth century

must be intelligible not in relation to us, but in relation to his contemporaries.[13]

In spite of certain similarities between them, Febvre's notion of mental equipment differs in a number of ways from the concepts that Panofsky developed at about the same time. First of all, the very word equipment (*outillage*) and the expression *outils mentaux* that Febvre sometimes used – which suggest the almost objectivized existence of a panoply of intellectual instruments (words, symbols, concepts and so on) available to thought – contrast with Panofsky's definition of mental habit as the set of unconscious schemata and internalized principles that give unity to an epoch's way of thinking, no matter what the object of thought might be. In the twelfth and thirteenth centuries, for example, these are the principles of clarification and reconciliation of opposites, which constitute a scholastic *modus operandi*, the application of which is not limited to theological construction. This first discrepancy leads to a second. Febvre sees the intellectual equipment that people of a certain time are able to manipulate as a stock of 'idea materials' (*matériaux d'idées*). This means that what principally distinguishes the mentalities of social groups is the degree to which they make use of the available 'tools': the most learned will put into play the quasi-totality of existing words or concepts, while the least able will use only a minute part of the mental equipment of their time, thus limiting, when they are compared with their contemporaries, what it is possible for them to think. Panofsky's stress is different (and paradoxically more social). In fact, for him mental habits point back to their conditions of inculcation, thus to the 'habit-forming forces' – for example, to the institution of the school in its various forms. This makes it possible for him to grasp, in their unified production, the homologies of structure existing among different intellectual 'products' of a given milieu. It also enables him to conceptualize the variations among groups as differences in systems of perception and appreciation, themselves issuing from differences in modes of formation. Marc Bloch approaches just such a conception in the chapter from *Feudal Society* entitled 'Modes of Feeling and Thought', where he describes a hierarchy of levels of language and cultural universes in terms of the conditions of intellectual formation.[14] Both Bloch and Febvre, however, lack the analysis (central in Panofsky) of the mechanism by which fundamental categories of thought within a given group of social agents become internalized and of unconscious schemata that structure all particular thoughts and actions.

Despite this theoretical limitation, it is quite clear that the position of the historians of the first *Annales* generation greatly influenced the evolution of French intellectual history. In fact, it changed its basic questions. What was important to understand was no longer audacities of thought but the limits of the thinkable. To an intellectual history based on unbridled minds and unsupported ideas, they opposed a history of collective representations, of mental equipment and intellectual categories available and shared at a given epoch. In Lucien Febvre's work, it is just such a project that establishes the primacy he accords to biographical study. Luther in 1928, Rabelais and Des Périers in 1942, Marguerite de Navarre in 1944 were so many case-studies for discerning how the perception and representation of the world were organized for the people of the sixteenth century, how the limits of the 'thinkable' were defined, how relations between religion, science and morality specific to the epoch were constructed. Thus individuals were returned to their times, since whoever or whatever they may be, they cannot exempt themselves from the determining forces that control their contemporaries' ways of thinking and acting. Intellectual biography as practised by Febvre is then in fact a history of society since it locates its heroes simultaneously as witnesses and as products of the collective conditioning that limits free and individual invention. The path was thus opened (once Febvre's personal bent for biography was put aside) for a history of the systems of beliefs, values and representations of an epoch or a group, designated in French historiography by an expression all the more encompassing for the fuzziness of its conceptual content: *l'histoire des mentalités*. It is this notion that we must now examine.

HISTOIRE DES MENTALITÉS AND HISTORY OF IDEAS

As of the 1960s, the notion of *mentalité* became current in French historiography to characterize a history that takes as its object neither ideas nor the socio-economic foundations of societies. More practised than theorized about, this history of *mentalités à la française* is informed by a number of conceptions shared (to a greater or lesser extent) by its adepts. [15] Jacques Le Goff has offered two definitions of the term: 'The mentality of any one historical individual, however important, is precisely what that individual shares with other men of his time.' And: 'The history of mentalities operates at the level of the everyday automatisms of behaviour. Its object is that which escapes historical individuals because it reveals the impersonal content of their thought.' Thus this constitutes as a fundamental object of historical study something that is the exact opposite of the object in the tradition of intellectual history. The always collective mentality that regulates the representations and judgements of social agents without their knowledge is opposed, term for term, to the conscious construction of an individualized mind. The relationship between consciousness and thought is therefore posed in a new way, close to the approach of sociologists in the Durkheim tradition, placing the accent on the schemata or contents of thought which, although they are expressed in the style of the individual, are in fact the internalized conditionings that escape conscious knowledge and cause a group or a society to share a system of representations and a system of values without the need to make them explicit.

Another point that such historians hold in common is a very broad definition of what is covered by the notion of *mentalité*. As Robert Mandrou wrote, it is 'what is conceived and felt, the field of intelligence and affect'. Thus attention is directed toward psychological categories at least as much as and probably more than toward intellectual categories, which leads to yet another distinction between a history of *mentalités* identified with historical psychology and intellectual history in its traditional definition. The merging of the *histoire des mentalités* and psychology is very evident in Febvre, who was an attentive reader of Charles Blondel (*Introduction à la psychologie collective*, 1929) and of Henri Wallon (*Principes de psychologie appliquée*, 1930).[16] It is also evident in Febvre's successors, in Mandrou, for example, whose *Introduction à la France moderne* (1961) was subtitled *Essai de psychologie historique*. This merging with psychology is fundamental to the thought of Ignace Meyerson, whose work has been of paramount importance for the transformation of Greek studies.[17] Well beyond the project of reconstituting the sentiments and sensibilities of the people of a past time (which is essentially Febvre's project), Meyerson is concerned with the essential psychological categories working to construct notions of time and space and observed in the production of the imaginary and collective perceptions of human activities as they vary from one historical period to another. An example of this approach can be seen in the notion of person as treated by Jean-Pierre Vernant, following Meyerson:

> There is not, and there cannot be, a perfect model of the individual, abstracted from the course of the history of mankind with all its vicissitudes and all its variations and transformations according to place and time. The purpose of the inquiry, then, is not to establish whether or not the individual personality existed in ancient Greece, but to seek to discover what the ancient Greek personality was, and

how its various characteristics differed from personality as we know it today. [18]

Starting from a similar intellectual position, Alphonse Dupront, at the International Conference of Historical Sciences at Stockholm in 1960, proposed the constitution of the history of collective psychology as a specific discipline in the field of the human sciences, giving it the broadest scope, since it was to include 'the history of values, mentalities, forms, symbolic systems, and myths'. [19] In reality, by defining collective psychology in this manner, he was suggesting a total reformulation of the history of ideas. One of the major objects of study in the history of collective psychology is the idea-forces (*idées-forces*) and the concepts that make up what Dupront calls the *mental collectif* of the people of an epoch. When ideas are grasped through the circulation of the words that designate them, situated in their social settings and considered as much in terms of their affective or emotional charge as of their intellectual content, they become, like myths or value complexes, one of the 'collective forces by which men live their times', hence once of the components of the 'collective psyche' of a civilization. This is one sort of fulfilment of the *Annales* tradition, both in its fundamentally psychological portrayal of collective mentality and its redefinition of what the history of ideas must be when it is reinserted into an inquiry into the whole of the *mental collectif*.

It is clear, moreover, that since the *histoire des mentalités* (considered as a part of socio-cultural history) takes as its object the collective, the automatic and the repetitive, it can and must employ quantitative methods: 'The history of collective psychology needs series that are, if not exhaustive, at least as broad as possible.' [20] We see then what this approach owes to the history of economies and societies, which, spurred on first by the great crisis of the 1930s, then by the post-Second World War crisis, became the 'heavy' sector of historical research in France, thanks both to the number of collective investigations and to the striking success of some among them. When in the 1960s cultural history emerged as the most popular and the most innovative domain in history, it did so by taking up and transposing the problematics and the methodologies that had assured the success of socio-economic history. The project was simple, as stated a posteriori by Pierre Chaunu:

The problem consists in attaining the third level [that of the affective and the mental] with the help of the statistical technique of regressions – that is, with the help of the mathematical analysis of time series – and of a dual interrogation of the document, first in itself, then in relation to its position in the homogeneous series in which the basic information is integrated. It amounts to as complete an adaptation as possible of the methods that were perfected first by economic historians and then by social historians.[21]

This pre-eminence accorded to the series, and therefore to the collection and to the treatment of homogeneous and repetitious data that lend themselves to comparison at regular intervals, has several implications. The most important is a preference for massive sets of documents that represent broad segments of society and allow the construction of a series of data over the long time-span. This opens the way to the reinterpretation and the renewed exploitation of sources traditionally used in social history (for example, notarial archives). It also results in the rediscovery of overlooked sources that permit the reconstitution of ways of thinking or feeling. Beyond methodological similarities, Chaunu's 'serial history of the third level' shares two sets of problems with economic and social history. The first is that of time-spans: how to co-ordinate and reconcile the long run of mentalities, which tend to be more or less immobile and inflexible, with the brusque changes and collective transfers of belief and sensibility of the short run. This issue (raised, for example, concerning the de-Christianization of France) parallels the central question of Fernand Braudel's *Mediterranean*: how to conceptualize the formation of hierarchies within the articulation and overlapping of the various time-spans – the short span, the conjuncture, the very long span (*longue durée*) – of historical phenomena.[22]

The second set of problems that cultural history has inherited is the manner of conceiving the relations between social groups and cultural levels. In fidelity to the work of Ernest Labrousse and the French 'school' of social history, the categorizations elaborated to classify variations in the *mentalités* have been based on hierarchies of wealth, sources of revenue and professions. Pre-established social and professional criteria have thus been used to reconstitute different systems of thought and cultural behaviour. This means that intellectual or cultural divisions have been made to follow social boundaries, whether such boundaries separated the common people from the notables or the dominated from the dominating or fragmented the social scale. This almost tyrannical pre-eminence of the social dimension, which predefines the cultural cleavages that are to be described, is the clearest trace of cultural history's dependence on social history in post-war French historiography. (I should note, however, that Febvre and Bloch are free of this dependence because they were more sensitive to either the commonly shared categories in a given time period or to differential use of available intellectual equipment.)

It is upon these methodological bases, stated or unstated, that the *histoire des mentalités* has developed in French historiography during the past fifteen years. Indeed, it has responded much more tellingly than intellectual history to French historians' new levels of awareness. The first of these levels is the recognition of a new equilibrium between history and the social sciences. When its intellectual and institutional primacy was contested, French historiography reacted by annexing the terrains and the modes of questioning of the closely related disciplines (anthropology and sociology) that had challenged its dominion. This shifted attention toward new objects of study – collective thoughts and actions related to life and death, beliefs and rituals, educative models and so on – which until then had been the province of ethnological investigation, and toward new questions, largely untouched by a social history that had been principally concerned with ranking the component groups in a given society. Second, historians recognized that social differences cannot be conceptualized solely in terms of wealth or dignity, but are either produced by or expressed in cultural differences. The unequal division of cultural competencies (for example, reading and writing), cultural goods (such as books) and cultural practices (attitudes toward life or death) thus provided a focus for a number of investigations using quantitative procedures and aiming at giving a new content to the formulation of social hierarchies, without questioning that formulation itself, however. Historians finally realized that traditional methodologies were inadequate for taking on these new domains. Consequently, as we have seen, historians have had recourse to an analysis of serial data in which testamentary formulas, iconographic motifs and what appeared in print replaced the price of wheat, or they have worked on language or languages, their interests ranging from lexical measurement to historical semantics, from a description of semantic fields to the analysis of 'utterances.'[23] Because it transposed the approaches and the problems that had pertained to socio-economic history and, simultaneously, shifted history's set of questions, the *histoire des mentalités* (as part or all of socio-cultural history) was able to occupy the front of the intellectual stage. Similarly (as Dupront implied), it managed to seem to reformulate – hence to disqualify – the older ways of pursuing the history of ideas.

A similar reformulation was under way within the field of intellectual history, however, where it resulted in positions completely contradictory to those of historians of mentalities. The major work here – which was, incidentally, well received by the *Annales* – is Lucien Goldmann's *The Hidden God*.[24] Goldmann's initial position is also distinct from the traditional biographical and positivistic orientations of the history of ideas. As with Febvre, and as with the *histoire des mentalités*, he is primarily interested in investigating the articulation of thoughts with the social domain. The concept of 'world vision' borrowed from Lukács makes such an approach possible. Defined as 'the whole complex of ideas, aspirations and feelings which links together the members of a social group (a group which, in most cases, assumes the existence of a social class) and which opposed them to members of other social groups',[25] this concept enabled Goldmann to do three things: to assign a social significance and social position to literary and philosophical texts; to understand the kinships among works of opposing forms and natures; to discriminate within an individual author's work the 'essential' texts (Goldmann's adjective) that make up a coherent whole and to which each particular work must be related. For Goldmann the concept of world vision takes on, simultaneously, the functions of mental equipment for Febvre and of the 'habitus' for Panofsky. *The Hidden God* offered a debatable but exemplary application of these propositions by construing Pascal's *Pensées* and nine of Racine's tragedies, from *Andromaque* to *Athalie*, as the corpus expressing most coherently 'a tragic vision of the world' identified with Jansenism and by connecting this collective conscience to a particular group, that of the legal and administrative office-holders, 'nobles of the robe' who were dispossessed of their political power, hence of their social leverage, by the construction of the absolutist state.

Whatever may be the historical validity of such an analysis, it introduced one crucial idea that is the complete opposite of one of the postulates of the *histoire des mentalités*. For Goldmann, it is the 'great' writers and philosophers who, through their essential works, express most coherently the conscience of the social group of which they are a part. It is they who achieve 'the maximum possible awareness of the social group whose nature they are expressing'. Hence the primacy Goldmann accorded to the major texts (newly defined by their equivalence to a world vision); hence its corollary: suspicion, if not outright rejection, of quantitative approaches in the field of cultural history. Well before the present-day mistrust of such approaches, which are based on an anthropological conception of culture, the tradition of intellectual history founded by Goldmann first alerted historians to the illusions of quantification. 'A sociological history of literature owes it to itself to privilege the study of the great texts,' Jean Ehrard wrote,[26] which was a way of saying, on the one hand, that it is in the singularity of these texts that shared ideas are revealed most clearly and completely and, on the other hand, that the counting of words, titles and collective representations is literally 'insignificant' and incapable of reconstituting the complex, conflicting and contradictory meanings of collective thought. Numerical collection of the superficial, the banal and the routine is not representative, and the collective consciousness of the group (which is for the greatest number a collective 'unconsciousness') can be interpreted only in the imaginative or conceptual work of the few authors who carry it to its highest degree of coherence and transparency.

The debate joined here touches upon the very definition of intellectual history, thus upon the constitution of the object of inquiry appropriate to it. Alphonse Dupront argued in 1960 against the history of ideas:

> The history of ideas, which in the final analysis is amorphous and capable of accepting a jumble of ideas that traditional history was disinclined to treat, leans too far toward pure intellectuality [and] the abstract life of the idea, often disproportionately isolated from the social milieux in which it took root and which gave it varying expression. . . . What is as important as the idea, perhaps even more important, is the embodiment of the idea, its meanings, [and] the use made of it.[27]

This attitude led to a call for a social history of ideas centring on their implantation and circulation. Writing ten years after Dupront, Franco Venturi challenged the pertinence of such a proposal, which, for him, missed the essential point.

> The risk of a social history of the Enlightenment, especially evident in France today, is that ideas may be studied when they have already been worked out and accepted and established and so become *structures mentales*. The moment of active creation slips by unobserved. The whole 'geological' structure of the past is examined, but not the soil in which the ideas themselves germinate and grow.[28]

Ideas versus mental structures: the opposition shows clearly the location of the divergences and the rejection of the supposed reductionism of the social (hence quantitative) history of intellectual production. Moreover, this reductionism has two faces. The first is sociological and brings the significance of ideas down to their definitions in social terms, either in the social position of the individuals or the milieux that produced them, or in the social area of their reception.[29] It should be noted that this criticism of the undertakings of cultural sociology does not impugn Goldmann's perspective but is, in reality, in his tradition. The notion of world vision both avoids simplistic equation in relating the significance of an ideological system, described in its own terms, on the one hand, and on the other, the socio-political conditions that cause a certain group or class in a given historical moment to share this ideological system, to a greater or lesser degree, consciously or unconsciously. We are far here from the summary characterizations that sacrifice the ideological to the social, for example in viewing the Enlightenment as wholly bourgeois on the pretext that the *philosophes* and their readers were for the most part of the various bourgeoisies. Confronted with the ideas – better, with the concepts – that people of a specific time utilized and to which they gave a content specific to that time, the historian of ideas needs to 'abandon the search for a determining cause in favour of the search for a *function*' – a function that will make sense only if one takes into account the entire ideological system of the epoch in question.[30]

In more recent years, the social history of ideas has come under attack for another reason involving another form of reductionism. Now it is less the reduction of an idea or an ideology to its conditions of production or reception that is criticized as it is the reification that equates the substance of thought to cultural objects. 'Serial history of the third level' necessarily involves just such a reduction, since its quantifying vocation supposes either that the cultural and intellectual entities analyzed are, from the outset, sets of objects – for example books or pictures, the subject-matter or themes of which can be inventoried statistically – or that collective thoughts, captured in their most repetitive and least personal expressions, can be 'objectified' and reduced to a limited number of formulas that need only to be studied in terms of their varying frequency in the diverse groups of a population. The sociological temptation here consists of considering words, ideas, thoughts and representations as mere objects to be counted in order to show their unequal distribution. This is tantamount to eliminating the social agent (individual or collective) from the analysis and to denying importance to the personal or social relationships that such social agents maintain with cultural objects or specific sorts of thought. A study centred exclusively on distribution is sure to fail to include the intellectual 'labour' of the use or appropriation of a product or an idea. As Carlo Ginzburg has said,

> As far as the quantitative history of ideas is concerned, only knowledge of the historical and social variability of the person of the reader will really lay the foundations for a history of ideas that is also *qualitatively* different.[31]

To continue in Ginzburg's line of thought, the intellectual use to which readers put their reading is a decisive question that cannot be answered either by thematic analyses of the printed works produced or by an analysis of the social diffusion of the various categories of works. Like forms of expressing tastes and opinions are more distinctive than these tastes and opinions themselves;[32] the ways in which an individual or a group appropriates an intellectual theme or a cultural form are more important than the statistical distribution of that theme or form.

Confident of their quantitative methodology, united behind a definition of the history of *mentalités* less imprecise than has been supposed,[33] French historians have long remained deaf to these challenges. By implication, their representation of the field of intellectual history viewed these criticisms as so many rearguard battles in the name of an outworn tradition. It postulated the absorption of the history of ideas into a broader categorization that could bear various labels: socio-cultural history, history of *mentalités*, history of collective psychology, social history of ideas and more. We can see today that according to this way of thinking, nothing had changed in the domain of intellectual history since the 1930s. It was wrong on two counts. First, this position failed to recognize the importance of the epistemological model offered by the work of Gaston Bachelard, Alexandre Koyré and Georges Canguilhem to the procedures of intellectual history. It is symptomatic to encounter in the *Annales* only one review of a work by Bachelard (two pages by Lucien Febvre in 1939 on the *Psychanalyse du feu*) and none on the works of Canguilhem or Koyré (the only article published by Koyré in the *Annales* did not appear until 1960). This extraordinary blindness was laden with consequences. It deprived French historians of an entire set of concepts that might have put them on guard against drawing overly simplistic conclusions from statistical inquiry and might have enabled them to abandon the disconnected description of the cultural products or thought contents of an epoch that quantitative research offers for a comprehension of the relations that exist at any given moment among the different intellectual fields. This approach might have made it possible to investigate what quantitative methods miss – the bonds of reciprocal dependence that unite representations of the social world, technologies and the state of development of different branches of knowledge. Furthermore, with the aid of such a notion as the epistemological obstacle (which echoes the most sharply focused aspect of the image of mental equipment), it might have permitted the drawing of connections between shared representations (the common stock of sensations, images and

theories) and advances in the knowledge designated as scientific.[34]
Had they listened to the epistemologists, French historians might
also have learned to put differently the problem over which all
history of *mentalités* stumbles, that of the reasons for and modalities
of change from one system to another. Establishing the existence of
changes by means of counts of objects or motifs fails to grasp the
processes of transformation at work, which can be understood only
by thinking, as Koyré has done, of both the dependence and the
autonomy of the various fields of knowledge. When this is done, the
passage from one system of representations to another can be understood at the same time as a profound break (in branches of knowledge but also in the very structures of thought) and as a process
made of hesitations, steps backward and obstacles.[35]

Not only did French historians fail to appreciate epistemology,
thus depriving themselves of the intellectual instruments that would
have enabled them to articulate what the social history of ideas
allowed them only to assert, but they also failed to appreciate the
new manner of conceiving of relations between works (in the
broadest sense) and society that had been proposed by historians of
literature and ideas, both with fidelity and distance *vis-à-vis* Lucien
Goldmann. Here the familiar historical problematic was modified in
two ways. First, by suggesting a non-quantitative conception of representativeness, and second, by isolating the ideological systems of
the society whose conflicts they were supposed to reflect, continue, or
express. This removal from the social context was not to affirm the
absolute independence of the ideological systems from the social; it
meant rather that this relationship is posed in terms of structural
homologies or broader connections. Historians of mentalities today
are rediscovering the validity of this line of inquiry, heretofore
neglected. This is perhaps because, having renounced the project of
a total history, they are not posing the problem of the connections
between intellectual choices and social position in the context of
well-defined segments of society or even at the level of the individual.[36] It is on this reduced scale, and possibly only on this scale, that
we can avoid deterministic reduction in grasping the relation
between systems of belief, values and representations and social
affiliations. Techniques of analysis fashioned for a history of thought
at the highest level are thus put to use on another terrain to comprehend how an 'ordinary' person or an 'ordinary' group appropriate
the ideas or beliefs of their time – in particular in ways that may
distort or even mutilate them. Intellectual history (understood as the
analysis of how specific ideological materials have been 'worked
out'), far from having run its course, thus annexes the terrain of

popular thought that had seemed to be the privileged domain of quantitative history. The relation between the *histoire des mentalités* and the history of ideas is thus infinitely more complex than French historians of the 1960s believed it to be.

CATEGORIZATION QUESTIONED

Beyond methods of analysis or the definition of disciplines, the fundamental issues in today's debates concern basic categories that until recently were generally accepted. These primary distinctions, usually expressed by oppositions such as learned/popular, creation/ consumption, reality/fiction, served as a common axiomatic basis for diverse ways of treating the objects of intellectual or cultural history. For several years now, however, these categories have come under convergent if not identical sorts of scrutiny. Little by little, historians have in fact become aware that the categories which so evidently structured their field of investigation that they often went unremarked were, just like the categories whose history they were writing, the products of changing and temporary delimitations. This is what prompts me to engage here in a critical re-evaluation of distinctions that are taken as self-evident but are in fact exactly what must be questioned.

The first such traditional opposition is between *savant* and *populaire*, high culture and popular culture. Presented as obvious, this opposed pairing implies an entire series of methodological corollaries. John Higham formulated their rationale in 1954 in these terms:

> The internal analysis of the humanist applies chiefly to the intellectual elite; it has not reached very far into the broad field of popular thought. The blunter, external approach of the social scientist leads us closer to collective loyalties and aspirations of the bulk of humanity.[37]

Many examples could be found in both France and the United States of this same opposition between the culture of the greatest number, which calls for an external, collective and quantitative approach, and the intellectuality of the highest forms of thought, which requires internal analysis to individualize the irreducible originality of their ideas. Explicitly or not, this dichotomy underlies the work of a number of historians who have explored the vast territory of popular culture – perhaps not the only interest but in any event a privileged focus of the *histoire des mentalités* in France and of a cultural history of anthropological inspiration in the United States.

In France, popular culture (which could be defined as what the discipline of intellectual history holds as pertinent to the common people) has been characterized in two ways. It has been identified, first, with a set of texts, the small books sold by peddling and known under the generic term of *Bibliothèque bleue*, and secondly, with a group of beliefs and acts taken as the components of a popular religion. In both cases the popular is defined in contrast to something it is not (scholarly and learned literature or the normative Catholicism of the Church). Also in both cases, the historian (whether 'intellectual' or 'cultural') is faced with a clearly defined body of materials whose themes must be inventoried.

But it is precisely the definition of the area of study that causes problems. First, the social attribution of cultural practices that until recently were classified as popular is now thought of in more complex terms. Is 'popular' religion the religion of the peasants, of the 'dominated' (as opposed to the elites), or of all laity (as opposed to the clergy)? Does 'popular' literature provide reading- (or listening-) matter to peasant society, to a public situated midway between the illiterate common people and a restricted minority of the literate? Or does it include a reading-matter shared by an entire society, which each group decoded in individual ways that ranged from simply spotting graphic signs to fluent reading? Debate on such difficult questions indicates that it is not easy to identify a cultural or intellectual level that represents the common people on the basis of a set of objects or practices. Second, all the cultural manifestations in which today's historians recognize people's culture appear always as virtually inextricable compounds of extremely diverse origins. The literature of the *Bibliothèque bleue* was produced by professional writers and printers, but it drew upon techniques of editing that subjected learned texts to transformations and forms of presentation foreign to learned editions. Readers stated their preferences through what they bought and in what number, and by that means their tastes influenced what texts were printed. Conversely, folk culture, on which the religion of the greatest number was based, was profoundly 'worked over' in every epoch by the norms or the prohibitions of the ecclesiastical institution. The question of whether we should define as popular what was created by the common people or what was contrived for their use is a false problem. It is more important to identify how differing cultural configurations crisscross and dovetail in practices, representations, or cultural products.

Despite appearances, these statements do not lead us away from intellectual history. It is clear that elite culture was itself constituted in large measure by operating on materials that did not properly belong to it. A similar and subtle game of appropriations, reutilizations and redirections established the relation, for example, between Rabelais and 'the peculiar culture of the marketplace',[38] or between the Perrault brothers and oral literature.[39] The relationship thus established between what elite culture was and was not concerns form as well as content and codes of expression as well as systems of representation – in other words, all of what has been recognized as the terrain of intellectual history. Such intersections must not be understood as external relations between two juxtaposed and pre-existent worlds (one scholarly, the other popular), but rather as encounters that produced cultural or intellectual 'alloys' the components of which were as solidly bounded together as in metal alloys. According to Mikhail Bakhtin, in certain epochs (such as the Renaissance), it was in works of literate or scholarly culture that popular culture expressed itself with maximum coherence and revealed its origins most completely. He writes:

> To help us penetrate the very depth of this matter, Rabelais is unique. In his creative world the inner oneness of all the hetero-geneous elements emerges with extraordinary clarity. His work is an encyclopedia of folk culture.[40]

'Encyclopedia' indicates here that beyond the utilization of words, images, or forms of the 'folk culture of humor', Rabelais's entire text turns around a carnivalesque conception of culture posited as the matrix of all popular expression.

Moreover, to question the separation of the popular and the learned also annuls the methodological differences postulated as necessary for treatment of these two domains. It is not necessarily in the nature of the 'popular' to be reserved for quantitative and external analysis by social scientists. Indeed, as Carlo Ginzburg has shown, when the documents permit it, it is entirely possible to grasp in detail how a man or woman of the people can think and use the disparate intellec-tual elements of literate culture that reach them through books and that filter through the interpretation they give to them. Here Bakhtin is turned upside-down, since fragments borrowed from scholarly and bookish culture found a system of representation that gave those fragments another meaning because the system was founded in another culture: 'We had identified, behind the books mulled over by Menocchio, a method he used in his reading; and behind this a solid stratum of oral culture.'[41] We cannot then postulate as necessary the connection established, for example by Felix Gilbert, between the broadening in social terms of the field of research in intellectual history and recourse to statistical procedures. [42] In reality, if under certain conditions it is legitimate to make use of the quantitative approach (internal or external) to deal with the more fully elaborated texts, conversely, when the archives permit it, the intellectual work of the most anonymous readers may be amenable to analytical procedures ordinarily reserved for the 'great' thinkers.

Doubts raised concerning the opposition of the scholarly and the popular lead us to question another of the distinctions that both historians of ideas and historians of *mentalités* hold as fundamental, the contrast between creation and consumption or between production and reception. Again, an entire series of corollaries is implicit in this first distinction. In the first place, it establishes a representation of cultural consumption which is opposed term for term to that of intellectual creation: passivity against invention, dependence against liberty, alienation against consciousness. The intelligence of the 'consumer' is (to borrow a metaphor from traditional pedagogy) like a soft wax tablet legibly inscribed with the ideas and images forged by intellectual creators. Another corollary follows from this: the study of intellectual diffusion, which would be the province of a retrospective cultural sociology, is necessarily a separate discipline from the study of intellectual production, which would be the prerogative of an aesthetic approach to forms or a philosophical comprehension of ideas. This total separation of production and consumption leads us to the postulate that ideas or forms have an intrinsic meaning totally independent of their appropriation by a social subject or group of subjects. Postulating this objective meaning, the historian often surreptitiously insinuates a personal 'consumption' and, without realizing it, holds it up as a universal category of interpretation. To act as if texts (or images) had intrinsic meanings independent of the readings that constructed them leads, whether we like it or not, to relating those texts to the intellectual (and sensorial) field of the historian who is analysing them and to decoding them by means of categories of thought of an unperceived historicity and which present themselves, implicitly, as permanent.

The restoration of historicity demands first of all that cultural or intellectual 'consumption' itself be taken as a form of production which, to be sure, manufactures no object, but which constitutes representations that are never identical to those that the producers (the authors or the artists) have introduced into their works. That is why Michel de Certeau's definition of the mass cultural consumption characteristic of Western societies today can be extended to a more general context. Certeau says:

> To a rationalized, expansionist and at the same time centralized, clamorous, and spectacular production corresponds *another* production, called 'consumption'. The latter is devious, it is dispersed, but it insinuates itself everywhere, silently and almost invisibly, because it does not manifest itself through its own products, but rather through its ways of using the products imposed by a dominant economic order. [43]

To eliminate the separation between producing and consuming is first of all to affirm that the work acquires a sense only through the strategies of interpretation that construct its meanings. The author's meaning is one among several and contains no unique and permanent 'truth' of the work. In this way the author can be restored to his or her just place. Authorial intention (conscious or unconscious) no longer embraces all possible understanding of the work, but neither is the relationship of artist and work rendered completely meaningless.

Defined as 'another production', cultural consumption – for example, the reading of a text – can thus escape the passivity traditionally attributed to it. Reading, viewing and listening are, in fact, so many intellectual attitudes which, far from subjecting consumers to the omnipotence of the ideological or aesthetic message that supposedly conditions them, make possible reappropriation, redirection, defiance, or resistance. Awareness of this should lead to a thoroughgoing rethinking of the relation between a public referred to as 'popular' and the historically diverse products (be they books and pictures, sermons and speeches, songs, photo-novels, or television programmes) offered for its consumption. The 'oblique' attention that for Richard Hoggart characterizes the contemporary popular decoding of these materials [44] is one of the keys to an understanding of just how the culture of the greatest number can at any epoch distance itself, make a place for itself, or establish its own coherence in the models imposed upon it, by force or by persuasion, by the dominant groups or powers. Such a perspective provides a counterweight to an emphasis on the discursive or institutional apparatus in a society that is designed to delimit times and places, discipline bodies and practices and shape conduct and thoughts by the regulation of space. These technologies of surveillance and inculcation must, in fact, compromise with tactics of consumption and utilization on the part of the men and women whom they had the task of shaping.

These remarks challenge an entire set of postulates implicit in contemporary socio-cultural history in France (in particular, in the interpretation of the Counter Reformation, the effects of which are supposed to have totally annihilated an ancient folk culture). They do not divert us from intellectual history, even strictly defined, since they incite us to situate all texts in their reading relationships. We need to guard against the notion, dear to historians of literature or philosophy, that a text conceals its meaning like an ore its mineral, thus making criticism the operation that brings to light this hidden sense. We need to remember that any text is the product of a reading and is a construction on the part of its reader:

> The reader takes neither the position of the author nor an author's position. He invents in texts something different from what they 'intended.' He detaches them from their (lost or accessory) origin. He combines their fragments and creates something un-known in the space organized by their capacity for allowing an indefinite plurality of meanings. [45]

When texts (and images of all categories) are conceived as leaving room for multiple readings, they cannot be apprehended either as objects whose distribution needs only to be catalogued or as entities with meanings that can be spoken of in universal terms. Rather, texts must be confronted within the network of contradictory utilizations that constituted them through time. Quite obviously, this raises two questions. What is reading? How can the older readings be restored? Answers are hardly guaranteed, but it is clear that intellectual history cannot long avoid searching for them. Provisionally, it is probably good methodology not to reject any of the insights that allow even a partial reconstitution of what readers made of their readings – direct grasp in statements incidental to a confession, written or oral, voluntary or extorted; examination of instances of rewriting and intertextuality in which the traditional separation of writing and reading is annulled, since here writing is itself a reading of another writing; [46] and finally, serial analysis of a limited body of works to show shifts in themes within a given genre (for example, works on *civilité* or preparation for death) that reflect the point of intersection of the producers' intentions and their public's reading of their works. [47] Without forcing it into the confines of a history of the social diffusion of ideas, intellectual history must give a central place to the relationship of the text and the readers, individual or collective, who construct it at each encounter – that is, who decompose it in view of recomposition.

But what is the status of these multiple recomposed texts that intellectual history takes as the objects of its analysis? Traditionally, their very function is presumed to give them unity. All in fact are supposed to constitute ways of representing a reality that they strive to apprehend by different means, philosophical or literary. The opposition between reality and representation is thus presented as primordial, both to distinguish types of history and to discriminate between types of texts. Unlike economic or social historians, who reconstitute what was, the historian of mentalities or ideas seeks not the real but the ways in which people considered and transposed reality. A division of materials appropriate to each corresponds to this historical division of labour. 'Documentary' texts, which reveal what ancient reality was like when subjected to proper critical inquiry, stand opposed to 'literary' texts which, since they are fictional, cannot be held as witnesses to reality. This fundamental split has been unaltered either by constructing statistical series on the basis of old 'documents', which only accentuates their truth value, or by historians' recent use of literary texts, since by that token the texts are reduced to the status of documents, admissible because they state in another way what social analysis has established by its own procedures. The individual text thus becomes a 'living' illustration of the laws of quantity.

It is these oversimplified compartmentalizations that historians sensitive to contemporary literary criticism or sociology are challenging today.[48] It is clear from the outset that no text, even the most apparently documentary, even the most 'objective' (for example, a statistical table drawn up by a government agency), maintains a transparent relationship with the reality that it apprehends. Never can a text – literary or documentary – disappear as a text – that is, as a system constructed according to categories, schemata of perception and appreciation and operating rules that go back to the very conditions of its production. The relationship of the text to reality (which can perhaps be defined as what the text itself posits as real by constituting it as an outside referent) is constructed in accordance with discursive models and intellectual categories particular to each writing situation. Thus fictional works should not be treated as simple documents or realistic reflections of a historical reality. Rather, we must recognize their specificity as texts situated in relation to other texts and with both rules of organization and a formal elaboration that aim to produce something other than a description. This in turn leads to considering that 'document-materials' also obey both construction procedures in which the concepts and obsessions of their producers are invested and the rules of writing peculiar to the genre of the text are inscribed. These categories of thought and these principles of writing are what must be brought to light before making any attempt at a 'positive' reading of the document.[49] Reality thus takes on a new meaning. What is real, in fact, is not (or is not only) the reality that the text aims at, but the very manner in which it aims at it in the historic setting of its production and the strategy used in its writing.[50]

If instead of texts taken in isolation or in restricted bodies of material, intellectual history examines the ideological system of a period or a group within a period, it finds itself face to face with a similar difficulty in articulating the representations and the social reality represented. Simplistic interpretations postulating the absolute autonomy of ideology or, conversely, attributing to it a function of social reflection must be replaced with another sort of comprehension, the principles of which Pierre Bourdieu has defined.[51] On the one hand, by postulating that the schemata of perception and appreciation that constitute the totality of representations of a group are the product of an internalization of the more fundamental oppositions of the social world, Bourdieu permits conceptualization of a relation between the principles of division or classification and the social divisions themselves: 'The cognitive structures which social agents implement in their practical knowledge of the social world are internalized, 'embodied' social structures.'[52] But, on the other hand, the relationship thus established is not one of dependence of the mental structures on their material determinations. The representations of the social world are themselves the constituents of social reality. Instruments of power, the stakes of struggles as fundamental as economic ones, the systems of classification or images of social order all transform this very order by modifying the demands (of wealth, title, or behaviour) attached to one position or another, by shifting the frontiers between groups, first in the imaginary realm and then in the factual, even by bringing into existence new groups or new classes.[53] Thus:

> The negotiations between antagonistic interest groups, which arise from the establishment of collective agreements and which concern, inseparably, the tasks entailed by a given job, the properties required of its occupants (e.g., diplomas) and the corresponding advantages, both material and symbolic (the name), are an institutionalized, theatrical version of the incessant struggles over the classifications which help to produce the classes, although these classifications are the product of the struggles between the classes and depend on the power relations between them.[54]

Has this sociological detour once again diverted us from intellectual history? No, if we allow that the decoding of texts or discursive compositions that make possible the interpretation of an ideology courts the same risks as the decoding of social facts, namely the negation of representations in the 'objective reality' they are presumed to reflect, or the identification of the reality of the social world with its representations alone, through the elimination of any referent outside the realm of ideology.[55] It is this double stumbling-block that historians of ideas have often not known how to avoid because they fail to give a central place to the reciprocal relations of conceptual systems and social relations in a given historical moment. From this point of view, a study like the one Georges Duby devoted to the threefold image of eleventh- and twelfth-century society is an excellent case in point. The model of the three orders, as it functions within a number of different texts, is understood in its relation to the social or political evolutions that justified its construction or its reuse and in the use, polemical or legitimizing, simultaneous or success-ive, that the different classes or powers (the bishops, the king, the aristocracy) made of it.[56] The entire realm of imagined social reality (*l'imaginaire*) of a given period thus forms a basic mental structure, a system of representations, the genealogy of which must be worked out, and a reality as real as the specific relations within a society.

IN GUISE OF CONCLUSION

Do not expect to find here, despite the imperatives of the genre, propositions stating what intellectual history must now be, as opposed to what it must no longer be.

The only definition of intellectual history presently admissible is probably Carl Schorske's, for he assigns it neither particular methodology nor obligatory concepts but simply indicates two directions for further work:

> The historian seeks . . . to locate and interpret the artifact temporally in a field where two lines intersect. One line is vertical, or diachronic, by which he establishes the relation of a text or a system of thought to previous expressions in the same branch of cultural activity (paintings, politics, etc.). The other is horizontal, or synchronic; by it he assesses the relation of the content of the intellec-tual object to what is appearing in other branches or aspects of a culture at the same time.[57]

Hayden White has a similar conception of the intellectual historian's task, and he proposes a dual model and a twofold line of questioning:

Gombrich and Kuhn have given us models of how to write the histories of genres, styles and disciplines; Goldmann shows us how to unite them on the broader canvases provided by social, political, and economic historians.[58]

Without necessarily saying so, historians in France who attempt to understand 'intellectual objects' (to use Schorske's term) concur in this definition of cultural space (and therefore of the terrain proper to their own study) as two-dimensional, which permits simultaneous conceptualization of an intellectual or artistic product within the specificity of the history of its genre or discipline, within its relation to other contemporaneous cultural products, and within its relations with various referents situated in other fields, socio-economic or political, of the whole of society. To read a text or decode a system of thought means, then, to embrace all the different questions which, when they are fitted together, make up what can be considered to be the actual object of study of intellectual history.

Behind its obvious strengths, however, such a definition conceals still more pitfalls. Two concepts generate trouble here and risk leading us astray: that of the 'intellectual object' and that of culture.

After Foucault, it is quite clear in fact that we cannot consider such 'intellectual objects' as akin to 'natural objects' that change only in their modes of existence through history. Madness, medicine and the state are not categories that can be conceptualized in terms of universals; every age makes their content unique. Behind the misleading permanence of historical terminology, we must recognize not objects, but objectifications that construct an original configuration each time. As Paul Veyne aptly writes: 'In this world, we do not play chess with eternal figures like the king and the fool [the bishop in chess]; the figures are what the successive configurations on the playing-board make of them.'[59] It is thus relations to objects that constitute these configurations in ways specific to each occasion and in accordance with groupings and distributions that are always unique. Intellectual history must not let itself be trapped by words, which can give the illusion that the various fields of discourse or practice are constituted once and for all and that they separate objects of study of varying contours, if not varying content. Quite to the contrary, it must depict the central importance of the discontinuities that cause knowledge and deed to be labelled, grouped together, or valued separately in different or even contradictory ways, according to the epoch. The object of study for intellectual history is thus

to relate the so-called natural objects to the dated and rare practices
that objectivate them and to explain these practices, not on the basis
of a single moving force, but on the basis of all the neighboring
practices in which they are anchored.[60]

This means reconstituting the 'submerged' or 'hidden grammar' (as
Veyne puts it) that underlies observable practices or conscious
discourse. It is by identifying the divisions and relations that have
constituted the object that it strives to apprehend that history (of
ideas, of ideological formations, of discursive practices – the label is
of little importance) will be able to consider that object without
reducing it to the simple status of a detailed instance of a supposedly
universal category.

The concept of culture is as parlous as the concept of intellectual
object. This is not the place for a full discussion of it. I might at most
note that one common representation (particularly striking in the
practice of 'serial history of the third level') constructs culture as an
instance of social totality situated 'above' the economic and social
domains that supposedly constitute the first two steps of the ladder.
This tripartite division, used for its convenience by quantitative
historians to distinguish different fields for the convenience of time-
series methods, in fact duplicates the Marxist categorizations systematized by Louis Althusser. This schema postulates, on the one
hand, that one of the elements – the economic – is determinant and
on the other hand, that culture and ideology form a level apart from
the social totality which is clearly identifiable and confined within
recognizable limits. This no longer seems admissible. In reality,
what needs to be considered is how all relations, including those that
we call economic or social relations, are organized according to
differing forms of logic that put into play and into operation the
schemata of perception and appreciation of a variety of social
subjects and consequently, the representations that comprise what
one can call a 'culture', be it common to the whole of a society or
particular to a limited group. The most bothersome thing about the
habitual definition of the world 'culture' is not so much that it
generally covers only the intellectual or artistic products of an elite
but that it leads us to believe that the 'cultural' inhabits only one
particular field of practice or production. To think in other terms of
culture, and therefore of the field of intellectual history, demands
that we conceive of it as a network of meanings that emerges from
the apparently 'least cultural' discourses and behaviours. As
Clifford Geertz says:

The culture concept to which I adhere . . . denotes an historically transmitted pattern of meanings embodied in symbols, a system of inherited conceptions expressed in symbolic forms by means of which men communicate, perpetuate, and develop their knowledge about and attitudes towards life.[61]

But as Geertz shows in his essay, 'Ritual and Social Change: A Javanese Example', to deny the representations of a society as a totality structured in hierarchical layers risks seeing the social domain dissolve into the meanings that are given it by social agents through their theoretical or practical knowledge of it.[62] It is thus a new articulation between 'cultural structures' and 'social structures' that must be constructed without superimposing either the image of the mirror, which makes the one the reflection of the other, or the image of the machine, in which every moving part reacts to an impulse given to the first link in the chain.

What is needed is to conceptualize both the king and the bishop, together with the space of their linked moves.

NOTES

This text was presented in 1980 at a colloquy held at Cornell University on problems in intellectual history. It has been published in English as 'Intellectual History or Sociocultural History? The French Trajectories', tr. Jane Kaplan, in Dominick LaCapra and Steven L. Kaplan, eds, *Modern European Intellectual History: Reappraisals and New Perspectives* (Cornell University Press, Ithaca, New York, 1982), pp. 13–46; and in French as 'Histoire intellectuelle et histoire des mentalités. Trajectoires et questions', *Revue de synthèse*, ser. 3, 111–12 (1983), pp. 277–307. The English translation has been edited.

1   See Felix Gilbert, 'Intellectual History: Its Aims and Methods', *Daedalus*, 100 (1971), pp. 85–97.

2   Jean Ehrard, 'Histoire des idées et histoire littéraire', in *Problèmes et méthodes de l'histoire littéraire*, Publications de la Société d'Histoire Littéraire de la France (A. Colin, Paris, 1974). pp. 68–80.

3   Robert Darnton, 'Intellectual and Cultural History', in Michael Kammen, ed., *The Past Before Us: Contemporary Historical Writing in the United States* (Cornell University Press, Ithaca, NY. and London, 1980), p. 337.

4   See Jacques Revel, 'The *Annales*: Continuities and Discontinuities', *Review: Journal of the Fernand Braudel Center for the Study of Economies, Historical Systems, and Civilizations*, 1 (1978), pp. 9–18; *idem*, 'Histoire et sciences sociales: Les paradigmes des *Annales*', *Annales ESC*, 34 (1979), pp. 1360–76.

5   Lucien Febvre, 'Guillaume Budé et les origines de l'humanisme

français. A propos d'ouvrages récents', *Revue de synthèse historique*, (1907), reprinted in his *Pour une Histoire à part entière* (S.E.V.P.E.N., Paris, 1962; Ecole des Hautes Etudes en Sciences Sociales, Paris, 1983), citation p. 708.

6   Lucien Febvre, 'Une Question d'influence: Proudhon et les syndical-ismes des années 1900–1914', *Revue de synthèse historique* (1909), reprinted in his *Pour une Histoire à part entière*, citation p. 785.

7   Lucien Febvre, 'Leur Histoire et la nôtre', *Annales d'histoire économique et sociale*, 8 (1938), reprinted in his *Combats pour l'histoire* (A. Colin, Paris, 1953), pp. 276–83.

8   Lucien Febvre, 'Etienne Gilson et la philosophie du XIVe siècle', *Annales ESC*, 1 (1946), reprinted in *Combats pour l'histoire*, pp. 284–8.

9   Erwin Panofsky, *Gothic Architecture and Scholasticism* (Archabbey Press, Latrobe, PA., 1951; Meridian Books, New York, 1957); published in French as *Architecture gothique et pensée scolastique* after his *L'Abbé Suger de Saint Denis*, tr. and concluding essay by Pierre Bourdieu (Editions de Minuit, Paris, 1967).

10   Lucien Febvre, *Le Problème de l'incroyance au XVIe siècle. La religion de Rabelais* (A. Michel, Paris, 1942; reprinted 1968), pp. 141–2 [*The Problem of Unbelief in the Sixteenth Century: The Religion of Rabelais*, tr. Beatrice Gottlieb (Harvard University Press, Cambridge, MA. and London, 1982), p. 150].

11   Ibid., p. 394 (Gottlieb tr., p. 424).

12   Lucien Lévy-Bruhl, *La Mentalité primitive* (Retz, Paris, 1922; 1976), p. 41 [cited from *The Primitive Mentality*, tr. Lilian A. Clare (George Allen and Unwin, London, and Macmillan, New York, 1923; AMS Press, New York, 1978), p. 32].

13   Lucien Febvre, *Amour sacré, amour profane. Autour de l'Heptaméron* (Gallimard, Paris, 1944; 1971), p. 10.

14   Marc Bloch, *La Société féodale, la formation des liens de dépendance* (Albin Michel, Paris, 1939; 1968) [*Feudal Society*, tr. L. A. Manyon (Routledge and Kegan Paul, London, 1962; 2 vols, University of Chicago Press, Chicago, 1964)].

15   See Georges Duby, 'L'Histoire des mentalités', in Charles Samaran, ed., *L'Histoire et ses méthodes* (Gallimard, Paris, 1961), pp. 937–66; Robert Mandrou, 'L'Histoire des mentalités', in *Encyclopedia Universales*, vol. 8 (1968), pp. 436–8; Georges Duby, 'Histoire sociale et histoire des mentalités. Le Moyen Age. Entretien avec Georges Duby', (1970), in *Aujourd'hui l'histoire: Enquête de la nouvelle critique* (Editions Sociales, Paris, 1974), pp. 201–17; Jacques Le Goff, 'Les Mentalités. Une histoire ambiguë', in Jacques Le Goff and Pierre Nora, eds, *Faire de l'histoire: Nouveaux problèmes* (3 vols, Gallimard, Paris, 1974), pp. 76–94 [*Constructing the Past: Essays in Historical Methodology* (Cambridge University Press, Cambridge and NY.; Editions de la Maison des Sciences de l'homme, Paris, 1985) pp. 167, 169]; Philippe Ariès, 'L'Histoire des mentalités', in Jacques Le Goff, Roger Chartier and Jacques Revel, eds, *La nouvelle histoire* (Retz, Paris,

1978), pp. 402-23; Roger Chartier, 'Outillage mental,' in Le Goff, Chartier and Revel, eds, *La nouvelle histoire*, pp. 448-52.

16 See Lucien Febvre, 'Méthodes et solutions pratiques. Henri Wallon et la psychologie appliquée', *Annales d'histoire économique et sociale*, 10 (1931), reprinted in his *Combats pour l'histoire*, pp. 201-6; *idem*, 'Une Vue d'ensemble. Histoire et psychologie', in *Encyclopédie française* (1938), reprinted in his *Combats pour l'histoire*, pp. 207-20; *idem*, 'Comment reconstituer la vie affective d'autrefois? La sensibilité et l'histoire', *Annales d'histoire sociale*, 3 (1941), reprinted in his *Combats pour l'histoire*, pp. 221-38.

17 Ignace Meyerson, *Les Fonctions psychologiques et les oeuvres* (J. Vrin, Paris, 1948).

18 Jean-Pierre Vernant, *Mythe et pensée chez les Grecs. Etudes de la psychologie historique* (La Découverte, Paris, 1967), pp. 13-14 [*Myth and Thought among the Greeks* (Routledge and Kegan Paul, London, Boston, Melbourne, Henley, 1983), pp. xiii-xiv].

19 Alphonse Dupront, 'Problèmes et méthodes d'une histoire de la psychologie collective', *Annales ESC*, 16 (1961), pp. 3-11.

20 Ibid., p. 8.

21 Pierre Chaunu, 'Un nouveau Champ pour l'histoire sérielle: Le quantitatif au troisième niveau', in *Mélanges en l'honneur de Fernand Braudel* (2 vols, Privat, Toulouse, 1972), vol. 2: *Méthodologie de l'histoire et des sciences humaines*, pp. 105-25.

22 Fernand Braudel, *La Méditerranée et le monde méditerranéen à l'époque de Philippe II*, 2nd edn (2 vols, Colin, Paris, 1966), vol. 1, pp. 16-17 [*The Mediterranean and the Mediterranean World in the Age of Philip II*, tr. Sian Reynolds (2 vols, Harper and Row, New York, 1972)]; *idem*, 'Histoire et sciences sociales. La longue durée' (1959), in his *Ecrits sur l'histoire* (Flammarion, Paris, 1969), pp. 41-83 [*On History*, tr. Sarah Matthews (University of Chicago Press, Chicago, 1980), pp. 25-54].

23 See Régine Robin, *Histoire et linguistique* (Colin, Paris, 1973).

24 Lucien Goldmann, *Le Dieu caché. Etude sur la vision tragique dans les Pensées de Pascal et dans le théâtre de Racine* (Gallimard, Paris, 1955) [*The Hidden God: A Study of Tragic Vision in the 'Pensées' of Pascal and the Tragedies of Racine*, tr. Philip Thody (Humanities Press, New York, and Routledge and Kegan Paul, London, 1964)]; Robert Mandrou, 'Tragique XVIIe siècle. A propos de travaux récents', *Annales ESC*, 12 (1957), pp. 305-13.

25 Goldmann, *Le Dieu caché*, p. 26 (Thody tr., p. 17).

26 Jean Ehrard, 'Histoire des idées et histoire littéraire', p. 79.

27 Dupront, 'Problèmes et méthodes', n. 19.

28 Franco Venturi, *Utopia e riforma nell'Illuminismo* (Einaudi, Turin, 1970), p. 24 [*Utopia and Reform in the Enlightenment* (Cambridge University Press, Cambridge, 1971), p. 14].

29 Jean Ehrard, 'Histoire des idées et histoire sociale en France au XVIIIe siècle: Réflexions de méthode', in *Niveaux de culture et groupes*

sociaux, Actes du colloque réuni du 7 au 9 mai 1966 à l'École Normale Supérieure (Mouton, Paris and The Hague, 1967), pp. 171–8.

30 Ibid., p. 175, and the comments of Jacques Proust, ibid., pp. 181–3.

31 Carlo Ginzburg, *Il formaggio e i vermi. Il cosmo di un mugnaio del' 1500* (Einaudi, Turin, 1976), pp. xxi–xxii [*The Cheese and the Worms: The Cosmos of a Sixteenth-Century Miller*, tr. John and Anne Tedeschi (Johns Hopkins University Press, Baltimore, 1980; Penguin Books, 1982), p. xxii].

32 Pierre Bourdieu, *La Distinction. Critique sociale du jugement* (Editions de Minuit, Paris, 1979), pp. 70–87 [*Distinction: A Social Critique of the Judgement of Taste*, tr. Richard Nice (Harvard University Press, Cambridge, MA. and Routledge and Kegan Paul, London, 1984)].

33 For example, by Robert Darnton (see his 'Intellectual and Cultural History').

34 Gaston Bachelard, *La Formation de l'esprit scientifique. Contribution à une psychanalyse de la connaissance objective* (J. Vrin, Paris, 1939).

35 Alexandre Koyré, *From the Closed World to the Infinite Universe* (Johns Hopkins University Press, 1958, 1968; Harper, New York, 1958).

36 See, for example, Ginzburg, *The Cheese and the Worms* and the essays of Natalie Zemon Davis collected in her *Society and Culture in Early Modern France* (Stanford, California, Stanford University Press, 1975), which make use of case-studies to pose the problem of the connections between religious choice and social rank.

37 John Higham, 'Intellectual History and its Neighbors', *Journal of the History of Ideas*, 15, 3 (1954), pp. 339–47, p. 346.

38 Mikhail Bakhtin, *Rabelais and His World*, tr. Hélène Iswolsky (MIT Press, Cambridge, MA., 1968), p. 4.

39 See Marc Soriano, *Les Contes de Perrault. Culture savante et traditions populaires* (Gallimard, Paris, 1968).

40 Bakhtin, *Rabelais*, p. 58.

41 Ginzburg, *The Cheese and the Worms*, p. 68.

42 Gilbert, 'Intellectual History', p. 92.

43 Michel de Certeau, *L'Invention du quotidien*, (Union Générale d'Éditions, 10/18, Paris, 1980), vol. 1: *Arts de faire*, p. 11 [*The Practice of Everyday Life*, tr. Steven F. Rendall (University of California Press, Berkeley, Los Angeles, and London, 1984), pp. xii–xiii].

44 Richard Hoggart, *The Uses of Literacy: Aspects of Working-Class Life with Special Reference to Publications and Entertainments* (Chatto and Windus, London, 1957).

45 Certeau, *Practice of Everyday Life*, p. 169. See also ch. 12, 'Reading as Poaching', pp. 165–76.

46 In the vast bibliography on the notion of intertextuality, see Julia Kristeva, *Semiotikè: Recherches pour une sémanalyse* (Editions du Seuil, Paris, 1969); Hans Robert Jauss, *Pour une Esthétique de la réception* (Gallimard, Paris, 1978).

47 Compare the views in Daniel Roche, 'Histoire littéraire et histoire

globale', in *Problèmes et méthodes de l'histoire littéraire*; *Colloque, 18 novembre 1972* (A. Colin, Paris, 1974), pp. 89–101.

48 See Jean-Marie Goulemot, 'Histoire littéraire,' in Le Goff, Chartier and Revel, eds, *La nouvelle histoire*, pp. 308–13.

49 See, for example, Michelle Perrot, 'Délinquance et système pénitentiaire en France au XIXe siècle', *Annales ESC*, 30 (1975), pp. 67–91; Roger Chartier, 'La "Monarchie d'argot" entre le mythe et l'histoire', in *Les Marginaux et les exclus dans l'histoire* (Union Générale d'Editions, 10/18, Paris, 1979), pp. 275–311. See also ch. 8 below, 'The Two Frances'.

50 See the remarks of Jean-Marie Goulemot in his introduction to Valentin Jamerey Duval, *Mémoires: Enfance et éducation paysanne au XVIIIe siècle* (Sycomore, Paris, 1980).

51 Pierre Bourdieu, 'Conclusion: Classes and Classifications', in *Distinction*, Nice tr., pp. 466–84.

52 Ibid., p. 468.

53 Luc Boltanski, 'Taxinomies sociales et luttes de classes. La mobilisation de la "classe moyenne" et l'invention des "cadres"', *Actes de la recherche en sciences sociales*, 24 (1979), pp. 75–105.

54 Bourdieu, *Distinction*, p. 481.

55 See Pierre Bourdieu, *Le Sens pratique* (Editions de Minuit, Paris, 1980), in particular ch. 9, 'L'Objectivité du subjectif', pp. 233–47.

56 Georges Duby, *Les trois ordres ou l'imaginaire du féodalisme* (Gallimard, Paris, 1978) [*The Three Orders: Feudal Society Imagined*, tr. Arthur Goldhammer (University of Chicago Press, Chicago, 1980)]; Jacques Le Goff, 'Les trois Fonctions indo-européennes: L'historien et l'Europe féodale', *Annales ESC*, 34 (1979), pp. 1187–215.

57 Carl Schorske, *Fin-de-Siècle Vienna: Politics and Culture* (Knopf, New York, 1980), pp. 21–2.

58 Hayden V. White, 'The Tasks of Intellectual History', *The Monist*, 53 (October 1969), pp. 606–26, p. 626.

59 Paul Veyne, 'Foucault révolutionne l'histoire', in his *Comment on écrit l'histoire: Suivi de Foucault révolutionne l'histoire* (Editions du Seuil, Paris, 1978), p. 236.

60 Ibid., p. 241.

61 Clifford Geertz, *The Interpretation of Cultures* (Basic Books, New York, 1973; and Hutchinson, London, 1975), p. 89.

62 Ibid., pp. 142–69.

2

ON THE RELATION OF PHILOSOPHY AND HISTORY

PHILOSOPHY AND HISTORY

This is not a subject that a historian approaches light-heartedly. First, there is the fear of awakening the ghosts of 'philosophy of history' in the style of Spengler or Toynbee – 'cut-rate philosophies', according to Lucien Febvre – that worked out their versions of universal history on the basis of a third-hand acquaintance with the rules and procedures of historical work. Worse, there is a sense of discomfort that arises from the evident gap between two spheres of knowledge for the most part foreign to one another. Historical practice today grants little importance to the time-honoured set of questions that philosophical discourse puts to it; philosophy's themes – the subjectivity of the historian, the laws and the ends of history – seem without functional pertinence. Historical practice is shot through with questions, doubts and hesitations that have little in common with an overall definition of what is the meaning of history, and this leads to an apparently unbridgeable gap between philosophical reflection on history, on the one hand (in which historians recognize little or nothing of their own practices and problems) and on the other hand, current debate within the historical profession on the definition, the conditions and the forms of historical intelligibility (in which many highly philosophical questions are posed, but without reference to formal philosophy).

THE PHILOSOPHY OF HISTORY AND THE HISTORY OF PHILOSOPHY

Any attempt to inaugurate a dialogue between philosophy and history presupposes a more precise assessment of the nature of and the reasons underlying their mutual miscomprehensions. For historians, there are two sides to philosophy, the history of philosophy and the

philosophy of history. Neither of these has an immediate relation to
the discipline of history as it has emerged from the last half century.
The history of philosophy, which might have provided the more
immediate meeting-ground for the two, has in fact (at least in the
French tradition) afforded opportunities for the widest divergences.
For Lucien Febvre and the historians of the early years of the
Annales, the philosophers' versions of the history of philosophy
illustrated the worst aspects of an ethereal intellectual history turned
in upon itself and devoted to vain exercises in pure ideas.[1]
Historians long felt ill at ease with a history of philosophy that
postulated the absolute freedom of intellectual creation totally
detached from a consideration of the conditions that made it possible
and the autonomous existence of ideas taken out of the contexts in
which they had developed and circulated.

In its major currents, the history of philosophy made no attempt
to bridge the gap with the historians' view of history. One might
even say that it did just the opposite when it defined its aim as 'the
objective analysis of [the structures of] a work' or laying bare 'the
demonstrative and architectonic structures of the work'.[2] Thus
defined, the history of philosophy was a specific history with no
common denominator with any other forms of historical knowledge
and no connection with knowledge of the 'world of realities' of which
Febvre spoke. This unique status, which totally removed philosophy
from the reach of ordinary historical interrogation, derived from the
fact that the history of philosophy was itself philosophy. According
to Hegel's dictum, the history of philosophy was 'essential for the
science of philosophy'. This unique and original relationship
between philosophy and its own history was the foundation for a
unique object that took the present state of the discipline as its point
of departure.

> The philosophical spirit can be said to be the creator of the history of
> philosophy, for it is its activity that here confers on the objects of
> history their value as *objects worthy of history*. . . . It is thus the
> philosophic thought of the historian of philosophy that erects the
> intrinsic doctrine into an object.[3]

This led, first, to the postulate of the specific nature of the
philosophical given present in every doctrine, a given that not only
was held impossible to reduce to the historical circumstances of its
appearance, but was also thought of as 'not strictly historical', thus
as denied or destroyed by any interpretation construing it as an
'event' taking place within history, subjected to a complex set of
determinants and connected to other 'events'.

The disassembly of all doctrines into elements of disparate and external origin, their resolution in a sum of influences, material circumstances, and individual or collective psychological needs, would make them appear as the epiphenomenal reflection of a moment in the life of humanity within the intellect of a historically determined man, and would thus destroy their very substance. [4]

As a corollary, the practice of the history of philosophy took as its task (one might even say its only task) the dismantling of the 'internal law specific to each doctrine' that organized the articulated demonstrations forming the very substance of all philosophical works.

The history of philosophy that was founded on this totally structural and 'internalist' basis developed within an absolute specificity that did much to keep history and philosophy apart, since it defined both its object and its methods in terms quite other than those of the historians. By constituting the history of philosophy on the basis of philosophical interrogation itself (and on that interrogation alone) and by asserting not only that philosophical discourse cannot be reduced to any determinant but also that the philosophical object cannot possibly be conceived in historical terms because to do so would be to destroy it, the philosophical history of philosophy, monopoly of the philosophers, launched a radical dehistoricization of its own practice. There is little doubt that this represents a wholly philosophical way to consecrate the eminent dignity of the position and the posture of philosophy, neither determined nor preoccupied by historical contingency, [5] although (or particularly since) this approach leads to an extremely rigorous reading of works guided only by a scientific interest in comprehending the order in their reasoning.

Historians (and others) may, however, have a different idea of the history of philosophy. Martial Guéroult gave a central place in the *Dianoématique* to questioning the conditions governing the determination of philosophical truth (the only way to establish the philosophical 'value' or 'reality' of certain doctrines, thus of the 'philosophizing thought'). For the historians the central question is that of the social conditions governing the production and the reception of discourses held to be philosophical in one specific system of discourse or another (the very question that is fundamentally unthought in all philosophy). Does this have practical value for the analysis of works? It is obvious that some of the attempts that have been made to connect philosophic discourse with the structures of the society in which it appeared have left uncomfortable memories of their hasty reductionism and their naïve determinism. Legitimizing a socio-economic interpretation of an intellectual system (to borrow a phrase of Jon Elster's from his book on Leibniz)[6] demands another approach than a direct parallel between a discourse and a social position. It is an approach that points out above all the transfer of paradigms from one domain to another (in this case, from economic discourse to philosophical discourse), or the use of analogies that bring together separate conceptual spheres (in the case of Leibniz, the social and the metaphysical). To envisage reinserting the history of philosophy within the history of the production of culture – thus within history itself – does not necessarily imply annulling the philosophical basis of philosophical discourse, but rather trying to understand its specific rationality in the historic nature of its production and in its relations with other instances of discourse. The various ways of understanding the history of philosophy quite obviously constitute important stakes in the relations between philosophy and history.

'RENOUNCING HEGEL'

A second and long-established antinomy joins the contrast between the philosophical history of philosophy and history. It opposes historical knowledge and the philosophy of history (or 'philosophical history', as Hegel called it). It is to Hegel, in fact, that we must turn in order to grasp accurately the distance that separates the practice of historians and the philosophical representation of history. The first outline for the introduction to the *Lessons on the Philosophy of History* (written in 1822) firmly established the distinction between all the forms of history practised by historians – the original history of classical antiquity or the medieval chroniclers, universal history in the style of Ranke, moralizing pragmatic history, critical and philological history, the special histories devoted to one particular domain – and the yet-to-be constructed philosophical history. This was the only true history, defined in Hegel's 1830 course as

> the expression of the divine and absolute process of the spirit in its highest forms, of the progression whereby it discovers its true nature and becomes conscious of itself. The specific forms it assumes at each of these stages are the national spirits of world history, with all the determinate characteristics of their ethical life, their constitutions, their art, their religion, and their knowledge. . . . The principles of the national spirits [*Volkgeist*] in their necessary progression are themselves only moments of the one universal spirit, which ascends

through them in the course of history to its consummation in an all-embracing *totality*.[7]

Necessity, totalization, finality: these fundamental notions have long furnished the scaffolding for philosophical discourse on history in varying degrees of fidelity to Hegel.

Concrete historical practice, which works with discontinuities, lags and differences, has for the last fifty years been constructed in precise opposition to this apprehension of historical reality. It is Michel Foucault who has expressed this disagreement in sharpest focus through a number of texts written in the later 1960s (the 'Réponse au cercle d'epistémologie' in 1968, *L'Archéologie du Savoir* in 1969, *L'Ordre du discours* in 1970). He contrasts term by term the idea of history common among the philosophers (and imbued with references to Hegel) and 'the effective work of historians'. History as it is practised involves the use of massive amounts of time-series data – Foucault cites sources such as *mercuriales* (official lists of food prices), notarial acts, parish registers and seaport traffic registers, alluding to the actual history devoted to economic, demographic, or social conjunctures. Concerning this history:

> The fundamental notions now imposed upon us are no longer those of consciousness and continuity (with their correlative problems of liberty and causality), nor are they those of sign and structure. They are notions, rather, of events and of series, with the group of notions linked to these [regularity, hazard, discontinuity, dependence, and transformation]; it is around such an ensemble that this analysis of discourse I am thinking of is articulated, certainly not upon those traditional themes which the philosophers of the past took for 'living' history, but on the effective work of historians.[8]

Foucault was an attentive reader of what in *The Archaeology of Knowledge* he called a 'new history' – the great theses and studies, generally monographic and set in the long term, that in France in the 1950s and 1960s were devoted to price and trade fluctuations, demographic changes, reconstituting family groups and reconstructing social evolutions. Foucault saw that such works, based in local research and by no means vehicles for an explicit theory of history, were original in two ways. They were new, first, in contrast to a global history intent on relating 'the continuous unfolding of an ideal history' that was the history of the philosophers and the Hegelians; and second, in contrast to a structural history that was supposed to have done away with both the event and ruptures or breaks. His analysis of history in the 1960s thus concentrated on a concept – discontinuity – that most distinguished history from the heritage of 'philosophical history'. Practising historians made a clear break with the thought that involved totality (which identified the one principle, the one 'substantial Spirit' universally present in the various 'forms' or 'spheres' in which that Spirit was incarnate at any given moment such as the State, religion, the law, mores and so forth) and with a continuity that postulated unity of the Spirit throughout its various, successive and necessary historical particularizations. 'Hands-on history' – *l'histoire sur le tas* – proceeded differently. It made 'an ordered use of discontinuity for the analysis of temporal series'[9] and it attempted to establish the interconnections among 'these diverse, intermingled, often divergent but not autonomous' series without tying them down to a universal principle penetrating all the particular spheres of life.[10]

New history versus 'philosophical history'; the *Annales* against Hegel – the fate of this dichotomy is an interesting one. On the one hand, philosophy itself gave up its Hegelian goals when it found it impossible to envisage or achieve the 'philosophy of universal history' that Hegel's 1830 course lectures promised. Rather than refuting Hegel, philosophy renounced him – or left him behind – by distancing itself from him and shifting its interests. According to Paul Ricoeur:

> What seems to us highly problematic is the very project of composing a philosophic history of the world to be defined by 'the effectuation of the Spirit in history'. . . . What we have abandoned is the workplace [of this history] itself. We no longer seek the formula on the basis of which the history of the world could be thought of as a realized totality.[11]

Thus the intelligibility of history was separated from any attempt at totalization, both on the level of each particular historical moment and on the scale of universal becoming.

As this renunciation or philosophical abandonment of Hegel was accomplished, historical practice, which had done much to make it possible, had itself changed profoundly. As history is written today, it is no longer (or no longer merely) the history on which Foucault wanted to anchor his analysis of discourse. The notion of series, central to a history freed from Hegelian influence, is the focus of contemporary revision. History is currently less fascinated by *mercuriales* and port of entry archives and freer to question the validity of the categorizations and procedures involved in the serial treatment of historical materials. Its criticism has been dual. First, it found illusory the serial history (and in French historiographical tradition the neologism 'serial' implies quantitative) of mental attitudes or forms of thought. Proposals of the sort were necessarily reductive and reifying, since they either supposed that cultural and intellectual entities were immediately present in countable objects or that they must be grasped in their most repetitive and least individualized expressions and, by that token, be brought down to a closed set of formulas. The historian's only task would thus be to study variations in their distribution in different places or milieux. It was in reaction to this sort of reduction and its over-simplified correlations between social levels and cultural indicators that a new view of cultural history was proposed centring more on practices than on distribution and on the production of meaning rather than the dispersion of objects. The notion of series is not necessarily expelled from this view of history. It persists, for example, in Foucault's sense of the 'series of discourses', each of them having its own principles of regularity and its systems of constraint. The new history is liberated, however, from the definition of series necessarily based on the statistical treatment of homogeneous and repeated data that was imposed in the construction of economic, demographic, or social series.

The interconnection of the various 'series' found in a given society presented a second problem. Its solution long consisted in apportioning these series among 'levels' or 'instances' that were presumed to structure society. This division, inherited from Marxism, seemed reinforced by a reading of Braudelian time-spans that set up a hierarchy among the long term of economic systems, the less lengthy conjunctures of social evolution and the short span of political events. This conception supposes a stable definition of the various 'instances', identifiable in all societies. It implies an order among determinants and it postulates that economic functions and social hierarchies produce mental and ideological representations rather than being produced by them. It is no longer an acceptable view, nor is it accepted. Historical research has attempted to interpret societies by using a variety of approaches, seeking ways to penetrate the web of tensions that make up society through an entry point that may be an event, major or obscure, the career of one individual, or the history of a specific group. The goal of all these various approaches has been to arrive at structures not by the construction of different series that are then related to one another, but on the basis of both a specific and a global understanding of the society in question through an event, an existence, or a practice. The programme outlined by Foucault (to determine what form of relation between the different series can legitimately be described) is now formulated in new terms that demand the elaboration of new questions lying on the borderline between the practice of history and philosophical reflection.

THE HISTORICAL OBJECT, OR, THE QUARREL OVER UNIVERSALS

'History is the description of the individual through universals,'[12] Paul Veyne states, clearly designating one of the primary tensions confronting historical knowledge, which once was accustomed to manipulating apparently stable, unvarying categories as if they were self-evident. Historical objects are not 'natural objects' varying only in their manifestations through time, however. There are no historical objects outside the ever-changing practices that constitute them, thus there is no field of discourse, no sort of reality that is defined once and for all, shaped definitively and traceable in all historical situations: 'Things are only the objectivations of determinate practices, the determinants of which must be brought to light.'[13] Thus historiography can envisage the objects that it chooses to study only by identifying how they are apportioned, what they exclude, and how they are related to other objects. Rather than particularized figurations of an allegedly universal category, they are 'individual and even singular constellations'.[14]

This calls for two comments. First, consciousness of this variation in historical objectivations must not be confused with evaluation of historians' concepts, which necessarily fluctuate because they are sublunary. Recognizing the mutability of the configurations that shape specific domains of practice, economies of discourse and social forms is not necessarily tantamount to postulating that the concepts manipulated for designating them are in essence false or ill-defined (unless, of course, they are still the generic or universal concepts of the traditional historical repertory). And second, there are obstacles to constructing historical objectivations, in all their variability, as correlated to practices. One of the more durable points of resistance is the distinction of reality in the social sphere – the historian's province – from what is not reality, which falls into the realm of discourse, ideology, or fiction. It was this differentiation that Michel Foucault attacked when he told historians:

> We have to demystify the global instance of *the* real as a totality to be restored. There is no such thing as 'the' real that can be reached by speaking about everything, or about certain things that are more 'real' than others and that one would fail to grasp, to the profit of inconsistent abstractions, if one kept to showing other elements and

other relations. . . . A type of rationality, a way of thinking, a programme, a technology, a set of rational and co-ordinated efforts, of definite and actively pursued objectives, instruments to attain this end, etc. – all that is of reality, even if it does not claim to be 'reality' itself or the whole of 'society'.[15]

Foucault contrasts this 'meagre idea of the real' generally held by historians, who equate reality uniquely with the social domain of lives lived or with reconstituted hierarchies, to an affirmation of the fundamental equivalence of all objects of history, without distinction by presumed levels of reality. It is thus no longer essential to distinguish between degrees of reality, the time-honoured basis for contrasting a socio-economic history that approached the real through documentary materials with another sort of history dedicated to products of the imagination. What is essential is to understand how patterns of practice and series of discourses are articulated to produce what can legitimately be designated as 'reality' and which is the object of history.

ON NARRATION: OR, THE PITFALLS OF THE TALE

One of the liveliest questions on the historians' agenda, the forms of historical writing, is another area that benefits from reference to philosophy. We are familiar with the debate launched by the assertion that the newer tendencies in history were a return to relation and narration and, as a corollary, involved abandoning the structural description of societies.[16] Two postulates underlie this judgement. First, this return to narrative signifies a renunciation of coherent and scientific explanations, in particular those furnished by notions of economic and demographic causality. And second, the choice of a particular mode of writing history – a mode that consists in 'the organization of material in a chronologically sequential order and the focusing of the content into a single coherent story, albeit with sub-plots'[17] – involves important changes. Simultaneously, the objects of history will shift from a concentration on social structures to sentiments, values and patterns of behaviour; methods of treatment will change from quantitative procedures to the investigation of particular instances; and in historical understanding the 'principle of indetermination' will replace determinist models.

This diagnostic, which has even been contested as invalid (is history today truly that 'narrative'?) is hasty for two reasons. First, where this criticism sees a return of the narrative in historiography, which is supposed to have disqualified and abandoned it, one can see, with Paul Ricoeur, the exact contrary. History in all its forms, even the least concerned with events or the most 'structuralist', belongs fully to the realm of narration. All truly historical writing is constructed, in point of fact, through the use of formulas it shares with narrative or with 'emplotment'. Various 'relay stations' or forms of transition exist to articulate the 'structures of historical knowledge . . . with the work of narrative configuration' and to link, in both sorts of discourse, the conception of causality, the characterization of the actors involved and the construction of temporality. [18] This means that history is always narration, even when it claims to be rid of the narrative, and its mode of comprehension remains dependent on procedures and operations that assure the emplotment of the actions represented. [19]

A second point needs to be considered. History belongs within the narrative genre, and the structural identity of fictional and historical writing rests on that fact. This does not exclude intelligibility, however. It is too simplistic to contrast explanations without narration and narration without explanations, since historical comprehension is constructed within narration and by means of the narrative, its arrangements and its compositions. But there are two ways of interpreting this assertion. First, it could mean that emplotment is in itself a sort of comprehension, thus that there are as many possible 'comprehensions' as there are constructable plots, and that the only measure of historical intelligibility is the plausibility of the story line. As Paul Veyne wrote, 'What is called explanation is nothing but the way in which the account is arranged in a comprehensible plot.' [20] Thus recounting always involves making something comprehensible. By the same token, historical explication is simply spinning a tale. Still, the proposition linking narration and explication can have another sense if it takes the information put in narrative form as so many traces or indications authorizing the reconstruction – always with a degree of incertitude but always subjected to verification – of the phenomena that produced them. Historical knowledge thus falls within a paradigm of knowledge that is neither made of laws capable of being expressed in mathematical terms nor restricted only to plausible narratives. [21] Emplotment should not be understood as an intellectual operation on the level of rhetoric but as a way of focusing on the possible intelligibility of the historical phenomenon, in all its ephemeral reality, by means of intersecting traces that are still accessible to us.

Once the false contradiction between historical knowledge and narrative configuration has been removed, the next problem concerns historiography's use of different modes of narrative writing and levels of narration. The compass of Braudel's *Mediterranean* is not the same as that of Le Roy Ladurie's *Montaillou*; 'microhistory' is written in a different key from social history, and a price curve is not equivalent to the rise and fall of an individual's career. It may be tempting to account for such differences by considering these as compatible techniques of observation (like the use of the microscope and the telescope) or by seeking connections with changes in narrative techniques in fiction in both print and pictures in our century. But there is doubtless more to the choice of one mode of narration over another. In particular, there is more to the interpretation of diverse and even contradictory representations of social phenomena when the social sphere is no longer thought of as a fixed and hierarchical whole structured into instances, but as a skein of complex relationships, all of which are constructed culturally, and in which the individual finds a place in multiple ways. [22] Thus it is clear that choices between the different possible modes of writing history – all of which belong to the narrative genre – construct differing modes of intelligibility for differently conceived historical realities. The major cleavages separating historians today, which coincide only partially with inherited and institutionalized oppositions, are formulated by such contrasts among the different ways of using historical materials, not in any didactic enunciation of theories of history, but in concrete practices of analysis.

HISTORY VERSUS STORY; OR, THE RULES OF TRUTHFUL NARRATION

One among many forms of narration, history is nonetheless singular in that it maintains a special relation to truth. More precisely, its narrative constructions aim at reconstituting a past that really was. This reference to a reality pre-existing the historical text and situated outside it, which the text has the function of bringing back as best it can, has not been abandoned by any of the various forms of historical knowledge. Even better, this is what constitutes history and keeps it different from fable or fiction. This very distribution of roles is what seems the least certain, however. There are two sets of reasons for this. First, the observation that history belongs to the sphere of narrative can lead to a near obliteration of the borderline between history and fiction, making history seem a 'literary artefact' or a 'form of fiction-making' that uses the same narrative categories and the same rhetorical figures as texts produced by the imagination. [23] This implies a shift in the criteria for the identification of modes of discourse, which will be classified according to the narrational paradigms that give them form, not by their relation or lack of relation to reality. There will be a related shift in the very definition of historical explication, no longer understood as accounting for a past event, but as a procedure for identifying and recognizing the modes and figures of discourse employed in narration. Even if such a view does not eliminate or deny the referential aim of history (how then could history be specific?) the accent is shifted to the fundamental rhetorical similarities between history and the novel and representation and fiction.

The second set of reasons for the unclear demarcation between historical and fictional narrative lies, to paraphrase Ricoeur, in the difficulties inherent in defining problems concerning the very concept of 'reality' as applied to the past. Here seemingly insoluble logical difficulties or historical naïveté doubtlessly derive from a continuing confusion between a methodological problem (as old as history itself) of the value and the meaning of the traces that permit indirect, mediated knowledge of the phenomena which produced them, on the one hand and, on the other (a practice that historians usually avoid as paralyzing) questioning the validity of the correspondence that historians demand and proclaim between what they write and the reality that they claim to reconstruct and make comprehensible.

'The question of proof remains more than ever at the center of historical research,'[24] but just how does one 'prove' historically? The question has long elicited a philological answer linking the truth of historical writing to the proper exercise of documentary criticism or the correct manipulation of techniques for the analysis of historical materials. The resulting historical statements can be verified or disqualified on a completely technical basis. If history is trimmed down to its most objective statements in this fashion it can be both differentiated from fable or fiction and validated as an objective reconstruction of the past that lies behind remaining traces of a reality discoverable through its vestiges. 'A reconstitution of this sort can be considered true if it can be reproduced by any other person who knows how to put into practice the techniques needed in the given connection.'[25] Even though the modalities of emplotment vary, even though historical writing is a literary artefact, thus a unique creation, the base on which historical knowledge rests is considered to escape these variations or this singularity since its 'truth' is guaranteed by controllable, verifiable and repeatable operations.[26]

This is all very well. Here lies the first constraint to historical discourse, recognized even by those who are least inclined to consider that discourse as scientific. To abandon its requisites would, in fact, destroy the very idea of historical knowledge. Nevertheless, experience clearly indicates that it is not enough to ensure the objectivity of the techniques proper to the discipline – be they philological, statistical, or in the realm of computer programming – to eliminate all uncertainties concerning the validity of the knowledge so produced, a knowledge that has been dubbed 'indirect, index-oriented, and conjectural'.[27] The question confronting history today concerns the shift from a validation of historical discourse based on its founding operations (which are not at all arbitrary) to another type of validation allowing us to hold possible, probable, or plausible the relationships that the historian postulates between documentary traces and the phenomena of which those traces are a sign – or, to use another vocabulary, between the representations that we can manipulate today and the past practices that they designate. When we formulate the problem of history as a true account in this way, we pose an entire set of questions which concern the pertinence and the representativeness of the accessible traces (a problem inadequately resolved by a paradoxical concept such as the 'normally exceptional'[28]) but which also concern the way in which representations of practices and the practices of representation intermesh.

The entire debate that has been launched (in Italy in particular) on the merits or drawbacks of the 'paradigm of the index'[29] seems to me to return to the dual operation underlying all historical discourse:

1 to constitute as representations all the various sorts of traces – those found in discourse, iconography, or statistics, among others – that point to the practices that make up all historical objectivation;
2 to establish a hypothetical relation between the various series of representations (constructed and used *as* representations) and the practices that are their external referent.

A number of consequences ensue. The first concerns the treatment of discourse, which constitutes the most massive (though not the only) body of historical materials. No document can be treated without being subjected to Foucault's critical and 'genealogical' questions on the conditions that made it possible and produced it and on its regularizing principles and its forms of exclusion, limitation and appropriation.[30] We need to place at the centre of documentary criticism – the most durable and the least contested characteristic of history – the set of questions and the requirements inherent in Foucault's proposal for the analysis of discourse as it applies to 'the effective work of historians' with the ultimate aim of ascertaining the constraints and the modes that govern the discursive practices of representation.

There are other consequences, however. When we conceive of the task of historiography as treating the relationship between representations and practices – and when we extend the same set of questions to other types of representation available to historians – we are stating that in principle all such relations are merely conjectural. It is illusory to think that we can contrast the certitudes of philological knowledge (restoring the 'true' or the 'real' on the basis of correct documentary criticism) and the incertitudes of hypothetical or arbitrary reconstructions based on indices. The pertinent question is what criteria permit us to hold possible the relationship that historical writing institutes between the representing trace and the practice represented (to parody the vocabulary of Port-Royal).[31] Carlo Ginzburg asserts that this relationship can be considered acceptable if it is plausible, coherent and explicative. It is evident that these terms are not easily founded or defined, the notion of 'explication' in particular. Nonetheless, they indicate points at which historical statements can be checked. The 'objectivity' of a historical statement can be tested when it is defined, as Maurice Mandelbaum said, as 'excluding the possibility that its denial can also be true' and[32] its possibility when compatibility with statements concurrently or previously made can be ascertained. Writing history subject to such categories (allowing for an irreducible margin of uncertainty and renouncing the very notion of proof) might seem a disappointingly far cry from the aim of truth that founded the discipline. There is no other way, however, barring the absolute relativism of a history indistinguishable from fiction or the illusory certitude of a history defined as a positive science, which surely no one would wish.

HISTORY AND PHILOSOPHY

For a historian, reflection on the relationship between the two disciplines requires first an answer to a purely utilitarian question relating to practice: how can philosophical thought permit us to better elaborate the problems that harass all concrete, empirical historical work today? Epistemological interrogation concerning history has perhaps long suffered from being little more than a generally normative discourse stating what history should or should not be or an explanation of how history should treat documents (or thought that it did treat them). This led to the elimination of questions essential to the discipline of history, questions on the delimitation of its objects, on its narrative forms and on its criteria of validation. To conceptualize problems such as these supposes an obligatory and profitable companionship with philosophy, since philosophy necessarily inserts methodological debate on whether historical techniques are licit or pertinent into a broader epistemological investigation of relations between the discourse produced by such operations and the referent that it claims to reconstruct. The task doubtless supposes that postures traditionally characteristic of both disciplines be abandoned – on one side, the contempt for the empirical that philosophy identified with history; on the other, the ostentation of a very real 'reality' that history considered reachable by documents and as readable as an open book (or an open archive).

It is not easy to undermine such certitudes. On occasion openly defended, more often they are spontaneously accepted as self-evident. The first step is to draw up a comparative history of their founding, thus of the establishment of disciplinary identity. The next step will be to construct the questions of philosophy in historical terms, starting with the question of its own history, and to elaborate in philosophical terms the difficulties of the practice of history.

NOTES

This text was written for the colloquy, 'Histoire et Philosophie' organized at the Centre Georges Pompidou in Paris in 1986. It has been published under the title, 'L'histoire a le récit veridique' in *et philosophie Histoire* (Centre Georges Pompidou, Paris, 1987) pp. 115–135. It owes much to the philosophical acuity of my wife, Anne-Marie.

1   Lucien Febvre, 'Leur Histoire et la nôtre,' *Annales d'histoire économique et sociales*, 8 (1938), reprinted in his *Combats pour l'histoire* (Paris: A. Colin, 1953), pp. 276–83; *idem*, 'Etienne Gilson et la philosophie au XIVe siècle', *Annales ESC*, 1 (1946), reprinted in Febvre, *Combats pour l'histoire*, pp. 284–8.

2   These formulas appear in the foreword to Martial Guéroult, *Descartes selon l'ordre des raisons* (Aubier-Montaigne, Paris, 1968), vol. 1: *L'Âme et Dieu*, p. 10 [*Descartes' Philosophy Interpreted According to the Order of Reasons*, tr. Roger Ariew, with the assistance of Robert Ariew and Alan Donagan (University of Minnesota Press, Minneapolis, 1984), vol. 1: *The Soul and God*, p. xviii].

3 Martial Guéroult, *Dianoématique*, (Aubier-Montaigne, Paris, 1979), bk II: *Philosophie de l'histoire de la philosophie*, p. 49. This work was written between 1933 and 1938, therefore before Guéroult's major works on Leibniz, Malebranche, Descartes and Spinoza.

4 Ibid., p. 46.

5 Pierre Bourdieu, 'Les Sciences sociales et la philosophie', *Actes de la Recherche en Sciences Sociales*, 47–8 (1983): 45–52.

6 Jon Elster, *Leibniz et la formation de l'esprit capitaliste* (Aubier-Montaigne, Paris, 1975), p. 16.

7 Georg Wilhelm Friedrich Hegel, *Lectures on the Philosophy of World History, Introduction, Reason in History*, tr. H. B. Nisbet (Cambridge University Press, Cambridge, London, New York and Melbourne, 1975), p. 65. [The insertion from the German is by Roger Chartier.]

8 Michel Foucault, *L'Ordre du discours* (Paris: Gallimard, 1970), pp. 58–9 ['The Discourse on Language', tr. Rupert Swyer, in *The Archaeology of Knowledge and the Discourse on Language*, tr. A. M. Sheridan Smith (Pantheon Books, New York, 1972), p. 230]. [The part of the extract in square brackets has been taken directly from the French edition.]

9 Foucault, 'Réponse au Cercle d'Epistémologie', *Cahiers pour l'analyse*, 9 (Editions du Seuil, Paris, 1968), pp. 9–40, p. 11.

10 Hegel, *Reason in History*, p. 102.

11 Paul Ricoeur, *Temps et récit*, (Paris: Editions du Seuil, 1985), vol. 3: *Le Temps raconte*, p. 297. The title of this section has been borrowed from this work.

12 Paul Veyne, *Comment on écrit l'histoire* (Editions du Seuil, Paris, 1971; rev. edn 1978), p. 87 [*Writing History: Essay on Epistemology*, tr. Mina Moore-Rinvolucri (Wesleyan University Press, Middletown, CT., 1984), p. 128].

13 Paul Veyne, 'Foucault révolutionne l'histoire', published in appendix to the rev. edn of *Comment on écrit l'histoire*, p. 217.

14 Ibid., pp. 231–2.

15 Michel Foucault 'La Poussière et le nuage', in *L'impossible Prison. Recherches sur le système pénitentiaire au XIXe siècle, réunies par Michelle Perrot. Débat avec Michel Foucault* (Editions du Seuil, Paris, 1980), pp. 29–39, 34–5.

16 Lawrence Stone, 'The Revival of Narrative. Reflections on a New Old History', *Past and Present*, 85 (1979), pp. 3–24. For responses to Stone, see Eric Hobsbawm, 'The Revival of Narrative. Some Comments', *Past and Present*, 86 (1980), pp. 3–8.

17 Stone, 'The Revival', p. 3.

18 Ricoeur, *Temps et récit*, (Editions du Seuil, Paris, 1985), vol. 1: [*Time and Narrative*, tr. Kathleen McLaughlin and David Pellauer (University of Chicago Press, Chicago and London, 1984)], in particular the chapter on 'Historical Intentionality', vol. 1, pp. 175–225, p. 182.

19 See Paul Ricoeur's interpretation of Braudel's *La Méditerranée*, where the very notion of the extremely long time-span (*la longue durée*) is

shown to derive from the event as it is constructed by narrative configurations (*Temps et récit*, vol. 1, pp. 289–304; McLaughlin and Pellauer tr., vol. 1, pp. 208–17).

20 Veyne, *Writing History*, p. 87.

21 Carlo Ginzburg, 'Spie. Radici di un paradigma indiziario', in Aldo Gargani, (ed.) *Crisi della ragione. Nuovi modelli nel rapporto tra sapere e attività umane* (Einaudi, Turin, 1979), pp. 56–106, tr. into French as 'Signes, traces, pistes. Racines d'un paradigme de l'indice', *Le Débat*, 17 (1981), pp. 133–6.

22 Carlo Ginzburg and Carlo Poni, 'Il nome e il come; scambio ineguale e mercato storiografico', *Quaderni Storici*, 40 (1979), pp. 181–90.

23 Hayden White, *Metahistory: The Historical Imagination in Nineteenth-Century Europe* (Johns Hopkins Press, Baltimore, 1973), introduction, 'The Poetics of History', pp. 1–42; *idem*, *Tropics of Discourse: Essays in Cultural Criticism* (Johns Hopkins Press, Baltimore, 1978).

24 Carlo Ginzburg, 'Prove e possibilità', in postface to the Italian tr. of Natalie Zemon Davis, *The Return of Martin Guerre* (Harvard University Press, Cambridge, MA., 1985), *Il ritorno di Martin Guerre. Un caso di doppia identità nella Francia del Cinquecento* (Einaudi, Turin, 1984), pp. 131–54, p. 149.

25 Krzysztof Pomian, 'Le Passé: De la foi à la connaissance', *Le Débat*, 24 (1983), pp. 151–68, p. 167.

26 See the position of Arnaldo Momigliano, 'L'Histoire à l'âge des idéologies', *Le Débat*, 23 (1983), pp. 129–46; *idem*, 'La retorica della storia e la storia della retorica: sui tropi di Hayden White', in his *Sui fondamenti della storia antica* (Einaudi, Turin, 1984), pp. 456–76. Momigliano indicates here that what distinguishes 'historical writing from all other types of literature is the fact that it is subjected to be checked by the facts' (p. 466) – that is, it is subjected to the obligatory disciplines of criticism and the interpretation of the documents.

27 Ginzburg, 'Signes, traces, pistes', p. 19.

28 The notion is from Edoardo Grendi, 'Micro-analisi e storia sociale', *Quaderni Storici*, 35 (1977), pp. 506–50.

29 See the debate centring on two books that proclaim themselves 'microhistory' and supporters of the paradigm of the index. On Carlo Ginzburg, *Indagini su Piero, Il Battesimo, il ciclo di Arezzo, la Flagellazione di Urbino* (Einaudi, Turin, 1981) [*The Enigma of Piero: Piero della Francesca: The Baptism, The Arezzo Cycle, the Flagellation*, tr. Martin Ryle and Kate Soper (Verso, London, 1985)], see the dossier 'Storia e storia dell'Arte: per uno statuto della prova indiziaria', *Quaderni Storici*, 50 (1982), pp. 692–727, with a criticism by Antonio Pinelli and a response by Ginzburg. On Pietro Redondi, *Galileo eretico* (Einaudi, Turin, 1985), see the article by Vincenzo Ferrone and Massimo Firpo, 'Galileo tra Inquisitori e microstorici', *Rivista Storica Italiana*, 1 (1985), pp. 177–238 ['Galileo: From Inquisitors to Microhistorians: A Critique of Pietro Redondi's Galileo eretico', *Journal of Modern History*, 58 (1986), pp. 485–524]; the response of Pietro Redondi,

'Galileo eretico: anatema', *Rivista Storica Italiana*, 3 (1985), pp. 934–56.

30 Foucault, *L'Ordre du discours*, pp. 62–72 (Swyer tr., pp. 230–7).

31 For one example of consideration of such criteria, see the discussion of Robert Darnton, *The Great Cat Massacre and Other Episodes in French Cultural History* (New York, Basic Books, 1984) in ch. 4 below and in Philip Benedict and Giovanni Levi, 'Robert Darton e il massacro dei gatti', *Quaderni Storici*, 58 (1985), pp. 257–77.

32 Maurice H. Mandelbaum, *The Anatomy of Historical Knowledge* (Johns Hopkins University Press, Baltimore and London, 1977), p. 150, cited in Ricoeur, *Temps et récit*, vol. 1, p. 248 (McLaughlin and Pellauer tr., vol. 1, p. 176).

3

SOCIAL FIGURATION AND HABITUS
Reading Elias

It might seem paradoxical to propose a historical reading of Norbert Elias's *The Court Society*, a work that opens with a sweeping criticism of historical procedure. In the introduction to his book Elias contrasts, point by point, sociology as he conceives and practises it, a discipline that produces certain, rigorous and cumulative knowledge, and history, which wanders among the dead-ends of relativism. For Elias, the historical approach to phenomena betrays three basic weaknesses: it generally supposes that the events it studies are unique; it postulates that individual liberty is the foundation of all individual decisions and actions; it credits the major evolutions of an epoch to the free intentions and the voluntary acts of those who hold power and authority. History, in this view, may think that it produces knowledge, but in fact it reproduces the ideology of the societies that it studies, which saw as central the will of a ruler which everything must obey and to which everyone must submit. Even when it is supported by inventiveness in handling documents and the demanding techniques of scholarship, such history can produce only an arbitrary knowledge made up of a succession of contradictory judgements that without exception reflect the interests and prejudgements of the historians who express them.

This is the procedure that Elias opposes to his own programme, which he calls sociology. It differs from history in ways that have nothing to do with the chronology of the phenomena considered. Sociology does not consist – or does not uniquely consist – in the study of contemporary societies, but must account for long-term (even very long-term) evolutions that allow us, by connection or contrast, to understand present-day reality. The object of this sociology is fully historical, in the sense that it is or can be situated in the past, but its procedures are not the historian's since it is not interested in individuals (supposed to be free and unique) but in positions that exist independently of individuals and of the rules of dependence that govern the exercise of their liberty. The basic principle of sociological analysis and its first point of difference with the historical approach, according to Elias, is that it studies not a particular king but the function of king; not the action of a ruler but the web of constraints within which that action operated.

Obviously, the traits that Norbert Elias attributes to history, which he considers one sole unvarying approach, are not those that the historians of the last twenty or thirty years would pick to characterize their practice. With the *Annales*, but also elsewhere, history has come a long way from the classical credos that Elias recalls and criticizes. The study of demographic and economic data in time series has shifted attention from the unique event to the repeated happening, from the exceptional political or military act to the cyclical rhythms of conjunctural movements. The analysis of societies, for its part, has offered a history of structures that is no longer that of individuals but includes comparison of group positions, a study of the mechanisms that assure social mobility or static continuity, and an analysis of the functioning of group dynamics that individuals in society could not perceive and on which their voluntary action had little effect. The evolution of new sets of problems in historical study has been something like an attempt to heed Elias as it studies with all possible rigour the determination of individual destinies and the phenomena that no will – not even the ruler's – could transform. Thus kings have been dethroned in historical preoccupations, and with them the illusion of the power of individual intentions.

Does this mean, though, that Elias's introductory statement has lost all pertinence and that today sociology as he practised it and history as it is practised are one and the same? This would be saying a bit too much. It would also miss the still-valid lesson in a work of an innovative vigour that has withstood the test of time. The very subject of Elias's book is an illustration of this: it can be understood as a study of the courts of the kings of France from Francis I to Louis XIV. This is an extremely classic and even somewhat archaic subject compared with historians' recent interest in the greater number, provincial societies and the lives of the people. Behind this appearance, however, Elias had completely different aims. He was not interested in understanding the court uniquely or even primarily as the site of an ostentatious collective life that was ritualized by etiquette and that existed as part of monarchical display. The object of his book is court society in both senses of the term. First, the court is to be considered as a society, as a social formation in which the relations that existed between social subjects are defined specifically and in which the many and reciprocal ties of dependence between individuals engendered original codes and patterns of behaviour. And second, court society is to be understood in the sense of a society the organization of which is based on the existence of a court (royal or princely). The court society thus constitutes one particular form of society, to be treated on a par with other great social forms such as feudal society or industrial society. The court plays the central role in this society because it organizes all social relationships, as do ties of vassalage in feudal society or industrial production in industrialized societies. Elias's aim is thus to understand society of the *ancien régime* on the basis of the social form that best qualifies it, the court.

Thus his subject is not the court, but the court society: not any particular court society, one must also add, even if his analysis is based on the example of the French court, which under Louis XIV offered the most thoroughly worked out form of court under the *ancien régime*. For Elias, this case-study permits us to reach the essential, which is the clarification of the conditions that make possible the emergence and perpetuate the existence of a social form of the sort. This explains the two-pronged research strategy of the work. On the one hand, it is a historical consideration of a specific situation, and by that token, a way of testing empirical and factual materials and a body of hypotheses and concepts. 'Sociological theories which are not borne out by empirical work are useless,' Elias states,[1] thus distancing himself from a brand of sociology more tempted by the construction of taxonomies of universal validity than by 'intensive analysis' of specific historical cases. In opposition to Weber's typology of forms of power subsuming all possible concrete situations, he offered a procedure that established the laws for the functioning of social forms on the basis of detailed examination of one instance of their realization in history.

In order to do this, however, a policy of comparison was an absolute requisite. Comparison was to be understood on three levels. The first allows us to define the different ways the same social form functions within comparable and contemporary societies. Thus on several occasions Elias contrasts court society in *ancien régime* France with situations in England, where the royal court was not the only centre of social authority, or in Prussia, where the use of the nobles as state functionaries prohibited the blossoming of a court culture that in France was the province of an aristocracy without professional activities.[2] Princely courts were not found uniquely in Western society between the sixteenth and the eighteenth centuries, however, and Elias sketches other comparisons with more remote

lands, for example, with the role played by the courts in Asiatic
societies. What is important here is to show the identical effects of
the same social form within societies remote from one another in
both time and space. The 'courtization of warriors' (the transformation of a military aristocracy into a court nobility) was one such
phenomenon that was engendered everywhere by the existence of
princely courts, and it seems to lie everywhere at the origin of the
'process of civilization' by which Elias means the pacification of
behaviour and the control of emotions.[3] Third, comparison for
Elias also meant highlighting contrasts in social forms and functions.
Thus bourgeois society of the nineteenth and twentieth centuries
serves as a counterpoint to court society, differing in its economic
ethic, the professional activities of its members and the constitution
of a private sphere separate from social existence.[4] Dichotomies that
we now take as self-evident (for example, between public life and
private life) and patterns of behaviour considered as the only
rational choices (for example, adjusting family expenses to available
revenues) can in this way be stripped of their putative universality
and brought back to the status of temporally circumscribed forms
produced by a new social equilibrium that was not that of court
societies.

THE COURT SOCIETY IN ITS TIME

It was thus both in order to justify the study from a sociological
viewpoint of a phenomenon ordinarily considered to be historical
and, he adds, at the request of the editors of the collection in which it
was first published in 1969, that Norbert Elias wrote the preface to
his book.[5] This date is misleading, however. *The Court Society* is a
work that Elias carried with him, thought through and for the most
part finished some years before, when he was Karl Mannheim's
assistant at the University of Frankfurt, a position that he occupied
from 1930 on. The work was his *Habilitationschrift*, a thesis that he
never defended, since when the National Socialists took power he
left for exile, first in Paris and then in London.[6] The book remained
unpublished until thirty-three years after it was written, when it
appeared with the addition of the preface.

Although commentators often forget it, the date of this work – the
beginning of the 1930s – is of great importance for its understanding.
First, it explains the referential base of the work, perceptible through
the authors discussed and the works used and cited. References in
The Court Society are of three different levels. There are, first, French

texts of the sixteenth, seventeenth and eighteenth centuries, which make up the documentary materials analysed. Saint-Simon is cited some twenty times, in both French and in German translation; the articles and plates devoted to hierarchy in the structure of dwellings in the *Encyclopédie* and the works of Charles Antoine Jombert and Jacques-François Blondel provide the material for the chapter 'The Structure of Dwellings as an Indicator of Social Structure' (in German, 'Wohnstrukturen als Anzeiger gesellschaftlicher Strukturen'); La Bruyère and Marmontel for the article 'Grands' in the *Encyclopédie*; Gratian in the French translation of Amelot de la Houssaie, Brantôme, *L'Astrée*; and the poets of the Renaissance are studied in the chapter entitled 'On the Sociogenesis of Aristocratic Romanticism in the Process of Courtization'.

The second group of references includes the classic authors of French historiography of the nineteenth and the first third of the twentieth centuries. Elias draws his information from the great syntheses of French national history, from scholarly working tools and from studies in social history. Taine's *L'Ancien régime* in his *Origines de la France contemporaine* and the volumes of Lavisse (in collaboration with Lemonnier and Mariéjol with Lavisse writing on the reign of Louis XIV) belong to the first category; Marion's *Dictionnaire des institutions*, published in 1923, to the second; Avenel's *Histoire de la fortune française* (1927), Sée's *La France économique et sociale au XVIIIe siècle*, translated in German in 1930 under the title *Französische Wirtschaftsgeschichte*, Normand's *La Bourgeoisie française au XVIIe siècle* and De Vaissière's *Gentilshommes compagnards de l'ancienne France* on country gentry, to the third. A few German historical works complete this bibliography, Ranke's *Französische Geschichte* being by far the most often cited. Elias borrows only partial bits and pieces of analysis from these historical works, all of which were published before 1930.[7] Above all, Elias uses such works as convenient collections of ancient texts that permit him to complete his first-hand readings.

In order to organize the historical data that he collected in his reading, Elias constructed a model of sociological interpretation that he intended as distinct from the dominant models in German sociology in the early thirties. We can see who were his favorite interlocutors in his references. The most frequently cited is, obviously, Max Weber. His book, *Wirschaft und Gesellschaft*, published in Tübingen in 1922, is cited on four occasions, and Elias discusses or offers nuances to several of its central theses, the theory of ideal types, the opposition between modes of rationality and the typology of the forms of domination that distinguish between and contrast patrimonial and charismatic domination.[8] Elias also cites Werner Sombart (in both positive and negative connections), borrowing his intuition of the political and cultural importance of princely courts but suggesting that his interpretation of their make-up was fragmentary.[9] He also cites Thorstein Veblen, whose 1899 *Theory of the Leisure Class* seems to him to miss its target in gauging the economic ethic of the aristocracy by the standards of bourgeois society.[10] Weber, Sombart, Veblen: these are Elias's sociological references in 1933, or at least those who seemed to him to count and to merit discussion. There are also allusions to Marx, whose manner of identifying historical discontinuities in terms of the passage from the quantitative to the qualitative Elias found dubious and Hegelian.[11]

In its writing, in its references and for the information it contains, *The Court Society* is thus an older book that was cast in nearly definitive form in 1933. This has a certain importance for understanding that in the intellectual universe in which it was conceived, which was still that of the nineteenth century, Weber dominated sociology and history. Although the work was not published until 1969, *The Court Society* was thus an earlier work than Elias's major work, *Über den Prozess der Zivilisation*, published in Basel in 1939.[12] Thus *The Court Society* should be taken as a first formulation of the concepts and the theses that Elias would develop on a broader scale in the two volumes of 1939. In contrast, a full understanding of the book supposes an awareness of the entire set of interconnected problems that gave it meaning and that put the court at the centre of both the constitution of the absolute state and the process of civilization that radically transformed the psychic economy of Western people between the twelfth and the eighteenth centuries. To read Elias's books properly, they must be read in connection with and in the context of the ages in which they were conceived and written, Weimar Republic Germany for *The Court Society* and exile for *The Civilizing Process*. It also supposes restoring the chronology of their translations, which took place late and out of order. The two works published under separate titles in French and in English (and under varying titles in English) are in fact inseparable parts of one work, *Über den Prozess der Zivilisation*.[13] *The Court Society* was, as we have seen, written earlier and published later than the two volumes of *Process of Civilization*.[14]

The Court Society is not only part of its age intellectually through its references. It is in fact difficult to read the pages in which Elias contrasts the domination of the absolute ruler and the rule of the charismatic leader without having it cross one's mind that they were written at the precise moment that one such leader was close at hand

and about to seize power. The characterization of the 'charismatic central group' as a possible place for social promotion, its definition as a group necessarily unified around a common objective (taking over power), the insistence on the importance of the authority and individual initiation of the leader, who has no apparatus of domination at his disposal outside his own group, can all well apply to National Socialism at its rise. Just as the court of Louis XIV was a privileged place in which to recognize general properties of court societies, it seems that Elias implicitly identified in Hitler's party the general characteristics of the domination of any charismatic leader observed 'during his rise to power' – which was, alas, the situation of Germany in the early thirties. [15] In an appendix written after reading an article that the historian Hans Mommsen published in *Der Spiegel* in March 1967, Elias returned – explicitly this time – to the National Socialist dictatorship. Writing under the title, 'On the Notion that there Can Be a State Without Structural Conflicts', [16] he asserts that the competitiveness and tensions existing in the Hitlerian state constituted a mechanism necessary to the perpetuation of dictatorial power and not, as historians often think, a sign of its incoherence or an index of its failure. On coming to power, the charismatic leader must both maintain an ideal ideological unity, cemented during the phase of his rise and transferred from the group of his loyal supporters to the nation as a whole and make use of existing rivalries in the inner circle governing the state. What was important, then, was to distinguish clearly the unifying ideology of dictatorship and a social reality that necessarily perpetuates conflicts among those who exercise that ideology.

FIGURATION, INTERDEPENDENCE AND BALANCE OF TENSIONS

Situating Elias's work within its era does nothing to blunt its innovative impact, which is, quite to the contrary, still intact today. It resides chiefly in the fundamental concepts that guide his analysis, and which he lists. These are notions 'that may seem unfamiliar' of figuration (*Figuration*), interdependence (*Interdependenz*), balance of tensions (*Spannungsgleichgewicht* or *Spannungsbalance*), social evolution (*Gesellschaftsentwicklung*) or the evolution of a figuration (*Figurationsentwicklung*). [17] Manipulation of these intellectual tools permits the definition of the object of sociology: 'How and why people are bound together to form specific dynamic figurations is one of the central questions, perhaps even *the* central question, of sociology'. [18] In *What is Sociology?*, published in 1970, hence contemporary with the new edition of *The Court Society* and the important preface for the republication of *The Civilizing Process*, Elias defines the object of sociological study as the 'webs of interdependence or figurations of many kinds' that people make up. [19]

The most important concept is *Figuration*, translated into French as *formation* (in the translation of *The Court Society*) or by *configuration* (as in the 1981 translation of *What is Sociology?*) and in English as 'figuration' or 'configuration'. Elias elaborates on its meaning in *What is Sociology?*[20] A *Figuration* is a social form of extremely variable extent (made up of a group playing cards together, the patrons of a cafe, a school class, a village, a city, a nation) in which the individuals involved are linked by a specific mode of reciprocal dependence and the reproduction of which supposes a mobile balance of tensions. As is evident, the notions of formation, interdependence and balance of tensions are closely linked, which enables Elias to shift several classic oppositions inherited from philosophic or sociological tradition, the contrast between liberty and determinism first among them. Elias refuses to operate on metaphysical grounds, where the only choice is between an affirmation of the absolute liberty of the human species or its total determination, according to the model of physical causality erroneously transferred to the historical plane. He prefers instead to think of the 'freedom' of each individual as part of a chain of interdependences linking people to one another and limiting individual possibilities of decision or action. Against the idealist categories of the individual *per se* (*Individuum an sich*) or the absolute person (*reine Person*) and against an atomistic representation of societies which considers them merely as aggregates of isolated subjects and the sum of instances of personal behaviour, Elias poses as central the networks of reciprocal dependence that make each individual action depend upon an entire series of other actions and, in turn, that modify the overall picture of social interplay. The image that best illustrates this permanent process of interlinked relations is that of the chess-board:

> As in a game of chess, each relatively independent act by an individual represents a move on the social chess-board which produces a counter-move by another individual – or frequently, in reality, by many other individuals – which limits the independence of the first and demonstrates his dependence. [21]

For Elias, the specificity of each social formation or configuration is defined by the variable modes of each of the chains of interdependence, which can be longer or shorter, complex or simple, constraining or loose. This is true whether the social formation occurs on the macroscopic scale of historical evolutions (such as court society or feudal society) or on the much smaller scale of the various formations, great and small, to be found within a society. This makes it possible to go beyond the opposition between a human being considered as a free individual and a singular subject and one considered as a social being integrated into multiple solidarities and communities. It also allows a way of thinking of intersubjective relations that avoids psychological categories (which suppose such relations invariable and consubstantial with human nature) and that see them in their historically variable modalities as directly dependent on the demands inherent in individual social formations. Finally, it also abolishes the distinction that ordinarily designates as 'concrete' or 'real' only flesh-and-blood human beings and treats the social forms that bind them to one another as abstractions. This is to Elias an unacceptable distinction. To illustrate his point he cites the example of a game of cards: the game has no existence of its own outside the players involved in it, but by that token, the individual behaviour of each player is governed by rules of interdependence implied in the specific 'formation' or 'figuration' of the game of cards. This enables him to conclude:

> The 'game' is no more an abstraction than the 'players'. The same applies to the figuration formed by the four players sitting around the table. If the term 'concrete' means anything at all, we can say that the figuration formed by the players is as concrete as the players themselves. By figuration we mean the changing pattern created by the players as a whole – not only by their intellects but by their whole selves, the totality of their dealings in their relationships with each other.[22]

Elias offers a counter to the impoverishing conception of the 'real' often encountered among historians, who take into account only the concrete existence of documentable individuals. His different manner of thinking held as equally real the relations (obviously invisible) that put these individual lives into association and thus determine the nature of the social formation into which they are set.

In all figurations the ties of interdependence existing between subjects or groups are distributed in series of unstable, mobile and balanced antagonisms that are the very condition of the continuing existence of the figuration. According to Elias, this is a universal and structural property of all social figurations, even if, to be sure, the balance of tensions has a specific purpose in each one:

> At the core of changing figurations – indeed the very hub of the figuration process – is a fluctuating, tensile equilibrium, a balance of

power moving to and fro, inclining first to one side and then to the other. This kind of fluctuating balance of power is a structural characteristic of the flow of every figuration.[23]

This is why the terms of this equilibrium must be defined, in court society in seventeenth-century France as well as in the dictatorial state of National Socialism. When the equilibrium of tensions that permitted the perpetuation of a social figuration is broken (when one of the adversaries or partners becomes too powerful, when a new group refuses to be excluded from power), it is the figuration itself that is jeopardized and eventually replaced by another, which rests on a new equilibrium of forces and on a new figuration of interdependence. A rupture of the first type refashioned all of social organization when the kings of France conquered pre-eminence and became absolute sovereigns, at the expense of their feudal rivals, producing court society. In turn (in France at least), pressure from social strata excluded from positions of domination by a balance of tensions that had become fixed in an antiquated form produced the Revolution, which installed the new configuration of bourgeois society.

The sociologist's task is thus primarily to identify and comprehend the different social figurations that have followed one another throughout the centuries. It is this task that Elias designates as 'the analysis of figurations'. The referential framework of this task is the distinction among three modes and rhythms of evolution in human societies: biological evolution (*biologische Evolution*), social evolution (*gesellschaftliche Evolution*) and evolution experienced on the scale of the history of the individual (*Geschichte* for Elias). The chronology proper to sociological analysis is that of social evolution, which is characterized by the linking of successive and temporary formations that are compared to the stability of the biological organization of the human species but that seem immutable when judged by individual existences. This distinction of three 'currents of evolution' is not intended to constitute an operative concept of historical temporality. Above all, it aims at defining two fundamental and structural properties of social figurations. First, the positions and relations that make social figurations specific exist independently of individuals who, one after the other, occupy those positions and find themselves within those relations. And second, contrary to animal societies, human societies are transformed without obligatory modification of the biological constitution of the individuals in them, which poses with particular force the problem of the very reasons for the appearance of a social figuration or its disappearance in favour of another.

Elias is not interested in a historian's articulation of the three time-spans that he identifies within a synchronic analysis. Rather, his purpose is to situate the duration and the rhythms appropriate to the evolution of social figurations, neither of which is perceptible by the subjects of any given formation. Their society seems to them an immobile and immutable system, all the more so as their existential scale of change is powerless to measure (save perhaps in times of crisis) modifications in social equilibrium.

Only these modifications – not the voluntary action of individuals, even individuals of absolute power – can account for the continued reproduction or the disappearance of figurations, however. The correct envisaging of the mechanisms that explain the evolution of social figurations thus implies a conceptual rigour that must be translated into lexical terms. This is why Elias rejects an entire series of notions that seem to him to obliterate what is essential, which is to clarify the conflictual interdependence and the tensions in equilibrium that characterize every social figuration in its unique way. The traditional vocabulary of intellectual history – for example, Burckhardt's notion of *Zeitgeist* – the newer lexicon of social history, which uses terms such as 'social conditions', the vocabulary of the sociology of behaviour that uses 'action' or 'interaction' all seem to him equally inadequate. Some of these supposed a dissociation between individuals and society as if the latter were a 'milieu', an 'environment' that existed in itself and was not made up by the network of the positions occupied by the individuals in it. Others implicitly made social evolution dependent on the voluntary action of one or more individuals, whereas such evolutions were the result of an equilibrium among the various groups in society that was installed, perpetuated, or broken by the very fact of the obligatory and multiple interdependences that linked them together. In fashioning a certain number of new, rigorously defined concepts, Elias proposed a new way of apprehending both social forms on all scales and the historical evolutions that created or destroyed these successive configurations.

THE ABSOLUTE STATE AND THE COURT

The figuration of court society is indissolubly linked to the construction of the absolutist state. In such a state, the sovereign has a double monopoly: a fiscal monopoly that centralizes tax-gathering and gives the ruler the possibility of rewarding his faithful supporters and servants in coin rather than in land, and a monopoly of legitimate violence that attributes military force to him alone and thus makes him master and guarantor of the pacification of the entire social area. This fiscal and military monopoly, which dispossessed the aristocracy of the traditional foundations of its power and obliged its members to live near the sovereign, dispenser of *rentes* (annuities), pensions and gratifications, was the result of a dual process that Elias studies in detail in *Power and Civility*, the second volume of *The Civilizing Process*.

First, the affirmation of the power of the absolute sovereign marked the outcome of a competition of many centuries' duration, opposing, in the same area, several units of domination. The hegemony of the most powerful of these implied, in reality, the progressive elimination of all its potential rivals and their reduction to a status of dependants. Elias formulates the law governing this evolution as a mechanism of monopolization (*Mechanismus der Monopolbildung*) on the basis of observation of economic changes in the twentieth century:

> If, in a major social unit a large number of the smaller social units which, through their interdependence, constitute the larger one, are of roughly equal social power and are thus able to compete freely – unhampered by pre-existing monopolies – for the means to social power, i.e. primarily the means of subsistence and production, the probability is high that some will be victorious and others vanquished, and that gradually, as a result, fewer and fewer will control more and more opportunities, and more and more units will be eliminated from the competition, becoming directly or indirectly dependent on an ever-decreasing number.[24]

Elias applies this law to political units struggling for hegemony where territorial conditions have given the process of monopolization its 'purest' form – in France between the eleventh and the sixteenth centuries. Free competition here gradually reduced the number of claimants to power. In the beginning of the fourteenth century, they were only five: the kings of France and of England, the dukes of Burgundy and of Brittany, and the count of Flanders. When the Capetians and then the Valois had firmly established their power, this first rivalry was paralleled by another rivalry within the ruling house (between the king and his kin) that was strengthened by the dismemberment of the royal domain into *terres apanagées* (endowed lands). In the early sixteenth century, after the elimination of his English rival and the defeat of rivals among his own kin, the king of France finally established his territorial and political domination.

As it puts down its rivals, external and internal, the unit of domination (become hegemonic) changes internally. The central lord

(*Zentralherr*) – king, prince, autocrat, or by any other title – takes over personal control of the monopoly of domination. A confiscation of power of the sort does not depend, either uniquely or basically, on his own political will, but rather on the equilibrium instituted among the most powerful social groups in the state:

> The hour of the strong central authority within a highly differentiated society strikes when the ambivalence of interests of the most important functional groups grows so large, and power is distributed so evenly between them, that there can be neither a decisive compromise nor a decisive conflict between them.[25]

The equilibrium of tension between the aristocracy and the robe – between the traditional *noblesse d'épée* and the holders of offices – was such that it created the most favourable condition for the construction of absolute power. The two dominant groups were sufficiently interdependent and had enough solidarity not to jeopardize the social figuration that assured their domination, but they were at the same time sufficiently in competition to make their alliance against the sovereign impossible. The king, weaker than the whole of society if it were to join together, was thus always stronger than each group taken separately. This assured his victory:

> A figuration with a balance of forces of this kind, in which two estates held each other more or less in an equilibrium in which neither group was able to attain permanent preponderance over the other, gave the legitimate king, who was apparently equidistant from all groups, the chance to appear as a peacemaker bringing the weary warriors the respite they all longed for.[26]

The antagonism that existed between the dominant social groups was thus, in the first place, the result of a differentiation of social functions that had reinforced the power of a bourgeoisie of office-holders and administrators that paralleled the traditional landed and military aristocracy. But this rivalry, the very condition of absolute power, could be and had to be perpetuated by the sovereign who, playing one group against the other, reproduced the 'balance of tensions' needed to create the personal form of the monopoly of domination. This meant, first, the parallel strengthening of the monarchical state and of the bourgeoisie of the robe, who took on the charges of justice and finance to counterbalance the claims of the nobility. Next, this meant that the royal will both protected and controlled the aristocracy as an indispensable counterweight to the power of the office-holders. The court became an institution essential to accomplish this end. On the one hand, it guaranteed

surveillance through proximity and thus assured the king's control
over his most dangerous potential rivals. On the other, it permitted,
through the granting of monarchical favours, the consolidation of
noble fortunes, imperilled not only by monetary depreciation but
by an economic ethic that regulated expenses according to the
demands of status, not on revenues – what Elias calls *status-
consumption ethos*. The court was thus a fundamental part of the
monarchical strategy of the ongoing reproduction of tensions:

> The tension and equilibrium between the various social groups and
> the resulting highly ambivalent attitude of all these groups to the
> central ruler himself, was certainly not created by any king. But once
> this constellation had been established, it is vitally important for the
> ruler to preserve it in all its precariousness. [27]

By preserving the aristocracy as a socially distinct group as well as
making it subject to the ruler, the court constituted the principal
mechanism that permitted the French kings to perpetuate their
personal power. Fiscal monopoly, military monopoly and court
etiquette were thus the three instruments of domination that
together defined this original social form that was court society.

An analysis of this sort elicits two comments. It emphasizes that
relations among social groups must not be understood exclusively
as class struggles. [28] Distancing himself from both the liberal
historiography of the nineteenth century and from Marxism, Elias
intended to show the ambivalence of all social relations. The rivalry
that existed between the nobility and the official class supposed their
common interest in maintaining a social configuration that assured
them positions of privilege. The monarchy's support of the bourgeoisie of the robe implied that aristocratic superiority was to be
preserved, and the proximity of the court nobility to the king, first
among 'gentlemen', relied on the submission of the Second Estate to
the absolute sovereign. Thus Elias rejected any perspective that
would make the absolutist state the simple instrument of a class designated as dominant (here, the aristocracy). The 'absolute
monarchy' was absolute precisely because the king was in no way
dependent on a given social group, but was in a position to
manipulate the balance of tensions which lay at the origin of his
power.

This manipulation of antagonistic groups not of his creation is
exactly what defines the area of the sovereign's personal action, by
which, for good or evil, he could individualize the function of king.
What Elias sketches here is a future set of interrelated problems
concerning the reciprocal influence between the inherent character-

istics of one social position or another and the specific properties of the various individuals who occupy such positions – to put it in other terms, between a post and its structural attributes, on the one hand, and the habitus and its particular dispositions. In this way, Elias treats Louis XIV's lack of charisma as a quality totally appropriate to a role that, at that moment in the evolution of the monarchy, demanded only (though necessarily) the perpetuation and regulation of existing tensions. This is why the king himself accepts the constraining rules of courtly domination instituted as a means to maintaining and signifying his absolute domination.[29]

COURT SOCIETIES AND THE CIVILIZING PROCESS

The establishment of the absolute power of the ruler, which was both the result and the beginning of a new social equilibrium, was accompanied by major changes, which Elias designates as constitutive of the civilizing process. In the West between the twelfth and the eighteenth centuries, sensibilities and behaviour were in fact profoundly modified by two fundamental facts, the state monopolization of violence, which obliged the mastering of impulses and thus pacified the social area, and the tightening of interpersonal relations, which necessarily implied more severe control on emotions and the affective sphere. The progressive differentiation of social functions, the very condition of the formation of the absolutist state, multiplied interdependence and thus elicited the mechanisms of individual self-control that are characteristic of Western societies in the modern age. Elias states the thesis that is perhaps the essence of his work thus:

As the social fabric grows more intricate, the sociogenic apparatus of individual self-control [*Selbstkontrollapparatur*] also becomes more differentiated, more all-round and more stable. . . . The particular stability of the apparatus of mental self-restraint [*Selbstzwang-Apparatur*] which emerges as a decisive trait built into the habits [*Habitus*] of every 'civilized' human being, stands in the closest relationship to the monopolization of physical force and the growing stability of the central organs of society. Only with the formation of this kind of relatively stable monopolies do societies acquire those characteristics as a result of which the individuals forming them get attuned, from infancy, to a highly regulated and differentiated pattern of self-restraint; only in conjunction with these monopolies does this kind of self-restraint require a higher degree of automaticity, does it become, as it were, 'second nature'.[30]

Thus the civilizing consisted, above all, in the individual's internalization of prohibitions that before were imposed from the outside, and in a transformation of the psychic economy that fortified the mechanisms of self-control exerted over impulses and emotions and allowed a shift from social constraint (*Gesellschaftliche Zwang*) to self-constraint (*Selbstzwang*).

In this long-term process, which concerned all individuals in Western nations (as a trend at least), court society – understood here in its sense of a specific social figuration distinct from the rest of society – constituted a central element that was both a laboratory of new sorts of behaviour and an area for the elaboration of new norms. Elias sees two essential moments in this role of courts: the seventeenth century, which in France if not elsewhere gave finished form to the monarchic court society organized for and by the absolute king, and the twelfth century, which marked a first stage in the civilizing process in the constitution of the great feudal courts. The first of these figurations is the subject-matter of *The Court Society*; the second provides material for several pages in the second volume of *The Civilizing Process*.[31] Here Elias shows how *courtoisie* designed a first set of transformations in behaviour patterns, expressed by the poetry of the *Minnesänger* and the troubadours and characterized by the respect of more constraining conventions, a better control over conduct, and less brutal relations between men and women. Within a warrior society that was still far from pacific or policed, the feudal courts, which underwent a first differentiation of the functions of government and a first tightening of interdependences, thus made islands of 'civilization' in which a new habitus found its first expression.

The definitive fashioning of this new habitus supposes another stage in social evolution and in the civilizing process – the court society of the absolutist states – and more severe requirements concerning the mastery of affect in *civilité*. Elias analyses the basis for this new social formation piece by piece. It lies in three main paradoxes. First, court society was a figuration in which the greatest social difference is manifested in the greatest spatial proximity. This occurred in the aristocratic *hôtel*, where masters and servants lived parallel and intersecting lives. It occurred in the court as well, where the king affirmed the absolute distance that separated him from his nobles while living constantly in their midst. This points to one of the fundamental and most original traits of court society, the confusion between private life and public life – or rather the absence of any such distinction in both practices and thoughts. For the king in his court as for the noble in his residence, all the acts and patterns of

behaviour that would be considered in the bourgeois social figuration as belonging to the sphere of the intimate, the secret, the
private were instead lived and manipulated as signs indicating a
social order in which public formalities showed everyone's place in
the hierarchy of conditions.

The second principle of court society follows from this: The social
being of the individual was totally identified with the representation
of that being given by that individual or by others. The 'reality'
of a social position was merely what opinion judged it to be: 'The
recognition of membership by others itself constitutes membership.'[32] This representation of rank by form had several important
implications. It founded an aristocratic economy of ostentation that
regulated expenditures by the demands of the rank that one wished
to hold; it constituted the hierarchies of etiquette as the standard of
social differences; it made of the various roles and places in the court
ceremonial the essential stakes in social competition. In this sort of
figuration, the construction of each individual's identity was always
at the intersection of that person's own self-representation and the
credit accorded or refused by others to that representation. In this
game the king carrried the most weight since, by modifying ranks in
the ceremonial, he could not only play with a balance of tensions
favourable to his own domination, but he also determined the 'real'
– that is, perceived and accepted – social position of each courtier.
Rivalry for the signs of prestige was thus at the same time a struggle
for the attributes and advantages of social power – what Elias called
Machtchancen.

The final paradoxical base of court society was that social superiority was reinforced in political and symbolic submission. It was
only by accepting the sovereign's 'domestication' and the subjection
to the constraining formalities of courtly etiquette on which he
insisted that the aristocracy could preserve the distance that
separated them from their rivals for domination, the bourgeoisie of
the higher administration offices. The logic of the court was thus a
distinction through dependence: by etiquette

> Court society represents itself, each individual being distinguished
> from every other, all together distinguishing themselves from non-
> members, so that each individual and the group as a whole confirm
> their existence as a value in itself.[33]

The king himself did not escape this logic, and it was only because
he too submitted to the etiquette that he imposed on the courtiers
that he was able to use it as an instrument of domination. This
explains the title Elias gave to one of his chapters: 'Die Verkettung

des Königs durch Etikette und Prestigechancen' ['The Bonding of Kings through Etiquette and Status Chances']. The king was himself 'chained' to the *mécanique* (the word can be found in Saint-Simon) that assured his power.

When life at court located distinction in proximity, reality in appearance and superiority in dependence, it required of those who participated in it specific psychological gifts that are not common to all, such as the art of observing others and oneself, the censorship of sentiments and the mastery of passions and the internalization of the disciplines that govern *civilité*. A transformation of this sort modified not only ways of thinking but the entire structure of personality and the psychic economy of the individual to which Elias gives an old name: the *Habitus*. The process of 'courtization' was also a remodelling of affectivity (*Affektmodellierung*) that subjected the courtier to a tight network of automatic self-controls reining in all spontaneous impulses and all immediate movements. This new psychic economy produced a unique form of rationality, which Elias calls *höfische Rationalität* and which was to regulate the exact proportion of each instance of behaviour to the relationship in which it was set and to assure that each gesture agreed with the aim it was to permit.

The new ways of feeling, experiencing and behaving also elicited what Elias designates by the term 'aristocratic romanticism', the nostalgic or Utopian valorization of a former noble life that was free, independent and natural. In the penultimate chapter of *The Court Society* he studies in detail and writes with brio of the different stages and expressions of this idealization of a chivalric and pastoral existence in which the nobility expressed its resistance to new dependences and constraints imposed by life at the court. In these pages, and in particular in his discussion of the *L'Astrée*, which he sees as an expression of acceptance of the new rules of *civilité* but also as a rejection of the court society that created them, Elias outlines a possible comparison of aesthetic forms and psychological structures. It is possible, he states, to establish correspondences between the two, but only on the condition of identifying the specific social figuration that produced the properties they hold in common. Thus it was the demands of court society that founded the relationships between classical tragedy and courtly rationality.[34] Before the age of classicism, the modes of existence of a nobility partially transformed into courtiers but still attached to chivalric values and behaviour patterns made the pastoral or sentimental novel – *L'Astrée* in this case – the expression of the social and affective frustrations of a group that had lost out to the monarchy.[35] It was the increasing urbanization and courtization of the aristocracy, separated physically and perhaps even more mentally from the countryside, that transformed the role of landscape in French painting 'from Poussin to Watteau'.[36] (Norbert Elias was fond enough of Watteau to have devoted an unpublished study to him.) In this manner, Elias discreetly proposes a historical reading of works that is aimed primarily at deciphering the traits of a specific psychological figuration in their forms, and by that token, at setting them within the social figuration that generated that psychic economy.

The Court Society is thus a book primarily devoted to a study of the genesis and the characteristics, social and psychological, of a figuration that existed in its broad traits in the Middle Ages in the great feudal courts, which gradually defined its forms in the Renaissance, and which reached its definitive nature in the seventeenth century, when a large body of men and women were stabilized in one place, courtly functions were highly differentiated and hierarchical and a specific noble culture purged of all feudal elements was constituted. The problem that Elias's work leaves aside regards the diffusion within other social strata of the models of behaviour and the psychological mechanisms worked out within court society. This is a central question if one admits that the civilizing process consists precisely in the generalization to the whole of society of the prohibitions, censures and controls once distinctive of the manner of being of men and women of the court. Envisaging this process is thus essential to Elias's overall purposes, and in the penultimate chapter of the concluding section of *The Civilizing Process* he discusses the question.[37]

Here Elias constructs a totally original interpretation of the circulation of cultural models, giving a central place to tension between distinction and divulgation. The general spread of behaviour patterns and constraints that at first were specific to court society is not to be understood as a simple diffusion that gradually reached the entire body social from the starting-point of a dominating elite. It was rather the result of a competitive struggle that led bourgeois strata to imitate aristocratic manners of being, which, in turn, obligated the court nobility to increase their demands for *civilité* in order to refurbish the value of this complex of manners and attitudes for the purposes of social discrimination. This competition for the appropriation – or, to the contrary, the perpetual confiscation – of distinction is the principal motivation of the civilizing process, since it leads to the increase of the refinements of *savoir-vivre*, to multiplying prohibitions and to raising even higher the threshold of censorship of behaviour.

The circulation of the models of comportment that reproduced cultural differences even within a process of imitation and social diffusion is to be envisaged on the same conceptual level as the shifts in the exertion of constraints of which Elias speaks at the end of *The Court Society*.[38] Here also one must take care to avoid all notions – power (*Herrschaft*) or authority (*Autorität*) – that might suppose that social constraint existed only from the higher toward the lower levels of society. Just as the attraction that court civilization held for the subordinate strata of society worked to make that very civilization more demanding, the constraints that the dominant groups exerted on the rest of the body social produced reactions to reinforce the mechanisms of self-constraint in the powerful. In characterizing each social 'figuration' or 'formation' on the basis of the specific network of interdependences that linked individuals to one another and to the group, Elias is able to comprehend the relations among the various groups in their dynamism and their reciprocity, and by that token, to avoid simplistic, one-dimensional, or static representations of social domination or cultural diffusion.

In France, the active rivalry between the court aristocracy and the official class of the bourgeoisie lasted only as long as the social formation that gave it existed. This is why Elias ends *The Court Society* with a final chapter 'Zur Sociogenese der Revolution' ['On the Sociogenesis of the French Revolution'], in which he outlines the process that led to the destruction of the absolutist court society. First, the balance among tensions that was maintained and manipulated by Louis XIV became fixed, as did the court ceremonials. When it lost all plasticity, the mechanism of domination was no longer able to integrate new social partners, but only to repeat the conflicts among the older ones – the king, the court aristocracy and the parlements. At the end of the eighteenth century, however, the social consolidation of bourgeois strata, until then excluded from a share in domination, set up a rupture between the apparent apportioning of power, taken over by the traditional elites, and the reality of the new equilibrium of forces. This made it impossible to conserve the old social figuration and equally impossible to reform it. This led in turn to the installation, by force, of a new figuration that reflected the new distribution of social positions. Elias's necessarily sketchy outline has the merit of not reducing the social process that ended in the Revolution to a simple opposition between the nobility and the bourgeoisie; in their *ancien régime* forms, the two groups felt just as much solidarity as rivalry (precisely because they were rivals). A second merit is that it does not interpret the Revolution as a simple victory of one of the dominant strata of traditional society, but as the establishment of a new social figuration, in which what had changed was not only the identity of the dominant group but the very figure of the balance of tensions among the groups and the links of inter-dependence among individuals. Thus we need to think in new terms of the last stage in the civilizing process – developed in the nineteenth and the twentieth centuries by a society marked by the universal obligation of work, a strict separation between private and public life and a hierarchy of values that gave priority to economic success.

PSYCHIC STRUCTURE AND SOCIAL STRUCTURE

In his 1939 work, Elias called for the constitution of a science that did not yet exist – 'historical psychology'. He defined its object in contrast to both the history of ideas and psychoanalytical studies, since it must be 'the whole human make-up' and 'the whole fabric of men's personality'.[39] That is, it encompasses both the conscious controls of the ego, which produces clear ideas and thoughts that are recognized as thought, and to unconscious and automatic controls of impulses. Elias reproaches the history of ideas, above all, with believing that the transformations that affect the very structures of human personality can be reduced to ideological transformations which the subjects themselves express in full awareness. This is his fundamental criticism of Burckhardt and his successors,[40] whom he accuses of unduly confusing innovations in the content of thoughts with changes in the psychological dispositions of individuals.

Elias reproaches psychoanalysis (and Freud, who is never named) with constituting something 'unconscious', conceived as an ' "id" without history'[41] as the most important element in the entire psychological structure. For him, to the contrary, there are no universal categories and no universal economy of the psyche, but only variable mechanisms, fashioned from the very start, in their definition and their articulation, by relations of interdependence characteristic of all social formations. He states in an important text in which he clarifies his disagreement with the Freudian lexicon and concepts:

Decisive for a person as he appears before us is neither the 'id' [*Es*] alone, nor the 'ego' [*Ich*] or 'super-ego' [*Überich*] alone, but always *the relationship* between these various sets of psychological functions, partly conflicting and partly co-operating in the way an individual steers himself. It is they, these relationships *within* man between the drives and affects controlled and the built-in controlling agencies, whose structure changes in the course of a civilizing process, in accordance with the changing structure of the relationships *between* individual human beings, in society at large. [42]

This led to the project that Elias defined in 1939: 'to investigate . . . the transformation of both the personality in psychic structure and the entire social structure'. [43]

Elias completed just such an enterprise in 1939 for one specific social formation, court society. He had applied the two linked approaches that gave his 1939 work its subtitle: the socio-genetic approach, which aimed at defining the mechanisms of formation and principles of structuration of one given social figuration, and the psychogenetic approach, which attempted to define the fashioning and the economy of the psychic habitus engendered by that figuration. Both cases attempted to analyse the whole of an entity, social or psychological; in both cases, a process was seized with all its unstable balances and its mobile tensions.

As is evident, behind the notion of 'historical psychology' Elias was defining an object that by far exceeded what is usually called the 'history of *mentalités*'. To be sure, history as it is practised today, in what it has acquired in the last fifty years and in its current research, has little in common with the history that Elias knew, criticized, or utilized in the early 1930s. Should we conclude that thus his books have lost their innovativeness and their gift for provocation? By no means. At a time when history has narrowed its field of study, favouring the monograph, the case-study, or 'microhistory', his works and those of certain others recall that some fundamental evolutions are comprehensible only on the very large scale, in the long term of the succession of social formations and the transformations in psychological structures. And at a time when history has fragmented its approaches and parcellized its objects, the work of Elias emphasizes the risk of this fragmentation, taking as its essential problem the ties between social forms, psychic habitus and aesthetic productions. *The Court Society*, written nearly fifty years ago, is thus a book that has much to teach us. We need to read it, like the classics, putting it into its own time, but also listening to it in the present.

NOTES

This interpretation of Elias's thought was published in preface to a new edition of *La Société de cour* (Flammarion, Paris, 1985), pp. i–xxviii, which includes translation of the author's preface, 'Sociologie et histoire' as well as of the text (first published in 1970).

1 Norbert Elias, *The Court Society*, tr. Edmund Jephcott (Basil Blackwell, Oxford, 1983), p. 22.

2 Ibid., pp. 96–8 (for England), pp. 188–90 (for Prussia).

3 Norbert Elias, *Power and Civility: The Civilizing Process, Vol. II*, tr. Edmund Jephcott (Pantheon Books, New York, 1982), pp. 225–7.

4 Elias, *Court Society*, pp. 53–4, 58–9, 114–16.

5 Norbert Elias, *Die höfische Gesellschaft. Untersuchungen zur Soziologie des Königtums und der höfischen Aristokratie mit einer Einleitung: Soziologie und Geschichtswissenschaft*, (Hermann Luchterhand Verlag, Neuwied and Berlin, 1969), Soziologische Texte, Band 54; new edns (Hermann Luchterhand, Darmstadt and Neuwied, 1975; Suhrkamp Verlag, 1983).

6 Norbert Elias, *Die höfische Gesellschaft. Untersuchungen zur Soziologie des Adels, des Königtums und des Hofes, vor allem in Frankreich des XVII ten Jahrhunderts* (Habilitationschrift en sociologie, University of Frankfurt, 1933).

7 The one exception is his mention of David Ogg, *Louis XIV* (T. Butterworth, London, 1933; and Oxford Press, London, 1951, 1967, 1969). Only two other references in the entire book are to texts published after 1930: a lecture by A. W. Southern in 1961, cited in the preface, and Wolf Lepenies, *Melancholie und Gesellschaft* (Suhrkamp, Frankfurt, 1969).

8 Elias, *Court Society*, pp. 121–2.

9 Ibid., p. 39.

10 Ibid., p. 67.

11 Ibid., p. 233.

12 *Über den Prozess der Zivilisation. Soziogenetische und psychogenetische Untersuchungen* (2 vols, Haus zum Falken, Basel, 1939). The work was republished with an important preface (Verlag Francke AG, Berne, 1969) and again (Suhrkamp Verlag, Frankfurt, 1978–9).

13 Norbert Elias, *La Civilisation des moeurs*, tr. Pierre Kamnitzer (Calmann-Levy, Paris, 1973) and *La Dynamique de l'Occident*, tr. Pierre Kamnitzer (Calmann-Levy, Paris, 1975). The English tr. was revised by Elias himself: Norbert Elias, *The Civilizing Process. Sociogenetic and Psychogenetic Investigations*, tr. Edmund Jephcott with notes and revisions by the author (Basil Blackwell, Oxford, 1978; 1982), vol. 1: *The History of Manners*; vol. 2: *State Formation and Civilization*. *La Dynamique de l'Occident* is quoted here from the edition of vol. 2 cited in note 3, *Power and Civility*.

14 Norbert Elias, *La Société de cour*, tr. Pierre Kamnitzer (Calmann-Levy, Paris, 1974); [*The Court Society*].

15 Elias, *Court Society*, pp. 123–31; 121; 122.

16 Ibid., pp. 276–83.

17 Ibid., p. 210.

18 Ibid., p. 205.

19 Norbert Elias, *Was ist Soziologie?* (Juventa Verlag, Munich, 1970) Grundfragen der Soziologie, Band 1; *Qu'est-ce que la sociologie?*, tr.

94   *Debate and Interpretations*

Yasmin Hoffman (Pandora, Paris, 1981); [*What is Sociology?*, tr. Stephen Mennell and Grace Morrissey (Columbia University Press, New York and Hutchinson, London, 1978), p. 15].

20 Elias, *What is Sociology?*, pp. 128–33.
21 Elias, *Court Society*, p. 144.
22 Elias, *What is Sociology?*, p. 130.
23 Ibid., p. 131.
24 Elias, *The Civilizing Process*, vol. 2: *State Formation and Civilization*, p. 106.
25 Elias, *Power and Civility*, p. 171
26 Elias, *Court Society*, p. 167.
27 Elias, *Power and Civility*, p. 198.
28 Elias, *Court Society*, p. 179.
29 Ibid., pp. 130–40.
30 Elias, *Power and Civility*, p. 234. [The insertions from the German are by Roger Chartier.]
31 Elias, 'On the Sociogenesis of *Minnesang* and Courtly Forms of Conduct', in *The Civilizing Process*, vol. 2, *State Formation and Civilization*, tr. Edmund Jephcott, or *Power and Civility* (from which quotations are taken here), pp. 234–5.
32 Elias, *Court Society*, p. 96.
33 Ibid., p. 103.
34 Ibid., pp. 109–12.
35 Ibid., p. 251.
36 Ibid., p. 230.
37 Elias, *Power and Civility*, pp. 229–333.
38 Elias, *Court Society*, pp. 263–6.
39 Elias, *The Civilizing Process*, vol. 2: *State Formation and Civilization*, pp. 284, 285.
40 Elias, *Court Society*, p. 244.
41 Elias, *Power and Civility*, p. 285.
42 Ibid., p. 286. [The insertions from the German are by Roger Chartier.]
43 Ibid., p. 287.

4

TEXT, SYMBOLS AND FRENCHNESS
Historical Uses of Symbolic Anthropology

Any French historian will find Robert Darnton's most recent book[1] an invitation to reflection, but – and let me make this clear from the start – that is what makes the work of such engrossing interest. An invitation to reflection, first, because it combines two purposes generally considered incompatible: understanding the radical foreignness of the behaviour and thought of people of three centuries ago and distinguishing a lasting French identity in that alien world. 'Frenchness exists', Darnton writes, discernible in peasant tales of the eighteenth century (or before), embodied in the heroes of a French national literature and present to this day in popular wisdom. How, though, is it possible to trace a continuity of this sort in texts or actions that Darnton himself qualifies as 'opaque' and likely to contain strong 'doses of cultural shock' for today's readers? This is the first question the book raises.

On another plane, the work is intended as a rigorous critique of French historiography, the history of *mentalités* in particular. Darnton offers two reproaches, both here and in other works, that a French historian is sure to find unsettling. First, he considers the very notion of *mentalités* woolly, vague and imprecise:

> Despite a spate of prolegomena and discourses on method, however, the French have not developed a coherent conception of *mentalités* as a field of study. They tend to load the term with notions of *représentations collectives* derived from Durkheim and the *outillage mental* that Lucien Febvre picked up from the psychology of his day. Whether *mentalité* will bear the load remains to be seen.[2]

Secondly, he strongly objects to the programme and the practice of the history of *mentalités* in its serial and quantitative form, defined by Pierre Chaunu as *histoire sérielle au troisième niveau* (the 'third level', after the economic and the social, being that of culture).[3] The history of *mentalités*, in this view, must be based on the collection of massive amounts of homogeneous, reiterated data treated in ways similar to the methods used for analysing economic, demographic, or sociological serial data. This leads Darnton to a diagnosis of French cultural history: 'The French attempt to measure attitudes by counting – counting masses for the dead, pictures of Purgatory, titles of books, speeches in academies, furniture in inventories, crimes in police records, invocations to the Virgin Mary in wills, and pounds of candle wax burned to patron saints in churches.' He objects to this method on two counts: first, 'cultural objects' are not of the same nature as the serialized data studied by economic history or demographic history, since they 'are not manufactured by the historian but by the people he studies. They give off meaning. They need to be read, not counted'. Secondly, culture cannot be considered as a 'level' of some social entity resembling a three-storey house because all interpersonal relationships are of a cultural nature, even those we qualify as 'economic' or 'social'. By their emphasis on counting and their 'undervaluation of the symbolic element in social intercourse' (p. 258), French historians have, in the last analysis, lost track of what is essential. Darnton's criticism is severe, but is it really pertinent to an understanding of what French cultural history in fact is? Is the programme outlined by Pierre Chaunu twelve years ago (following his reading of Michel Vovelle's thesis on Provençal wills) a fair expression of what French historians are producing today? Darnton's aim is true and he hits the bull's-eye, but what is his target worth?

Darnton's book is presented as an essay in historical anthropology – better, as an 'anthropological mode of history' – capable of going beyond the insoluble contradictions in which the history of *mentalités* '*à la française*' has come to be imprisoned. Anthropology has much to offer the historian: an approach (gaining entry into another culture by starting from a seemingly incomprehensible, 'opaque' rite, text, or act); a programme (to 'Try to see things from the native's point of view, to understand what he means, and to seek out the social dimensions of meaning' [p. 260]); and a concept of culture as a 'symbolic world' in which shared symbols, 'like the air we breathe', serve thought and action, mould classification and judgement and furnish warnings or indictments. To understand a culture, then, is above all to retrace the significations invested in the symbolic forms culture makes use of. There is only one way to do this: to go 'back and forth between texts and contexts'; to compare each specific and localized use of one symbol or another to the world of significance that lends it meaning. Such a programme is different from that of historical anthropology as it has come to be defined within the *Annales* tradition, which consists essentially in a historical treatment of anthropological objects. For Darnton, reference to anthropology has a different status, since it purportedly offers 'the historian what the study of *mentalité* has failed to provide: a coherent conception of culture'.[4] This 'coherent conception' bears a signature, however – that of Clifford Geertz, with whom for six years Darnton presented a seminar at Princeton University (from which *The Great Cat Massacre* sprang) on the topic 'History and Anthropology'. *The Great Cat Massacre* uses the concept of culture in a strictly Geertzian sense, as expressed, for example, in *The Interpretation of Cultures* as 'an historically transmitted pattern of meanings embodied in symbols, a system of inherited conceptions expressed in symbolic forms by means of which men communicate, perpetuate, and develop their knowledge about and attitudes toward life'.[5] Under what conditions can a historian legitimately make use of a definition of this sort? What attitude does it imply *vis-à-vis* texts that give access to the 'symbolic forms' that functioned in ancient societies? Is it sufficient to the founding of a new way of writing cultural history, freed from the incertitudes of a defunct history of *mentalités?* These are questions that the book encourages us to pose as clearly as possible.

Before turning to these questions, however, we need to state what the book is. It contains six essays connected by a good many echoing motifs and joined by a common principle placing any specific 'text' into the 'context' that makes its interpretation feasible. In the first essay, the text is furnished by French popular tales, as collected by folklorists between 1870 and 1914. These presumably offer a written form of versions of the same tales that were passed on orally during the seventeenth and eighteenth centuries – versions independent of and pre-dating the more 'learned' written tales of Perrault, Madame d'Aulnoy, or the comtesse de Murat. In order to understand these tales, which contain surprising amounts of crudity and cruelty, we need to relate them to the social experiences and daily practices of the world in which they circulated, the peasant society of the *ancien régime*, now fairly familiar to us through regional and general studies that have appeared in the last twenty-five years. Darnton's interpretation is that French tales communicate, in a specific and national manner, a body of learnings concerning the social world and precautions to be taken or rules to be followed to make one's way in that world. 'Frenchness exists', and in this case it consists in a moral code of guile, in a celebration of ruse, the only recourse in an unfeeling, unjust and brutal society. In this view, the way peasants construed the world is expressed in such tales in a thought not formulated in clear and distinct ideas, but arising out of the manipulation of a repertory of symbols in story form.

This is the process described in 'The Great Cat Massacre', the essay that gives the book its title and its jacket design (an engraving from William Hogarth's series on the *Stages of Cruelty*, emblazoned with the French colours). The 'text' is the story of a massacre of cats carried out by apprentice and journeyman printers on the rue Saint-Séverin in Paris in the 1730s. The episode is related by one of the massacrers, who later became first a *prote* (foreman) and then an engraver, in a manuscript entitled *Anecdotes typographiques*, bearing the date 1762. Ill-fed by their master and kept awake by neighbourhood cats, the apprentices and journeymen decide to take revenge. First they harass the master and his wife with nocturnal meowings near their bedroom window, then they carry on (at the master's request) a veritable cat-hunt including la Grise, the mistress's adored pussycat, which they smash to pieces with an iron bar. The slaughter ends in a parody of justice when some of the feline victims are condemned to be hanged after a mock trial. The scene infuriates the master, throws the mistress into despair when she realizes that la Grise is dead and sends the workers into fits of laughter. It all seems to them so comic that they are still laughing over it long after, spurred on by the talent for mimicry of one of their number, who replays the scene, acting out the master's fury and the mistress's distress.

Why all this laughter over a horrible massacre? We need to turn to the 'context' to see. Here it is of three sorts: social, involving tensions existing between master printers and journeymen in Paris; festive, borrowing from the rituals of Carnival and *compagnonnage*; and symbolic, endowing the cat with multiple significance to make it an incarnation of the Devil, a stand-in for the household, and a symbol of female sexuality. By playing on these plural meanings, the journeyman printers could attack their bourgeois master and his wife without resorting to physical violence. The mistress is cast in the role of a witch with no need to put it into words; her womanly honour is attacked without raising a hand to threaten her virtue. The metonymic aggression that directs to the cats the violence symbolically aimed at the masters (who are helpless to respond) is so clever and so well carried out that it necessarily leads to laughter – hearty and long-lasting laughter.

In his first two essays Darnton follows the model of 'thick description' to the letter. The massacre of Parisian cats is like the cockfight in Bali: it is a point of entry that gives us access to the comprehension of a culture in its entirety. It is one 'text' among others that make up this culture. It provides us with an interpretation which that culture gives of itself. Once their symbolic forms are deciphered, the folk-tales or the ritual can reveal the significances it is their task to manifest and the statements concerning society with which they have been invested. This approach, now classical, is fertile, but it nevertheless raises a question: is it legitimate to consider as 'texts' actions carried out or tales told? To be sure, the old tales can be known only through the fixed written form folklorists have given them, and the cat massacre would never have been heard of if Nicolas Contat, the author of the *Anecdotes typographiques*, had not written of it thirty years after the event took place. But can we qualify as a text both the written document (the only remaining trace of an older practice) and that practice itself? Is there not a risk here of confusing two sorts of logic, the logic of written expression and the logic that shapes what 'practical sense' produces? Metaphorical use of terms like 'text' or 'reading' is always risky, and it is even more so when the only access to the object under anthropological investigation is a *written* text. Not only does it obliterate the ways of speaking or acting that gave the tale or the rite as much significance as its literal meaning (or even more); above all, a real text with a status of its own stands between the observer and this oral or festive supposed 'text'. In this sense, the massacre of the cats is not the cockfight: in relating it and interpreting it the historian is dependent on a report that has already been made of it and a text that is already in existence, invested with its own specific ends. This text exhibits the event, but it also constitutes the event as the result of the act of writing. 'The funniest thing that ever happened in the printing shop of Jacques Vincent, according to a worker who witnessed it, was a riotous massacre of cats' (p. 75), Darnton writes at the start of his essay. The whole question, obviously, lies in the status to be given this 'according to': it may very well refer to an eyewitness, but it quite certainly refers to a text-maker.

The two initial essays are followed by four others that appear to deviate somewhat from the principles stated in Darnton's introduction. It is immediately evident that the texts on which they are based belong to another cultural level than peasant tales or a printer's yarn. They include an anonymous description of the city of Montpellier written by a local bourgeois in 1768; a series of 501 reports written between 1748 and 1753 by Joseph d'Hémery, *inspecteur de la librairie* (inspector of the book trade), on the men of letters of his time; the 'Système figuré des connaissances humaines' from the *Encyclopédie*; and letters addressed by a La Rochelle merchant, Jean Ranson, to the director of the Société Typographique of Neuchâtel, Frédéric-

Samuel Ostervald, in which Ranson places book orders and comments on his reading. In the analysis of these documents the relationship between text and context becomes somewhat hazy; at the most we might speak of intertextual comparisons, for example, between Ranson's letters on Rousseau and the thoughts of other readers of Rousseau's works, or between the branching investigations of the *Encyclopédie* and similar 'trees of knowledge' proposed earlier by Bacon or Chambers. In these four studies, the text is always taken in itself and for itself and analysed for its intentions and mechanisms. Darnton concentrates on the categories and representations that lie behind the descriptions given; on the rhetorical strategies that aim at imposing a new order (to the advantage of pre-Revolutionary burghers in the Montpellier text or of the Philosophes in d'Alembert's 'Discours préliminaire'); and on the ways in which the various authors use the written word, as they read it or produce it, to construe and construct their own existence. Can intellectual and affective forms taken in this sense really be called 'symbolic'? And can an approach that aims at reconstructing the categories and classifications at work within texts to describe or select and set up hierarchies among people and items of knowledge be called anthropological? This seems doubtful, unless we accept an extremely broad definition of symbolic forms – so broad that it would lose all specific content, at which point it becomes difficult to see what would be excluded from the category of the symbol.

Even though Darnton's intention is to interpret 'a massacre of cats in the same vein as the *Discours préliminaire* of the *Encyclopédie*' (p. 7), there is an incontestable rupture in the book between the first two essays and the last four. The first two aim at recreating a situation on an anthropological terrain; hence they take the written texts only as a means of access to the spoken tale or to the act of the massacre. The remaining four attempt to show how both a position within society and an intellectual stance are expressed by means of a piece of writing (descriptive, administrative, philosophical, or epistolary). A common question underlies both groups, to be sure: how do people organize and manifest their perception and evaluation of the social world? But whereas the views and judgements of the peasants who told or heard the tales and of the workers who did away with the cats are accessible only through the mediation of texts relating what they are supposed to have heard, said, or done, the views of the burghers, administrators and Philosophes are available to us in the first person in texts wholly organized according to strategies of writing with their own specific objectives (recasting social order, keeping track of the literary world, substituting the authority of the Philosophes for that of the theologians, remaking individual lives through a reading of Rousseau). This perhaps explains the contrast between Darnton's treatment of Contat's narration, which is obliterated as a narration and held to be a transparent account of the massacre it recounts, and his treatment of the other texts, considered, to the contrary, in their full textuality and analysed for their conceptual categories and the rhetorical formulas that shape their intended effects.

We can now return to the three questions posed earlier, beginning with the one raised by Darnton's attempt to define a French identity on the basis of practices or texts that he qualifies as alien to us and opaque. This objective might appear astonishing and provocative, given that it aims at tracing national continuity in cultural forms that owe nothing either to the centralized state or to a sense of homeland. French historians, ill accustomed to associating popular culture and national history, might well find this unsettling. The heritage of a social history that gave priority to regional and local divergences and an awareness that the same rituals or the same motifs existed in the various societies of other European *anciens régimes* have helped remove the study of cultural practices from the framework of the state. More recently, the return to national history that inspires several projects presupposes an emphasis on the role of the state in centralizing and unifying the country, while cultural traditions may well appear, in this view, as holding back or shackling the foundation of a feeling of belonging to a nation. Darnton's objective is thus more novel than it seems when he calls for a re-evaluation of the national traits that make French folk-tales different from their German or Italian counterparts based on the same story, for example. What is still difficult to sustain, however, is the double and contradictory affirmation of a radical discontinuity between old and new ways of thinking about the world and of acting on it and a discernible continuity of a French 'cultural style'. Either this continuity exists, in which case the old ways of thinking are not so strange, or else those old ways were truly different from our own, in which case they could never be found in our present world. 'Frenchness exists', *sans doute*, but certainly not as an entity that spans the centuries.

The second question Darnton's book raises is whether a strict conformity to a programme for *histoire sérielle au troisième niveau* is a necessary characteristic of French cultural history. A pronouncement of the sort seems to take little account of the discussions under way or the fields of research under investigation today. Some of the scholars most firmly rooted in the *Annales* tradition have themselves raised questions concerning the choice of categories and the methods once considered obligatory to the study of *mentalités*. A quantification that reifies what is contained in thought has been criticized as illusory, since this supposes either that cultural and intellectual entities are immediately available in quantifiable objects, or else that collective thought must be seized in its most repetitive and least personal expressions, thus reduced to a limited set of formulas to be studied merely as present in a given society in greater or lesser number. To combat this reduction of thoughts to objects or to 'objectivations' – to counter a simplistic sociologism that establishes strict correspondences between the various social levels and cultural forms – a definition of history primarily sensitive to inequalities in the appropriation of common materials or practices has come into being. Serial data can and should continue to be collected, if only to give a preliminary notion of the extent and distribution of cultural objects and practices (Darnton's own highly quantitative recent studies on late eighteenth-century best sellers are perhaps the best example of this). Nevertheless, it is indisputable that the most pressing question inherent in cultural history today, not only in France but *also* in France, is that of the different ways in which groups or individuals make use of, interpret and appropriate the intellectual motifs or cultural forms they share with others. Hence the complex of shifts in the historian's task to focus attention on individual careers, to revoke or cast doubt on the canonical separation between the popular and the learned and to attempt a reconstruction of practices on the basis of representations given of them and objects manipulated in them.[6] This may not be the 'anthropological mode of history' that Darnton aspires to, but it decidedly is not, or is no longer, the cost accountant's history that he claims is typical of the French.

Darnton's criticism has two parts, however: he speaks of 'over-commitment to the quantification of culture' but also of 'undervaluation of the symbolic element in social intercourse'. We need to think a moment about this 'symbolic element' and about the definition of culture as a 'symbolic world'. The notion of symbol is taken in its broadest sense, following Geertz's definition, as 'any object, act, event, quality, or relation which serves as a vehicle for a conception'. Is this in any true sense a workable definition? Let us look at the question 'from the native's point of view' and open one of the older dictionaries, Furetière's, for example, in its 1727 edition. *Symbole* is given as:

sign, type, sort of emblem, or representation of some moral thing by the images or the properties of natural things. Figure or image that serves to designate some thing, either by means of painting or sculpture, or by discourse. The lion is the symbol of valour; the ball that of inconstancy; the pelican that of paternal love.

It is clear, then, that the symbol is a sign, but a specific, particular sign, which implies a relation of representation – for example, the representation of an abstraction by a figure. In order to be qualified as 'symbolic', the relation between a sign and what it makes known to us, which is invisible, supposes that this sign is put in the place of the thing represented, that it is the representing thing. Thus for a person of the seventeenth and the eighteenth centuries, hieroglyphics, enigmas and emblems were symbols *par excellence*.

Although symbols are signs, however, not all signs are symbols, to the extent that the relation that connects them to the things of which they are the 'indication' or the 'mark' is not necessarily a relation of representation. Under the word *signe*, Furetière's dictionary lists several of these other possible relationships between the signifier and the signified: identification through a recognition of the whole by means of a part ('This child, who had long been lost, was recognized by a sign he bore on his thigh'); diagnosis in which a state is deduced from a property (as in certain or probable 'medical signs'); prediction or presage that deciphers the future on the basis of the present. These acceptations, ancient and common, in a dictionary of the French language reflecting and popularizing the theory of the sign as it had been formulated by the logicians and grammarians of Port-Royal, stand as a first warning against too broad a use of of the term 'symbol'. In point of fact, they clearly indicate that not all the signs manipulated in a given culture are by any means symbols, which necessarily require a relationship of representation between the visible sign and the referent signified. To be sure, the historian or the anthropologist is not obliged to remain prisoner of the thought categories of the people he studies, and he has a perfect right to draw up his own analytical vocabulary. I recall this older sense of 'symbol' for a particular reason – to note that anyone concerned primarily with reconstructing the way in which men and women of the eighteenth century conceived of and expressed their relations with the world should pay strict attention to the definitions that they themselves gave of the term to designate the mode held to be essential to this way of thinking and of speaking. And to remark – once more in contrast to too loose a definition of the term 'symbol', which by broadening the notion makes it less readily comprehensible – that the old definitions better enable us to formulate a working meaning of the term by founding such a meaning in a particular type of relation between the sign and the signified in the relation of representation.

Even when defined more precisely, the notion is not easy to use. First, we can hardly postulate stability in the relationship connecting the symbolic sign and what it represents and presents to our eyes. Variation springs from many sources: regarding the sign, a plurality of meanings can be carried by any given symbol; regarding circumstances, a sign may or may not be invested with a symbolic function, depending on the conditions of its use; regarding comprehension, it is inevitably highly uneven from one group or one individual to another. It seems risky, then, to claim that symbols are 'shared, like the air we breathe'. Quite to the contrary, their significations are unstable, mobile, equivocal. They are not always easily decipherable and not always well deciphered. Therefore it seems difficult to postulate that at a given moment and in a given place, a particular culture (for example, that of Parisian printing workers in the beginning of the eighteenth century) is organized in accordance with a symbolic repertory the elements of which are documented at various dates between the sixteenth and the nineteenth centuries and in multiple sites. Furthermore, how can one postulate that symbolic forms are organized into a 'system'? This would suppose coherence among them and interdependence, which in turn supposes the existence of a shared and unified symbolic universe. During the *ancien régime*, in any event, such a system and such a unity seem highly doubtful, given the multiple cleavages in French society, fragmented by differences in age, sex, status, profession, religion, residence, education and so forth. Have we then a right to think that, beyond this discontinuity of particular cultures, each of which secreted its own 'pattern of meaning', there existed a symbolic culture that could be held to englobe the others and to propose a system of symbols accepted by everyone? The errors of one particular form of the social history of culture, which attempts at any cost to correlate every form and every bit of raw data with a specific social 'level' (usually identified in dryly socio-professional terms), are insufficient to persuade us, without reservations, of the validity of a 'general idiom' capable of accounting for all single expressions. Here again, metaphorical use of the vocabulary of linguistics comports a certain danger.

Ascertaining the status of symbolic forms is not to be taken for granted, then, and although the traditional vocabulary of cultural history is hardly satisfactory, borrowings from anthropology do not in themselves resolve all uncertainties. They may even create a few problems of their own by destroying the 'textuality' of texts that relate the symbolic practices being analysed. The now famous cat massacre is a case in point. We know of it from a manuscript text entitled *Anecdotes typographiques. Où l'on voit la description des coutumes, moeurs et usages singuliers des compagnons imprimeurs*, dated 1 September 1762, dedicated to d'Hémery, *inspecteur de la librairie*, and signed 'Mxxx (Le Brun) Ancien Prote, Graveur et Auteur'. The title page bears an address, 'A Bruxelles. Chez Pierre Hardy, A la Vérité', that is doubly fictitious, since the text was not printed and no such printer existed.[7] Giles Barber has managed to trace the author: 'Le Brun' was one Nicolas Contat, a wood-engraver who began his career in 1737 as an apprentice to the printer Vincent on the rue Saint-Séverin. Jean-Michel Papillon mentions the change of name in his *Traité historique et pratique de la gravure en bois* (1766) but offers no explanation for it: 'The so-named Contat, called Le Brun, formerly a Printer or Worker in Letters, has always worked in wood engraving.' Thus the text has an indentifiable and identified author. Is this reason enough to conclude, with Darnton, that his work belongs in 'the line of autobiographical writing by printers that stretches from Thomas Platter to Thomas Gent, Benjamin Franklin, Nicolas Restif de la Bretonne, and Charles Manby Smith' (p. 78)?

This text with no 'I' makes a curious autobiography. It presents a hero named Jérôme who is not immediately present (he appears only at the end of chapter 3) or continuously present and who never speaks as the grammatical subject of a statement but is always the object of description. The procedure followed in the text is to give a succession of general statements that are either pronouncements of supposed universal verities concerning the printing trade or descriptions of what happens to Jérôme and his companions. In neither case is the enouncing subject clearly designated. This gives the text an odd tone: the reader never really knows who is speaking, and the various adventures that befall the hero are as if neutralized, set off at a distance and stripped of their reality by the author's use of the present indicative or the historic future. None of the usual marks of autobiography can be found in this text, and its editor, Giles Barber, remarks that it is possible neither 'to find any precise motive for the writing of the *Anecdotes typographiques*, nor to establish the exact status of the text and to know for whom it was intended'.

I would like to hazard a hypothesis: Contat's *Anecdotes* belong in the time-honoured tradition of texts that purport to reveal to the public the secrets and the practices, true or supposed, of particular professional, ethnic, or religious communities. As in such texts, Contat first presents the differentness of the world he intends to unveil. For him, the *enfants de l'Imprimerie* constitute 'a people, or rather a republic that lives separate from the other nations' – a republic with its own laws, government and language, which the text is about to exhibit before the eyes of all. It is hardly surprising to find the same elements as in the literature of revelation such as, for example, works published since the later Middle Ages promising to divulge the secrets of sham beggars' organizations. First the various degrees of initiation are related, then the various sorts of apprenticeships are described and a dictionary translates terms specific to the trade. Rather than to autobiographies, then, the text seems close to works that owed their success (on occasion a resounding one, as in the case of the *Jargon ou langage de l'Argot réformé*, which describes the monarchical and corporative organization of the beggars' and vagabonds' kingdom) to the divulgation of the secrets, real or imaginary, of communities held to be to some extent mysterious.

During the eighteenth century, there were two genres that breathed new life into this sort of literature. First, there were descriptions of crafts and trades. Contat alludes to these directly in his 'Avis au lecteur en forme de préface':

> A Dictionary and an exact description of the instruments that serve for the crafts and trades has just won your suffrages, what must a faithful portrait of the instruments of the author and of the conservator of the arts [printing] produce and excite in you; of those men who generously spend their days to procure for us the beautiful engravings [that are] the fruit of their wakeful nights?

A second model for the work, travel accounts, is more implicit. The subtitle of the *Anecdotes typographiques*, 'in which one sees the description of the customs, mores, and usages singular to the Journeyman printers', imitates the title of many a travel account. Contat plays on this parallel to announce that he is about to transport the reader to an isolated people, exotic in its own way, but close at hand.

Although it is clear that the entire text is founded on personal experience and on an intimate knowledge of the printing trade, the work is not primarily autobiographical in nature. Its announced intention is dual: 'to pique the public's curiosity' by proposing 'anecdotes', a 'description', and an account (*une histoire*) of a trade rich in secrets; and to use this publicity to defend the independence and the tradition of the community of print workers, threatened, according to the 'Avis au lecteur', by the government, which, 'armed with all its despotic authority attempted to make changes and disunite the Companions'. This perhaps explains the choice of a particular mode of discourse that uses the various anecdotes as *exempla* charged with the incarnation of universal verities. Thus a description of the printing trade that both publicizes and argues in favour of the profession is interwoven with narrative elements, grouped around the character of Jérôme, that dramatize the life of this community and enliven the text with anecdotic tales.

I do not mean by this judgement that the *Anecdotes* has no relation to social reality or that what it relates is pure fiction. My interpretation of the text should lead us to raise questions, however, concerning the *discursive* function attributed to each anecdote or episode and to avoid hasty conclusions concerning their 'reality'. The cat massacre is one of the *exempla* to illustrate the tricks the weak play on the strong and the revenge of the wily on those who torment them. In this it resembles the plot of French folk-tales celebrating ruse and the ingeniousness of the lowly turned against the masters. Did the massacre ever take place? Probably. As Contat tells of it? We cannot know and will never know. But it is clear that for us it remains a massacre in writing. Thus we need above all to decipher its function in the text.

But, someone might object, what difference does it make whether symbolic manipulations fall into the category of acts that actually took place or into that of imagined writing? Is not the same hostility toward the master expressed in both cases? Is he not attacked in the same way, using an animal and using parody, both charged with symbolic meanings? The objection is valid, even if, as is obvious, the social effects of a collective act or an individual's invention are not the same. It obliges us to return to the detail of the narration itself. Darnton sees in it three 'ceremonial and symbolic themes' that turn the scene into a witch-hunt (with the printer's wife as the witch), a charivari, and a carnival mock trial (pp. 96–8). For him, the presence of the 'theme of sorcery' is attested by the text's choice of words in expressions such as '*Des chats endiablés font toute la nuit un sabbat*' ('Some bedeviled cats celebrate a witches' sabbath all night long'); '*Le lendemain Monsieur Leveillé fait son sabbat et passerait pour sorcier si on ne le connaissait pas*' ('Leveillé stages a sabbath the next night and the night after that. If you didn't know him, you would be convinced he was a witch'); or '*Il est décidé que ce sont des chats envoyés, que l'on a jeté quelque sort*' ('The word spreads that there is witchcraft afoot and that the cats must be the agents of someone casting a spell').[8] The whole problem here is to discern the semantic charge of this vocabulary of sorcery within the culture of Paris artisans of the early eighteenth century. Is it unthinkable that such terms had lost much of their original force to become a neutralized, weakened vocabulary that no longer necessarily implied the images or the ideas that they bore a century earlier? Let us turn once more to Furetière: *Sabbat* 'is said by extension of a great noise, of shouting such as one imagines is made at the Sabbath. There are the cats, beginning their *sabbat* in the gutters'. Hence the word had come some distance from its first referent, passing, as the linguists say, from denotation to simple connotation. Contat attests to this himself when he calls the cook who mistreats the apprentices and journeymen '*diable incarné habillé en femme*' ('The Devil incarnate dressed as a woman'). Must we necessarily conclude that when he speaks of her in these terms he really thinks the cook a sorceress as the seventeenth century understood the term? Similarly, the allusion to a spell cast, of which the parish priest is aware, does not seem sufficient evidence on which to decide that the cat-hunt was ordered by the master as a substitute for an exorcism, nor that the mistress is accused of being herself a witch. Words are just as mobile as symbols and are charged with meaning to unequal degrees. It is not at all certain that the use of terms taken from the vocabulary of sorcery set off the same associations among Parisian printers as a hundred years earlier in peasant culture.

Is the massacre a charivari? Darnton thinks it is, on the basis of allusions to relations between the master printer's wife and the young abbé who tutors their two sons. The master is thus cuckolded, 'So the revelry of the workers took the form of a charivari' (p. 97). But is this a legitimate term for a 'festivity' in which none of the elements that characterize the charivari are present? To return to Furetière: '*Charivari*: Confused noise that the common people make with pans, basins, and pots to show offense to someone. One makes charivaris in derision of people of highly unequal age who marry.' The massacre of the rue Saint-Séverin hardly corresponds to this definition, either in its forms (there is no parade and none of the noise-making common to charivaris) or in its supposed motivation, since adultery did not usually give rise to charivaris, which mocked either remarrying widows or henpecked husbands. The allusion to the mistress's infidelity when she deceives her husband with the young abbé probably has another function in the text. When we couple it with another intrigue between Marion, the printer's daughter, and an abbé attached to Saint-Germain l'Auxerrois, it adds a joking, entertaining touch of anticlerical satire to the narration.

To finish the series, can the parodic trial of the cats that crowns the massacre be fully likened to carnival festivities? The *mardi gras* execution included one essential element missing here: the fire in which the effigy of carnival is burned. On the rue Saint-Séverin there is no pyre and no glowing coals, but only hanging cats – which is a far cry from both the carnival ritual and the typical festive use of the cat, in which (for example, in Saint John's Eve festivities) it is thrown into the fire. The mock trial, as Darnton indicates, echoes a cultural form common among typographic workers and practised, for example, at the Feast of Saint Martin. There is therefore no reason whatsoever to see in it a strictly carnival rite. The massacre, as Contat describes it, is thus not easy to place among folklorists' classical categories, and it is perhaps wiser to avoid trying to make it conform with the canonical forms of carnival festive culture or of the charivari. When they do away with the cats, the mistress's pet in particular, the *compagnons* make a clear statement of their animosity toward the people who use them badly. They do so by wreaking their violence on the animal who best symbolically (in the sense given above) represents the household and the lady of the house. But although it is probable that urban artisan culture attached to the cat the significance that is manipulated in the narrative and in the macabre ceremony (if it indeed took place), it is more doubtful that this culture was really playing with the full repertory of diabolical and carnival motifs that Darnton attributes to it. This would suppose that the collective action that takes place on the rue Saint-Séverin carries with it an entire set of beliefs, rites and behavior difficult to imagine as simultaneously inhabiting the mind of urban printshop workers of the eighteenth century.

This analysis of Contat's text – which is itself open to dispute – is intended only to point out three ineluctable demands on anyone who sets out to decipher the symbolic system that underlies a text: first, to take the text as a text and to try to determine its intentions, its strategies and the effects produced by its discourse; next, to avoid supposing a stable, full value in its lexical choices, but to take into account the semantic investment or disinvestment of its terms; finally, to define the instances of behaviour and the rituals present in the text on the basis of the specific way in which they are assembled or produced by original invention, rather than to categorize them on the basis of remote resemblances to codified forms among the repertory of Western folk-culture. If we keep these injunctions in mind we can measure the risk involved in a linguistic comparison that designates as a 'general idiom' the symbolic system of a certain culture and as particular statements localized uses varying from one given set of circumstances to another. It is not a simple task for the historian to situate the statement in relation to the idiom or to measure the gap, the amount of 'play', existing between the forms held to be characteristic of a culture and the individual actions or

sayings – written or spoken – he finds before him. We need rigorous
verification of the signs considered to be sure and clear indices of
manners of thinking and feeling, and we need an explicit description
of the operation by means of which a singular event is accepted as
revelatory of a totality. In this sense Darnton's book, and the essay
on the massacred cats in particular, brings a welcome addition to the
ongoing reflection on both the nature and the status of historical
proof and the relationship between the exception and the normal, or,
as Edoardo Grendi writes, 'the normally exceptional'.[9]

This discussion of Robert Darnton's book is perhaps a bizarre
way to do justice to his talents. His is not a book on theory or
epistemology but, as is Darnton's wont, a work in which the society
of *ancien régime* France springs to life, in which men and women of
300 years ago become flesh-and-blood beings who think and suffer,
cry or laugh. No reader, unless of a particularly bilious and carping
nature, could possibly resist this sensitive and subtle quest for a lost
humanity. But at the same time, the book is also intended as a
'defence and illustration' of a new way of conceiving of and writing
about cultural history. For this reason, I hope I shall be forgiven for
turning aside for a moment from the seductive picture Darnton
paints to the unavoidable grisaille of a discussion of concepts and
methods.

NOTES

This text was published as a review article in *Journal of Modern History*, 57, 4
(1985), pp. 682–95. Subsequent discussion on it with Pierre Bourdieu and
Robert Darnton was published in *Actes de la Recherche en Sciences Sociales*, 59
(1985), pp. 86–93, and it has prompted a reply in Robert Darnton, 'The
Symbolic Element in History', *Journal of Modern History*, 58 (1986),
pp. 218–34. May it stand as proof that intellectual debate is not necessarily
incompatible with friendship.

1 Robert Darnton, *The Great Cat Massacre and Other Episodes in French
   Cultural History* (New York: Basic Books, 1984), pp. 298. Page
   references in text refer to this work.
2 Robert Darnton, 'Intellectual and Cultural History', in Michael
   Kammen, ed., *The Past before Us: Contemporary Historical Writing in the
   United States* (Cornell University Press, Ithaca, NY and London,
   1980), pp. 327–54, esp. p. 346.
3 Pierre Chaunu, 'Un nouveau champ pour l'histoire sérielle: Le
   quantitatif au troisième niveau', in *Mélanges en l'honneur de Fernand
   Braudel* (2 vols, Privat, Toulouse, 1973), vol. 2: *Méthodologie de l'histoire
   et des sciences humaines*, pp. 105–25.

4   Darnton, 'Intellectual and Cultural History', p. 347.
5   Clifford Geertz, *The Interpretation of Cultures* (Basic Books, New York, 1973), p. 89.
6   For further critical re-evaluations of the history of *mentalités*, serial and non-serial, see ch. 1. See also Roger Chartier 'Culture as Appropriation: Popular Cultural Uses in Early Modern France', in Steven L. Kaplan, ed., *Understanding Popular Culture: Europe from the Middle Ages to the Nineteenth Century* (Mouton, Berlin, New York, Amsterdam, The Hague, 1984), pp. 229–53.
7   This text has been published, with an introduction and notes, by Giles Barber in the Oxford Bibliographical Society Publications, (Oxford, 1980), n.s., vol. 20.
8   Darnton's translations, pp. 102–4.
9   Carlo Ginzburg, 'Signes, traces, pistes: Racines d'un paradigme de l'indice', *Le Débat*, 6 (1980), pp. 3–44; Carlo Ginzburg and Carlo Poni, 'La Micro-histoire', *Le Débat*, 17 (1981), pp. 133–6. See ch. 2, notes 21 and 28.

Part II

REPRESENTATIONS OF THE SOCIAL

Four Case-studies

5

THE WORLD TURNED UPSIDE-DOWN

The nightmare of the world turned upside-down struck the more notable citizens of Romans, in south-east France, during Carnival in 1580. The draper turned magistrate and the *peuple mécanique* ran through the streets crying out their inmost fantasies of butchering the rich, selling their flesh for roasts and then sharing out their ex-masters' wives and wealth. Begun as a joke, the artisans' and crafts-men's game took a more serious turn to become a revolt in which they threw over social status. The powerful were no longer men but meat (at least in words), and the poor seized treasures and powers. The affair ended badly: the rebels' leader was killed at dawn on *mardi gras* and his effigy was displayed, hanging head down to show that the world had been righted once more.[1] Symbolic role reversal, as this occurrence illustrates, harbours dangers for the dominant and holds out hope to the oppressed, and it can frequently be found in traditional French society. It lay at the very heart of the crowds' glee when an altar boy was elected bishop at the Feast of Fools, at Carnival when the buffoon was crowned king, at *chevauchées de l'âne*, when the henpecked husband was set to ride backwards on a donkey. The exchange of functions and places, certainly an essential characteristic of festive behaviour in the early modern age, was not limited to a repertory of actions. It also invaded the representations, visual and other, that were part of carnivalesque festivities and feasts of fools. In the morality plays the actor who played the role of the World was invited to change his clothes or put them on upside-down; in liars' competitions the interlocutors strove to outdo one another in inventing the impossible. These *concours de mensonges*, which figure prominently in the medieval *sotie*, can also be found in popular culture. In these jocose dialogues, often attributed to a particular group of men, such as the sawyers of Magnards in the Nivernais or the copper-smiths of Villedieu-les-Poêles in Normandy, the formula 'I saw' introduced some highly improbable happening. They can still be found today in the oral traditions of several regions of France.

THE MOTIFS IN PRINT

Popular fancy in the *ancien régime* took pleasure in symbolic reversals in another manner, however. From the sixteenth to the nineteenth centuries the *imagiers* (image-makers) devoted a large share of their output to depictions of the world turned upside-down. Throughout western Europe prints of this sort presented a series of motifs (sometimes many, sometimes few) that gave visual form to what the medieval farces or the spinners of tall tales offered orally. The titles of these broadsheets varied little, both through time and from one language to another. Thus we find *Così va il mondo alla riversa* or *Il mondo al rovescio* in Italy, *Die Widerwertige Welt* or *Die Verkehrte Welt* in Germanic lands, *De Verkeerde Wereld* in Flanders, and *Le Monde renversé, à l'envers*, or *à rebours* in French imagery. This body of works, which has been examined by Giuseppe Cocchiara and by Jacques Cochin [2] seems to us worthy of study for two reasons. First, in its literate inventiveness, which developed the motifs of these prints, joins with popular culture, which made them its own, possibly because their motifs corresponded to time-honoured traditions. And second, these images reveal archetypes that transcended frontiers, but they also created new series of representations. Only a limited number of images (twenty-eight in all) have been considered here, both because we have drawn only on the collections in Paris at the Musée National des Arts et Traditions Populaires and at the Bibliothèque Nationale, and because a great number of these popular prints have doubtless disappeared for ever. Still, even though our investigation, to be truly exhaustive, should have included all European print collections, the provisory conclusions presented here are not biased, since they draw authority from the geographic diversity and chronological range of their materials.

To begin with the most obvious: certain specific themes of the world turned upside-down have roots deep in the past. *The Hunter taken by the Rabbits* can be found in a manuscript of the fourteenth century. At the end of the fifteenth century, the engraver Israël van Meckenem shows the same hunter, roasted this time. A woodcut from Antwerp from the beginning of the sixteenth century shows the wolf guarding the sheep. The grouping of various sorts of reversal on one plate seems to have arisen first in Italy in the mid-sixteenth century. Ferrante Bertelli, publisher of the first Italian atlas, put out an engraving with the 'world turned upside-down' title in 1560 in Venice. The catalogue of prints put out by the great Roman printer–bookseller Antoine Lafréry in 1572 (the first of its kind in Italy) includes a 'world turned upside-down', a 'cage of fools', a 'Land of Cockaigne', and a 'Triumph of Carnival' – titles that give a good indication of the general context of motifs of reversal. Of the first nine items in the corpus of images studied here, which range from the sixteenth to the end of the eighteenth century, three are Italian. Symptomatically, they are also the oldest. Germanic and Flemish models emerged from this original matrix to enjoy wide success, but they rarely appear in French libraries. The stock of Michel De Groot of Amsterdam (1643–80) included at least one 'world turned upside-down', and the firm of J. Noman de Zalt Bommel, which had acquired around 1815 the entire print stock of Stichter in Amsterdam, listed no fewer than five, three of them dating from the seventeenth century. An anonymous copperplate engraving made in Nuremberg around 1650 confirms the homogeneity of this subject-matter and doubtless attests to the circulation of prints everywhere between the United Provinces and the Italian peninsula.

The second and largest group in our corpus (fourteen images) ranges in date from the end of the *ancien régime* to the mid-nineteenth century. For the most part French, these broadsheets show the continued vitality of the theme, first among the *imagiers* of the rue Saint-Jacques (five examples from Jean and Noël Basset), next among provincial print-makers, particularly in Lorraine, who at the time reached their height: Desfeuilles in Nancy, Pellerin in Epinal, Dembour and Gangel in Metz. Belgium is represented here with two images, one from Brepols, the other from Glénisson, typical of the famous firms in Turnhout and often reprinted in succeeding centuries.

After this high point (and this may be an impression resulting from better conservation) came the decline. During the second half of the nineteenth century Epinal and Metz were the only French cities in which images on this theme were still being reprinted (two examples apiece). This near eclipse may be linked to a growing interest in subjects that derived from the world turned upside-down but noticeably modified its original meaning. Such were the *Réformes du ménage* [Household Reforms], widely sold by Pellerin, which focused on reversal of sex roles and, by that token, inherited traits of the older *Dispute pour la culotte* [Dispute over Wearing the Trousers] or the *Réformes de messieurs les écoliers* [Reforms of the Gentlemen Schoolboys] that reversed the master/student relationship. The ironic use of the term *réformes*, borrowed from contemporary political vocabulary, like the systematic use of the future tense in the explanatory legends, eliminated once and for all the violence that the motif had contained to bring it back within an improbable and ridiculous 'right-side up' future time. We can see the theme gradually losing its substance as it evolved from the context of the carnivalesque Feast of Fools and the general hilarity of the *chevauchée de l'âne* to sarcastic drawings of an irony approaching Daumier's. Political imagery is revealing in this regard. At the end of the sixteenth century propaganda posters such as *La Marmite renversée des Huguenots* [The Huguenots' Cook-pot Overturned] or the *Renversement de la grande marmite* derive directly from the world turned upside-down. In 1789 the peasant who rides a composite mount, half cleric, half noble, exclaiming '*J'savois bien qu'jaurions not'tour*' ['I knew we would get our turn'] reverses the older traditional image of Jacques Bonhomme collapsing under the weight of the nobility and the clergy. Similarly, the *Tiers état dépeçant le monstre des privilégiés* [Third Estate Cutting Up the Monster of the Privileged] recalls certain scenes of butchery in the world turned upside-down. Nothing of the sort appears, on the contrary, in nineteenth-century iconography – one symptom of the decline of themes that still had had immediate validity in revolutionary France.

Borrowings should be noted as well as overall chronology. As always in popular imagery, the print-shops copied one another and reprinted older models that thus continued for several centuries. To cite one example, Mondhar, an *imagier* of the rue Saint-Jacques in the mid-eighteenth century, recopied quite exactly in *La Folie des hommes ou le monde à rebours* (Men's Folly, or the World Upside-down) eight topsy-turvy world motifs from the seventeenth century in which both the settings and the text of the legends are strictly identical. Eight other motifs very likely follow an original lost today. Mondhar's prints circulated widely outside Paris, and they served as a model for woodcuts by Leloup in Le Mans at the end of the eighteenth century and by Rabier-Boulard in Orléans at the beginning of the nineteenth.[3] These two print-shops worked in a much rougher style than the Latin Quarter print-shops. By tracing the Parisian prototype directly onto their wood blocks, both Leloup and Rabier-Boulard reversed the scenes right to left, thus in their unsophisticated techniques they paralleled the reversal in the subject-matter represented. The only liberty they took with the Parisian versions was for reasons of modesty: in both Orléans and Le Mans, the son no longer teaches his father 'how to live' by a good spanking on his bare posterior, but teaches him to read, thus substituting the pedagogy of literary reason for the violence of corporal punishment. [4]

The disposition of the image on the page was stabilized fairly early. The oldest print in our corpus (Bologna, sixteenth century) presents a single scene with two centres of interest: centred at the top of the page is the globe upside-down; in the centre, a standing woman dressed in man's clothing holds a sword and a lance, while the man, seated and wearing a dress, spins. Quite soon, however, the dominant model shows a series of smaller pictures separated from one another and disposed in superimposed bands. The globe upside-down occupies the centre of the image (Rome, sixteenth century; Milan, 1720) or else constitutes the first motif (Paris, seventeenth century and Mondhar, eighteenth century). The globe disappears in the nineteenth century. The scenes seem to obey no particular order as they succeed one another, which is fitting for a topsy-turvy world. If there is order, it is established by the law of facility: the engraver links aquatic scenes on one band, thus bathing his figures in the same element (Rome, sixteenth century) or groups together animal hunts, reducing the décor to its simplest expression (Nuremberg, seventeenth century).

THE TRAJECTORY OF A REPERTORY

The twenty-eight images (or series of images, since certain of them take up several sheets) are carefully set apart to isolate each iconographic entity. For the most part, this separation follows the straight line with which the engraver has framed each of the motifs, but in the oldest images he has had to zig-zag somewhat in order to do so. There are thus 411 vignettes, and, as some of them contain two themes, 418 units enter into the count. The eight categories used for classification have been defined by the locus of the reversal: social relations, sex roles, adult/child relations, relations between people and animals, relations among animals, order among the elements of nature and the position of things and people. This latter category is the most disparate as it constitutes a world of the absurd (which finds echoes in some surrealist paintings) in which objects are pictured upside-down, men walk with their legs in the air and the cart is put before the oxen. Man even becomes an object. Pinot in Epinal printed an image at the end of the nineteenth century, *La Brouette met le sac sur le dos de l'homme devenu brouette* [The Wheelbarrow Puts the Sack on the Back of the Man, Become a Wheelbarrow]. The motif of the globe turned upside-down is a category in its own right, usually showing the globe carried by two men, at times by a man and a woman or by a white man and a black man.

A distribution chart of this corpus, divided into three periods (see table 5.1) shows both lasting and shifting traits. In each of the chronological brackets, the role reversal between people and animals accounts for the highest number of motifs. Its advance is only moderate from the sixteenth to the eighteenth century, but with the nineteenth century it invades the world turned upside-down to account for more than half the images. This gain is at the expense of two other categories, in particular, relations between animals. The thematic repertory, which often reflects the plots of animal fables, was established early. Nineteenth-century plates make use of it without showing great inventiveness. The Bolognese image of the sixteenth century, *Como va il mondo alla riversa*, places a proliferating bestiary in the empty spaces separating the principal motifs to show the weak attacking the strong, in imitation of reversals taken from the human world. Here the cub guides his mother and the male is ruled by the female. Only some such pairs had both a long past and a durable posterity: the mouse and the cat (who is pursued and sometimes devoured), the cock and the hen (the object of a number of variations in which the hen mounts the cock, the cock lays an egg, or the cock lays an egg while the hen crows), and the sheep and the wolf (in which the devourer is devoured). The taste for attributing to certain animals qualities belonging to others seems to have been a legacy from the Middle Ages. This is obvious, in fact, in the formulas from liars' competitions in the *soties* in which the pairs shown in our images often appear, as in the *Sotie des menus propos*, where one character announces:

> Je verraye volontiers couris
> Une brebis après un leu.   .
> [I would love to see a sheep run after a wolf.]

When we leave the *ancien régime* for the early nineteenth century, the decline in the number of images involving exchange of social roles is even more striking. The theme was well established from the sixteenth to the eighteenth centuries, among the Italian engravers as well as with François Guérard, who operated on the rue Saint-Jacques between 1672 and 1715. It took the form of exchanged social symbols in the image showing the king going on foot and the peasant on horseback. Above all, it involved a reversal in the hierarchy of learning in which the rustic teaches the scholars, the sick care for the doctors, the client counsels the lawyer and the serving-maid tells the gipsy's fortune. Between 1790 and 1850 these motifs almost totally

Table 5.1 Distribution of motifs in images of the 'world upside-down'

Locus of reversal	1500–1790 (9 images)		1790–1850 (14 images)		1850–1900 (5 images)		Totals	
Human-animal relations	55	30.6%	87	56.1%	42	50.7%	184	44.0%
Relations among animals	38	21.1%	14	9.1%	8	9.7%	60	14.4%
Social relations	28	15.6%	4	2.6%	10	12.1%	42	10.0%
Age hierarchy	18	10.0%	13	8.4%	7	8.4%	38	9.1%
Elements of nature	15	8.3%	12	7.7%	5	6.0%	32	7.7%
Sex roles	11	6.1%	12	7.7%	5	6.0%	28	6.7%
Absurd positions	9	5.0%	9	5.8%	5	6.0%	23	5.5%
Upside-down globe	6	3.3%	4	2.6%	1	1.2%	11	2.6%
	180		155		83		418	

disappear in our sample, for reasons difficult to ascertain. The *imagiers* censor out of their production, consciously or unconsciously, anything that might threaten the delicate balance of the social order, even when offered in jocular fashion. Clearly, the function of the world turned upside-down was to conserve social order, since the reversal of hierarchies is presented as just as impossible and absurd as to see sky and earth or air and sea change places.[5] At the beginning of the nineteenth century, however, the situation changes. It seems as though the image merchants did not want to risk having their images misunderstood: taken literally they might be an invitation to subversion. This fear dissipated in the second half of the century, when the reversal of social relations reappears in the images. Even then social reversal, for the most part, takes only two forms. It is domestic, where the master or the mistress serves his valet or her serving woman; or it is military, and we see conscripts commanding the generals or the officers doing fatigue duty. The peasant has abandoned a place that the industrial worker will never occupy. Now reversal is shown only in situations in which it remains innocuous and in which order seems unassailable.

In the nineteenth century, the 'world turned upside-down' was thus above all a world in which animals put people at their mercy and ruled over them. Here inventiveness is almost inexhaustible, fragmented into a multitude of images. Most animals are domestic, with the horse and the ass sharing the highest number of occurrences, followed by the ox, the dog, pigs, poultry and sheep, in that order. Although on occasion the victims of these reversals are persons of substance – travellers obliged to pull the coach while the horse rides, or horsemen saddled, bridled and mounted by their steeds – more often they are country people. Plowmen and farmers' wives, millers and shepherds are the slaves of farm animals. Some images had a particularly strong hold on imaginations and persisted through the centuries. People are reduced here to human 'beasts of burden' weighed down by barrels, bales, baskets of vegetables, or – the most frequent case – sacks of grain to be milled. Or they are 'plow-men' pulling the plow (the *charrue* in the North or the more rudimentary *araire* in the South of France). This inversion on the level of daily chores extends to rustic pleasures, producing the classic figures of the hunter hunted by his quarry or the fisherman caught by a fish. One of the most obsessive motifs of this imagery perhaps reveals part of its meaning: the man decapitated, hacked to pieces, grilled, or turned on the spit by animals who would normally be his victims. The theme returns time and again and with many variations. Mondhar's *La Folie des hommes ou le monde à rebours* [The

Folly of Men, or, the World Backwards) presents a good many of them:

> Voyez pour se vanger de celui qui l'Ecorche
> Jean Lapin à son tour tourne l'homme à la broche.
> [See how Johnny Rabbit takes revenge on his flayer when he
> in turn turns man on the spit.]

> Les cochons affaméz par des traits inhumains
> Egorgent font griller dépiècent les Humains.
> [The pigs famished by inhuman treatment slit the throats,
> grill, cut up the humans.]

> Quel objet plen d'horreur un boeuf tout en boucherie
> Fait d'un Homme écorché sanglante boucherie.
> [What a horrid object an ox makes in slaughtering in bloody
> butchery a flayed man.]

We might add to this repertory of prospects painful for the butcher, the hunter, or the roast-purveyor the cook stewed by the goose and the farmer roasted by the turkey. What pierces through in these images of blood and fire is the fear of unleashing animal forces that have been mastered only with great pains. The power ratio between humans and beasts is upset, and once again one cannot help but think that even if the image is presented only as a joking fable it suggests something unsettling and worrisome. Worlds turned upside-down open the door to George Orwell's animals and Alfred Hitchcock's birds. Like them, the *imagiers* did not go to the bestiary of exotic beasts for the destroyers of man's supremacy. Wild animals are in fact rare in these images. When present, they are animals that are normally hunters' quarry, circus animals making their trainers dance, or zoo animals mocking caged keepers. One print is a somewhat mysterious exception to this. Put out by one of the Bassets between 1790 and 1805, it is entitled *Les Tigres tuent l'homme qui les dévorait* [Tigers Kill the Man who was Eating Them]. Here the man is not so much disguised as a beast as he *is* a wild animal, shown eating big game raw, and the tigers who kill him with a dagger appear as guardians of the normal order of nature. The reversal here is too subtle to decode easily, but its very opacity clarifies the meaning of other and more banal portrayals of the phantasm of a loss of human qualities and a return to savagery.

The relative share of the whole set of themes illustrated in our sampling remains nearly the same over three and a half centuries. This does not mean, however, that the motifs remained static. The reversals in age hierarchy illustrate this. In the older images, the world upside-down parodies the ages of man, one of the most wide-spread themes in popular imagery. In an exchange of their usual attributes, the old man gets the toys and the child gains wisdom. An image from sixteenth-century Rome and a German broadside of the mid-seventeeth century show these two motifs side by side. A group of oldsters run along flying streamers and twirling whirligigs, while the child, ensconced in a professorial chair, lectures to a group of greybeards. Later on, the reversal of ages appears less frequently as exchange of roles between the teacher and the taught, except as the tutor whipped by his pupil. Age reversal shifts to centre on parents and children, and from the portrayal of their 'upside-down' relations we can infer the familial relations that usually pertained. The key is given in the two most frequent images, often joined in one vignette: *La fille donne ici la bouillie à sa mère.* [The daughter gives her mother her porridge.] *Le fils à coups de fouet apprend à vivre à son père.* [The son whips his father to teach him how to behave.] Here we see not only age reversal but how parental roles were assigned. The mother is primarily giver of nourishment and the father disciplinarian. There is also a psychological sex difference that contrasts the gentleness of the little girl to the violence of the boy.

This same opposition appears in role reversals between man and woman. All that is needed to masculinize the woman is to give her a weapon – a sword, a musket, or even, as with Pellerin in Epinal in the second half of the nineteenth century, a cannon. Feminization of the man does not necessarily rely on his wearing a skirt. A distaff and a spinning-wheel suffice, particularly if a child is also placed on his knee. The exchange of attributes, hence of activities, often involves an exchange of operating space: the woman moves outdoors and the man inside the house. Women with guns leave for the open country to hunt or go on patrol, while the man remains at home to spin, cradle a child, or, as in one of Desfeuilles's prints, to *ébrener* [wipe clean] an infant. The distribution of tasks between husband and wife and the ridiculous alterations thereof furnished inexhaustible subject-matter for prints sold by the *imagiers*. Other titles include *Le mari battu* [The Beaten Husband; only one example in our corpus], *Le Querelle du ménage* [The Domestic Quarrel], or *Les Réformes du ménage* [Domestic Reforms]. Innovations appear, as in the Milanese print of the beginning of the eighteenth century entitled *Il mondo al roverscio ossia il costume moderno* [The World Upside-down, or, Modern Custom], in which two women serenade under a man's window. This motif reappears only once again, in modified form, in a Flemish image:

L'année est bissextile
L'homme est courtisé par la fille.
[This is leap year: the man is courted by the girl.]

Contrary to other forms of representation, the popular print tended to conserve the traditional functions of the sexes, perhaps because it was addressed to a public for whom complementary tasks within the home were the very condition of survival for the family group.

Unfortunately, sketching the general outlines of this corpus of images of the world turned upside-down is of little help in measuring their effect on the sensibilities of their buyers. Since the print-makers stood between print and public, it is only extremely indirectly, by surveying change or stability in themes, that we can gauge the public's reactions. These images attract us but no longer make us laugh, which presents us with the problem of their great success. Their intention seems clear: to show an order in which both nature and society are equally inviolable. This contrary vision has the one purpose of dissolving subversion in general laughter, just as the Feast of Fools or Carnival limited the temptation to overturn social order to a few festive days. Laughter was possible for the viewers of these prints only if the motifs represented remained without impact on an unchangeable reality and if they kept deep anxieties from rising to consciousness. We can only suppose that this is how the images of the 'world turned upside-down' were perceived in those centuries, even though now and again the apprehensions or the desires that they aimed at obliterating broke through. For we who know more about the fears and the tensions that inhabit a society, this imagery reveals what it thought to conceal, and by that token it loses its comic power. It takes on another and fascinating power, however, since it often occupies a narrow territory in which dividing-lines vacillate and categories blur.

NOTES

This brief text was written in collaboration with my friend Dominique Julia for an issue of the review, no longer published, *L'Arc*, 65 (1976), pp. 43–53, devoted to the work of Emmanuel Le Roy Ladurie.

The principal works used are: A. Martin, *L'Imagerie orléanaise* (Duchartre and Van Buggenhoudt, Paris, 1928); Achille Bertarelli, *Le stampe popolari italiane* (Rizzoli, Milan, 1974) [*L'Imagerie populaire italienne* (Duchartre and Van Buggenhoudt, Paris, 1929)]; Emile Henri van Heurck and Gerrit

Jacob Boeknoogen, *L'Imagerie populaire des Pays-Bas, Belgique-Hollande* (Duchartre and Van Buggenhoudt, Paris, 1930); Paolo Toschi, *Stampe popolari italiane dal XV al XX secolo* (Electa, Milan, 1964) [*L'Imagerie populaire italienne du XVe au XXe siècle* (Editions des Deux Mondes, Paris, 1965)]; Jean Adhemar, *Imagerie populaire française* (Electa, Milan, 1968); Maurits de Meyer, *Volksprenten in de Nederlanden, 1400–1900* (Scheltema and Holkema, Amsterdam, and Standaard, Antwerp, 1970); Wolfgang Brückner, *Populäre Druckgraphik Europas. Deutschland von 15 bis zum 20 Jarhundert* (Callwey, Munich, 1970); and two catalogues of exhibits at the Musée National des Arts et Traditions Populaires (Paris): *Cinq siècles d'imagerie française* (1973); Jean Cuisinier, *Mari et femme dans la France rurale traditionnelle* (1973). Note: The corpus that served for this analysis includes twenty-eight prints. A certain number of them are reproduced in the works of Bertarelli, van Heurck, Martin and Brückner. The others (the vast majority) are either in the Print Room of the Bibliothèque National in Paris or in the Iconothèque of the Musée National des Arts et Traditions Populaires.

1 Emmanuel Le Roy Ladurie, *Les Paysans de Languedoc* (Flammarion, Paris, 1966) [*The Peasants of Languedoc*, tr. John Day, George Huppert, consulting ed. (University of Illinois Press, Urbana, Illinois, 1984)]. Emmanuel Le Roy Ladurie later devoted an entire book to the event: *Le Carnaval de Romans. De la Chandeleur au mercredi des Cendres, 1579–1580* (Gallimard, Paris, 1979) [*Carnival: A People's Uprising at Romans, 1579–1580*, tr. Mary Feeney (George Brasiller, New York, 1979)].

2 Giuseppe Cocchiara, *Il mondo alla rovescia* (Boringhieri, Turin, 1963; 1981). The corpus of works studied by Jacques Cochin – 'Mondes à l'envers, mondes à l'endroit', *Arts et traditions populaires* (1969) vol. 17 – begins only at the end of the eighteenth century and is almost exclusively limited to French territory. It contains an analysis of the relationship of image to legend that we have only suggested here.

3 Rabier-Boulard's print, which dates from 1820, is doubtless a reprinting of a wood-block of Sevestre-Leblond, an Orléans *imagier* (1751–1805) that had been used subsequently by Jean-Baptiste Letourmy (active in Orléans 1775–1800).

4 All the problems of filiation cannot possibly be outlined here. Let us recall simply that print-houses ran the same plates at regular intervals, especially in the nineteenth century, even when the owner of the shop had changed. We have counted each press-run as an entity in our counts, however.

5 See Jacques Revel, 'L'Orient d'une culture', in Jean-Paul Aron, ed., *Qu'est-ce que la culture française?*, (Denoël-Gonthier, Paris, 1975).

6

TIME TO UNDERSTAND
The 'Frustrated Intellectuals'

What were the effects upon a given population of intellectuals and on the society in which they lived of an imbalance between a more restricted number of positions that society offered university graduates and the greater number of those graduates? The problem that I intend to treat here historically, and which falls within the history of intellectual positions, lies at the heart of contemporary debate concerning the multiple effects of the devaluation of university degrees in the labour-market.

This question was first introduced among the problems that concern historians in connection with England. In an article that has become a standard reference, Mark H. Curtis suggested that English universities had contributed greatly to social disequilibrium between 1600 and 1640 by preparing a great many more graduates than there were posts, lay or ecclesiastical, in the government or in the Church of England, to which these men could aspire and in fact did aspire. [1] In the reign of Elizabeth I important ecclesiastical positions – those of bishop or vicar – were open to holders of university degrees. Under the first two Stuarts the situation changed and the number of students as potential candidates for an ecclesiastical benefice (excluding the sons of the gentry and the nobility), ran on the order of one hundred more each year than the number of available posts. When these unsuccessful candidates were blocked from becoming vicars, they had to accept other employment as curates, lecturers (preachers) and schoolmasters. Such posts all paid less, were more unstable and carried less prestige than a vicariate. A similar bottleneck existed in the market for lay administrative posts, the price for which rose sharply and which were passed on from father to son. This meant that a number of university graduates were blocked from state service even though intellectually and psychologically they had been prepared for it. As a result there arose in England between 1600 and 1640 a population of intellectuals whom Curtis qualifies as 'discontented', 'dissatisfied' and 'alienated'. Joined by their frustration and their bitterness, these 'alienated intellectuals', who Curtis gives as representing between 15 and 20 per cent of students at Oxford and Cambridge during this period, subsequently fomented radical social and political criticism, Puritan or republican.

Thus the problem of the 'alienated intellectual' was first posed on the basis of a concrete historical situation, England under the first Stuarts. If we raise it again today, however, we need to take into account the way sociologists have shifted the problem in order to understand the mechanisms that governed the educational system of the time and the social effects of that system. The basic situation has not changed. It still involves an imbalance between diplomas and posts; between subjective aspirations and objective chances. The accent is now less on the ideological evolution of frustrated intellectuals and more on a transformation in the very definition of the positions that they occupy, thus on changes brought to the social arena as a whole. The first mechanism for change is the devaluation of secondary and university diplomas: 'Bearing in mind that the volume of corresponding jobs may also have varied over the same period, one may assume that a qualification is likely to have undergone devaluation if the number of diploma-holders has grown more rapidly than the number of suitable positions.'[2] The social effects of this devaluation are accentuated by being misunderstood – that is, by an attachment to outdated representations of the value of such degrees. And the lesser is the cultural capital of the social agents, the wider is the gap between the degree's real value in the labour-market and their representation of its value. When this imbalance between titles of study and posts becomes perceptible, it engenders reconversion strategies aimed at using the titles that are held to obtain a post equivalent to the one that such degrees formerly guaranteed. This leads next to a redefinition and re-evaluation of a certain number of posts and positions from the simple fact of a change in the scholastic and social qualifications of the people who occupy them, and that in turn leads to the creation of new positions or new professions in the more flexible sectors of the social arena. By means of these strategies (which are never completely calculated nor totally mastered by the social agents involved), the devaluation of educational titles generates modification in the social structure so that a shift in the definition of professional positions accompanies the perpetuated gaps between them. The divorce of subjective hopes from objective chances of social success thus reproduces social distinctions. Transfer is founded on a keen competition in which

reconversion strategies, although they modify the social sphere profoundly, fail both to narrow the gaps and to stop the advance of
those who had dominated the market in titles of study and posts
before.[3]

This model for the comprehension of the problem of the 'alienated
intellectuals' should lead us to pose the problem on two levels. First,
we need to explore the degrees of adequacy or illusion in the way
various groups represented the market in social positions and the
reasons for their frustration, and also the strategies used to avoid
disqualification. And second, we need to ascertain what transformations took place in social structure – changes unperceived or poorly
perceived by the social agents involved and induced by resistance to
the devaluation of university degrees or to the lowering of the
prestige of positions. Above all, what we need to do is to understand
how social space relates to the images of society – '*l'imaginaire social*'
– and to grasp the ways in which systems of representation spoke of
and affected changes in society.

UNIVERSITY ATTENDANCE

Before we can ask such questions of Europe in the seventeenth
century we need to test whether Curtis's findings can be taken as
universally valid. Was it true throughout Europe that the university
found itself in a conjunctural situation of notable increase in both
university attendance and degrees granted and if so, at what
moments in the century? Was the closing of the market in administrative positions and church benefices coveted by holders of
university degrees that was typical of the English situation to be
found everywhere? To answer the first of these questions we can
turn to the data contained in time-series studies published in the last
ten years that firmly establish university enrolment in four regions.[4]
In the nineteen universities of Castille (among which Salamanca,
Alcalá and Valladolid account for the lion's share) annual registrations reached a high early in the seventeenth century. After the
all-time high in 1590 of nearly 20,000 registered students, the years
1610–20 show a secondary peak, after the various plagues, that
oscillates between 13,000 and 14,000. These highs are followed by a
decline that continues, almost without respite, for a century, to
reach its lowest point at the beginning of the eighteenth century with
fewer than 5,000 students registering annually. If we calculate that
newcomers made up one-fourth of the students in attendance each

year, 5.4 per cent of young men aged from 18 to 19 years entered the Castillian universities at the end of the sixteenth century, as against 2.2 per cent in the middle of the eighteenth century.[5]

If we compare figures for first year students at Oxford and Cambridge we can see a first peak in the 1580s (an annual average of 445 entering students at Oxford, 465 at Cambridge), followed by an all-time high in the 1620s at Cambridge (513 entrants) and the 1630s in Oxford (530 entrants). The figures collapse with the Civil Wars, and recuperation in the 1660s reaches a lower peak, only to be followed by a constant decline in admissions until the mid-eighteenth century, when we see an average of 182 entering students in Oxford each year in the 1750s and 115 in Cambridge in the 1760s.[6] If we add to the entering students in these two universities those admitted to the Inns of Court, we have 2.7 per cent of the cohort of young men of age to enter the university who began university studies in the 1580s, 2.4 per cent in the 1630s and only 1.5 per cent in the 1690s.[7]

Annual university registration of entering students in the German Empire can be calculated on the basis of overall annual registration, taken as ten-year averages and corrected for the effects of multiple registration of students, a frequent occurrence in an epoch in which the *peregrinatio academica* was a widespread habit. By applying a registration coefficient varying from decade to decade to overall registration, Willem Frijhoff has recently provided a reliable graph of new students in the universities of the Empire.[8] He shows three clear peaks: if the years 1576–85 are taken as index 100, the years 1616–25 are at index 133; the years 1646–55 at index 160; and the years 1696–1705 at index 190. After this high, the number of new registrations declines continuously during the entire eighteenth century.[9] There are 1.4 per cent of young men of seventeen years of age who entered the university in the 1620s, 2.7 per cent toward 1650, 2.1 per cent around 1700 and 1.2 per cent in the 1770s.[10]

In the United Provinces the number of students who earned diplomas, in both local and foreign universities and given in twenty-five year averages, shows a continual rise during the seventeenth century. Forty-two students graduated yearly between 1600 and 1624, 72 between 1625 and 1649, 105 between 1650 and 1674, and 123 between 1675 and 1699. This was followed by a drop to 100 graduates yearly between 1700 and 1750.[11] The ratio of graduates to all males surviving to the average age at which university titles were granted (which varies between twenty-one and twenty-four years of age in different epochs), shows a curve similar to the one for the other countries, peaking in the last quarter of the seventeenth century (0.72 per cent) before declining to its low point in the mid-eighteenth century (0.57 per cent between 1725 and 1749). [12]

Three judgements concerning university students in the seventeenth century can be made on the basis of these data. First, it is clear that a high point in university recruitment was reached during the century. The number of students was higher than for both the sixteenth and the eighteenth centuries, and at a time in which the political situation was far from peaceful and the economic situation far from favourable. Secondly, university enrolment peaked in Castille in 1590, in England in 1630 and in the Empire and the United Provinces in 1690, which confirms that southern Europe preceded northern in this onslaught of the faculties. Finally, the high points in university attendance relative to the population in general (which require adjusting for shifts in the overall population) come somewhat earlier, at the end of the sixteenth century for Castille and England, in the mid-seventeenth century for the Empire. The conclusion seems clear: in the seventeenth century, the universities of Europe took in more students and prepared more graduates than they were to do in the following century and even during the first half of the nineteenth century, when they competed with a proliferation of schools of a more strictly professional nature. Since we lack any firmer way to identify 'intellectuals' than by attendance at a university and the possession of a degree, such data will have to serve to justify saying that at various moments each of these nations experienced a notable expansion of its intellectual population during the seventeenth century. What do we know, however, about the evolution of the market in the social positions to which these graduates aspired?

THE MARKET FOR POSITIONS

Unfortunately, the information available on this important question is still largely incomplete, and it is extremely difficult to measure the number of offices or benefices that were open to university graduates each year. Obviously, this number depended on two variables, the total number of ecclesiastical or administrative and judiciary positions existent at any given moment, and the degree to which they were subject to open competition or reserved for hereditary transfer. Hard data regarding both of these variables can be ascertained for only a few places, which at best permits a body of hypotheses to be verified. In Castille, it is clear that after 1560 the number of administrative positions open to university graduates did not rise. This is the case, for example, for the *plazas de asiento* that were the most lucrative and the most prestigious of the positions to which the hierarchy of *letrados* could aspire, since they were primarily as officials in the royal councils and courts. Between 1500 and 1560 their number tripled, passing from 48 to 132. Afterward the increase slowed, with 148 such positions in 1600, and 166 in 1691.[13] Moreover, after the end of the sixteenth century these posts were monopolized by a minority of families who used the six *colegios mayores* of Salamanca, Alcalá and Valladolid to assure their place in society (two-thirds of the posts in the chancelleries and the royal councils were in the hands of graduates of the *colegios mayores*).[14]

The situation in Holland a hundred years later seems analogous. To take one example, until the middle of the century, fewer lawyers from provincial areas were admitted to the Court of Holland than the number of law graduates from those same provinces, but between 1650 and 1665 the ratio was reversed and the number of Hollander lawyers at the court was greater than the number of graduates. After 1665 the situation was again reversed, and an increasing imbalance was set up between the number of those who held degrees and those who filled posts. The gap widened the most when the number of graduates was the highest.[15]

These two case-studies can perhaps help to draw up a multiphase model.

1 First, the increase in employent opportunity offered by both the growth of the churches in times of reform and in national and colonial bureaucracies set off an increase in the student population, since more young people could aspire – and aspire legitimately – to convert their university degree into a professional post and an enhanced social position.

2 When this increase in university registration and in degrees earned attained its maximum, the market in the coveted posts had *already* become saturated. This is what happened in Castille in the 1580s and in Holland a century later.

3 This entailed a transformation in an entire set of professional positions that were occupied by graduates unable to satisfy their social ambitions. This is what occurred, for example, with the profession of schoolmaster in England before the Civil War. Many graduates and *literati* (university students without degrees) turned to teaching school. In the diocese of Norwich in the 1580s, 47 per cent of the new schoolmasters were *literati* and 30 per cent graduates.[16] In Cambridgeshire between 1574 and 1604, two-thirds of the schoolmasters at the grammar school level, but also

one-third of primary school masters had a university degree.[17] In the diocese of London between 1627 and 1641, one half the schoolmasters in grammar schools held a diploma.[18]

The invasion of the lower levels of the teaching profession by university graduates had several consequences. The social groups that provided a recruitment pool for schoolmasters shifted to the minor gentry, commercial milieux and the wealthier yeomen. The very definition of the function of schoolmaster changed as the requirements for diplomas and experience attached to the position rose, while at the same time the way was closed off to those who previously could aspire to such positions. The teaching profession became the seat of profound social and economic dissatisfaction – economic because the revenue of a grammar school master was only one-half to one-fourth that of a vicar, and social because it brought less prestige. One text dated 1663 defined the school-master's position as 'the least remunerative and the least considered'.[19] A schoolmaster who held a university degree viewed teaching in an ordinary petty school or grammar school as a purgatory to be undergone before obtaining a post of master in a more prestigious urban grammar school or winning a church benefice. In fact, in Warwickshire and Worcestershire between 1601 and 1640, 56 per cent of schoolmasters in grammar schools entered into the ecclesiastical career, but after a wait of upwards of ten years.[20] Those who exercised the profession of schoolmaster because other social opportunities were unavailable viewed it as a prolonged frustration.

4 There was a lag – a 'time to understand'[21] – between when degrees fell out of balance with the posts available and when people recognized that such an imbalance existed. This means that there was necessarily a lag before changes became apparent in two conjunctural situations, in the number of available positions (which was the first element to react) and in university registration (which reacted later). Once the process of disinvestment in the university as an institution was set off, however, it continued, leading either to the choice of other educational possibilities or to a rejection of upper-level studies.

FORMULATING A REPRESENTATION: THE SURPLUS OF INTELLECTUALS

This schema for the comprehension of the question is still provisory and hypothetical. Nevertheless, it serves to account for similarities in situations encountered at varying moments of the seventeenth century in all European countries. It also offers a way to conceptualize the creation of a population of intellectuals frustrated of their social aspirations as a disharmony between a system of representations that long continued to grant to university degrees an efficacy they no longer had, on the one hand, and on the other, to grasp a functioning social situation that devalued degrees, due to the increase in the number of degree-holders.

As we have seen, however, this discrepancy, which at first was misunderstood, hence aggravated, was at length perceived by social agents. It then founded an entire set of representations to attempt to define it, denounce it, or account for it. What we need to understand now is how, in the seventeenth century, a new ideological motif came to be fashioned to give expression to a concerned awareness of what was designated as an over-production of graduates or a surplus of intellectuals. This ideological motif (just like iconographic motifs) was formulated in different ways and expressed by different means according to the various national traditions. In Castille, it appears in literary fiction in the picaresque novel, which can be read (among other ways) as a portrayal and denunciation of a proliferation of students that was producing the new *déclassés*. One example of this literature is the *Guzmán de Alfarache* of Mateo Alemán, the first part of which was published in 1599 and the second in 1602, at the moment of the most severe discrepancy between university enrolment and possible access to a bureaucratic career. Alemán's fictional account reverses his own situation: he himself was a university graduate who became *déclassé*. He earned his degree of Bachelor of Arts at the University of Seville in 1564 and began the study of medicine at the University of Salamanca the following year. The death of his father, a never-ending series of debts and, beneath it all, his origin as a *converso* (a converted Jew) dashed his hopes for a career in the liberal professions and turned him into a marginal figure (at least in his own mind) by obliging him to follow the calling of money-handling, scorned in Spain of the Age of Gold. He held a post in the Treasury, but also and primarily he was an inveterate financial trader.

In his novel, Mateo Alemán objectifies his dashed ambitions, but by inversion, since his hero, Guzmán, is a beggar who becomes a student. After many wanderings that had taken him from Spain to Italy and then from Rome back to Madrid, widowed and much reduced, Guzmán the *picaro* decides to 'make himself a churchman':

> I say to myself, 'I have [notions of] the humanities, I want to make use of them now. I'll go to Alcalá, which is three steps from here, where I'll do my philosophy and my theology, then I'll take my

degrees. Perhaps I have a talent for getting up in the pulpit, and between masses and sermons, I'll have earned my bread. At the worst I can become a monk and always be sure of a pittance.'[22]

In Alcalá, Guzmán becomes Master of Arts (as did Mateo Alemán) and then studies theology. He falls in love, however, and gives up his orders and pursuit of his degrees, making the seven years of study in Alcalá wasted. This stroke of fate, which deprives Guzmán of the position to which he had aspired, can perhaps be taken as an expression of the frustrations of an entire group. He exclaims:

> Guzmán, Guzmán! What happened to all those sleepless nights, all that solicitude, all those early morning risings, and so much time spent in the schools – so many deeds, so many degrees, and so many ambitions? I have already told you when I was young that everything ends up in a basket and I tell you now that all of my sort end up rotting in a tavern. God willing they stay there![23]

By reversing his own fate and that of many like him in the career of his hero, Mateo Alemán turns his fiction into an inverted configuration of a social reality. He speaks here, in the style of a book made up of parallels and reversals – of poverty and wealth, error and punishment, heredity and free will, sin and grace,[24] – for the dashed hopes of the 'alienated intellectuals' of Spain under Philip II.

In France in the early seventeenth century an abundance of texts point to the overly large number of universities and colleges and deplore the effects of increased enrolment. The arguments put forward, both by political figures such as Cardinal Richelieu in his *Testament* or by the administrators who wrote one memorandum after another on university reform, turn around three principal points.[25] First, an over-supply of university or secondary school students was contrary to social utility. When those who might otherwise have devoted themselves to commerce and the arts and crafts turned instead to administrative posts and ecclesiastical benefices, it threatened the productive capacity of the realm. By this token, following good mercantilist logic, it forced the kingdom into economic dependency since it set up a trade deficit, thus sapping the nation's monetary reserves and undermining its political power. Secondly, the escape toward government offices and church benefices that was made possible by earning a university degree or acquiring Latin-based culture increased beyond measure the number of clerics and officials, major and minor, thus increasing the number of people exempt from taxation. Thus the risk of disturbing social equilibrium was immense, particularly because taxation by assessment, the rule in France, raised the share that the productive sector had to pay to make up for the parvenus who defected to the Church and the legal and administrative professions. Finally, super-abundance of the literate threatened social order. It blurred social distinctions by holding out hopes to many people of a status incongruent with their place in society, thus destroying the strict reproduction of family position on which society was founded. Imbalance in the pyramid of 'estates' and an excessive frequentation of schools and universities (or what was judged as such) contradicted notions of social stability in which birth, talents and aspirations should show perfect harmony.

There were occasional attempts to transfer this ideology into educational policy. Whether such reforms were instituted under Richelieu, Colbert, or Louvois, their underlying principles were the same. First, it was important to lower the curriculum level in the *petites écoles* in order to remove the humanities from elementary education. In the words of a *Mémoire des raisons et moyens de la réformation des universités* dated 1667 and resulting from a survey of the *intendants* taken by Colbert:

> In these schools only reading and writing, ciphering and counting will be taught, and at the same time those who are of low birth and inept for learning (*les sciences*) will be obliged to learn a trade, and those whom Providence has caused to be born into a condition to labour the earth will be excluded from writing and taught only reading, unless the seeds of enlightenment and of a gift for the sciences be remarked in them, for which they might merit being excepted from the common law. [26]

Eliminating excess literates required pruning back the school system as well, eliminating the *collèges* and universities in smaller cities in order to make access to higher education more difficult. The 1667 *Mémoire* says as much explicitly:

> Their elimination will render studies more difficult because the peasants who through the convenience of proximity send their children to a near-by university and who keep them easily with their own produce would be unable to keep them in the larger cities where it is much more expensive to live and where they could not send their own provender because of the distance involved. Having fewer students of this sort, there will consequently be less complaint and quibbling, fewer priests and fewer do-nothing and ignorant monks and, to the contrary, much more money and more persons in commerce, [and] many more to labour the earth and to serve the King and the State in the armies. [27]

Neither Colbert nor Louvois achieved their ends, however, as city governments and urban populations insisted on their schools and firmly opposed any policy of striking educational institutions off the map. The fact remains that throughout the century the elites of the French administration agreed on viewing an over-production of literates as a mortal danger for the state and society.

In the German states in the mid-seventeenth century this collective representation took the form of a coherent theory, designated by the term *Uberfüllungsthese* (thesis of career overcrowding). Its ideological basis was the same as in France, but it was backed up by a greater commitment to observation and measurement. It drew support, first, from an awareness of a spectacular proliferation of universities and secondary schools, tied to a strengthening of political power in the various German states and to their confessional exclusiveness; and secondly, from a clear perception of a growing imbalance between the university degrees expected of candidates for public office and the scholastic requirements traditionally demanded for such posts. Awareness of an over-production of graduates and excessive enrolment in the universities had two effects. First, measuring variations in the student body based on registration counts initiated a preoccupation with university statistics. Thus with the eighteenth century we see a first description of university populations based on data in time series. Second, the notion of an excess of intellectuals underlies a body of thought that aimed at limiting access to the universities by a strict adjustment of the number of students to the number of available positions (*ne plures civium literis incumbent quam cujusvis status ratio requirit* Paul Grunewald wrote in 1677) and by instituting severe entrance examinations. [28] In the Empire at the turn of the eighteenth century, the thesis of an over-production of intellectuals reflected and expressed (in its fashion and not necessarily in full awareness) the two peaks in enrolment in institutions of higher education in German lands, one in the mid-seventeenth century and the other in the decades 1690–1710.

THE *LONGUE DURÉE* OF AN IDEOLOGICAL MOTIF

Once the various forms of the idea of a surplus of intellectuals had been firmly established in the seventeenth century, when university enrolment was on the upswing, it took on a force of its own and was manipulated for political or polemical ends in a wide variety of educational and social situations. It underlay the hostility that French administrators of the eighteenth century showed toward schooling for the people. [29] It underlay debate on the educational

system in France and Germany in the first half of the nineteenth
century.[30] East of the Franco–German borders, the over-production
of intellectuals unable to find employment in the state, the Church,
or the liberal professions was used as an argument against the
classical curriculum of the *Gymnasium*. To the west, it was used to
criticize what was taught in the *lycées*, the faculties of letters and the
Ecole Normale. The idea that the number of students enrolled in
letters and in law was too great entered into a way of thinking about
society that came to be largely independent of its social context. It
was even strong enough to resist statistical surveys that belied it.
This was the case, for example, in France under the July Monarchy
when the Minister of Public Instruction, Villemain, writing a report
in 1843 and citing statistics, stated that enrolment in the *collèges* was
higher in 1789 than in their royal and communal counterparts in his
own time. What is remarkable is that his statement was disbelieved
not because it might be false (as was shown later) but because it went
against a representation, held to be self-evident, that was deeply
rooted in a fear of the proletariat of dissatisfied former students.[31]
Thus we need to try to understand what lent credence to the notion
of a surplus of frustrated intellectuals and gave it a life of its own,
unrelated to objective, statistically measurable changes in the
student population.

The notion implies a fixed conception of society that is radically
opposed to the liberal and meritocratic ideology that has wrongly
been considered the only social ideology of the nineteenth century.
The denunciation of an excess of intellectuals was in point of fact in
no way liberal, since it implied the need to work to match the
number of prepared young men with the number of positions
available to them. It was not meritocratic since it founded this one-
to-one ratio on the perpetual reproduction of the dominant class.
The motif of excess intellectuals is doubtless one of the most evident
indications of the strength of the social ideology of the *ancien
régime* society that saw sons as duplicating their fathers and the *collège*
or the university as an endless bucket-line dipping into the same
source to supply the dominant classes. Those who transgressed the
rules of this game constituted a possible menace to order. Opening
up studies and university degrees to those whose condition should
have kept them away jeopardized all of society. Victor Cousin's
report on the vote for the School Act of June 1833 spells out the
reasons for this:

> In general these young people who do not feel themselves destined for
> a high career carry on their studies negligently; and when after

mediocre successes they return, around eighteen years of age, to the profession and the habits of their families, since nothing in daily life recalls to them or keeps up their past studies, several years efface the little classical knowledge they had acquired. Often also these young people contract relations and tastes in the *collège* that make it difficult or nearly impossible for them to return to the humble careers of their fathers. This produces a race of restless men discontent with their lot, with others, and with themselves, enemies of a social order in which they feel out of place, and ready to throw themselves, with a smattering of knowledge, with genuine talent, and with unbridled ambition into all the ways of servility and revolt.[32]

This text, along with many others, expresses a widely shared fear of intellectuals who were doubly *déclassé* – both because their studies failed to harmonize with their condition, and because their employment did not conform with the hopes to which their degrees allowed them to aspire. Different from their fathers but nonetheless forced to accept their fathers' social status, these parvenus who had become learned in vain could only blame society for their personal disappointment and live out their unhappy fate in restlessness and discontent, as Cousin said. For conservatives in nineteenth-century Europe, they served as reserves in the armies of revolt. They formed an 'intellectual proletariat' even more dangerous than its industrial counterpart since they had momentarily thought to upset the hierarchy of social status and could put their meagre store of learning to the service of subversion. This idea, stated with such clarity by Victor Cousin, gained new strength from the Revolutions of 1848, which were imputed (as was the English Revolution two centuries earlier) to alienated and frustrated intellectuals. This new attitude resembled an amplified version of an image that ran throughout the literature of the Enlightenment to denounce the danger of a growing force of writers who Voltaire called '*la canaille de la littérature*' ['hack writers'].[33] In the microcosm of the world of letters, legitimate writers – the ones who held the posts and the offices – viewed such thwarted ambitions and aborted careers in the same terms as society as a whole saw the bitterness of the proletariat of the graduates who lacked school certification.

The motif of the alienated intellectuals not only bore with it a fixed conception of society and a depreciated image of the intellectual; it also contained a representation of learning that saw its divulgation and dissemination as a profanation. European societies in the modern age shared in the idea that the operative value and the symbolic efficacy of learning strictly depended upon its mastery by a narrow elite that held it out of the reach of the commonality. Carlo

Ginzburg has demonstrated the two ways in which this monopoliz-ation of knowledge worked.[34] The first of these was Christian, and it made clerics the only authorized interpreters of the secrets of God, of nature and of power (*arcana Dei, arcana naturae, arcana imperii*). When traditional forms of knowledge were shattered in the scientific revolution of the early seventeenth century, the frontiers of knowl-edge were pushed back and traditional prohibitions disappeared, but the control of learning by a restricted minority – the *respublica literatorum* – who alone were capable of handling it without im-perilling faith, law, or order was in no way changed. At the very moment when Icarus and Prometheus became emblematic of this unlimited search for knowledge, it became clear that it was the province of a new sort of cleric. Conrad Vorstius, the Arminian professor of theology at the University of Leiden, put it most succinctly: '*Hic vero libertas aliqua inquirendi, aut etiam dissentiendi doctis omnino concedenda est*' ['We have to give some freedom of inquiry and even of dissent, above all to intellectuals'].[35] A century later, Kant founded his distinction of the uses of reason on a similar division:

> Which restriction [on freedom] is an obstacle to enlightenment, and which is not an obstacle but a promoter of it? I answer: The public use of one's reason must always be free, and it alone can bring about enlightenment among men. The private use of reason, on the other hand, may often be very narrowly restricted without particularly hindering the progress of enlightenment. By the public use of one's reason I understand the use which a person makes of it as a scholar before the reading public. Private I call that which one may make of it in a particular civil post or office which is entrusted to him.[36]

Even if every citizen is supposed to be able to exercise both of these uses of reason, it is clear that its *public use*, which supposes mastery of scholarly writing, is by that token reserved for a minority of those who submit their ideas to the judgement of readers.

To the contrary, an uncontrolled divulgation of knowledge risked its perversion. This argument was used from the outset in the sixteenth century by the adversaries of printing. When it dis-seminated knowledge, the printed book disseminated an illusion as well, since it was of such immediate access that it led to misunder-standing the true labour of learning. It also threatened authority because it gave everyone the impression of being as learned as the scholars.[37] It was probably here that the ideological roots of this thesis of intellectual over-production ran deepest. The unbridled increase in scholarly literates and in university graduates could indeed be perceived as destructive of both knowledge itself (scattered, perverted, or travestied) and the symbolic and social position of its self-appointed guardians. It is this representation that lay behind all the others, and it long provided intellectuals with a self-image, even when their discourses seemed to deny it.

Thus the question posed at the outset has been shifted. What we need to understand is not so much whether an intellectual representation and a university conjuncture matched one another, but what were the conditions under which that representation was stated and manipulated. It is clear that the motif of an excess of intellectuals belongs within the very long time-span of a concept of static social hierarchies and of a monopolistic appropriation of knowledge. This gives it relative independence from the fluctuations of university recruitment and the number of the degreeless *literati*. It is also certain, however, that the theme took on unusual force every time those who held power and reserved knowledge to themselves perceived – rightly or wrongly – that their position was threatened by too large a body of parvenus. This is what occurred in the seventeenth century when university graduates failed to find employment in the market of administrative offices and church benefices; this is what occurred at the time of the revolutions of the first half of the nineteenth century. Thus we need to identify the social groups in each concrete historical situation who affirmed the thesis of the overproduction of intellectuals; we need to define the social and political strategies that utilized this notion; and we need to understand how it was reformulated each time. There were important stakes involved. A representation of the sort, although it did not reflect the situation in the universities exactly, was nevertheless tied to that conjunctural situation and was in a position to influence it when it grew strong enough to be expressed in educational policy. This was the case in the seventeenth and the nineteenth centuries. It is perhaps still true in the twentieth.

Postscript

Preparation for the Fourth Franco-Swiss Meeting on Economic and Social History held in Geneva in May 1982 led me to return to the first draft of this study. That and the discussions connected with this meeting in turn lead me to offer several further comments and some additional data.

I One problem of prime importance is whether it is possible to reconstitute a long-term view of university recruitment in France comparable to overviews of the sort already drawn up for Castille, England, the German Empire and the United Provinces. The difficulties are not few. On the one hand, French sources are by far inferior to those available in neighbouring countries. Enrolment records were rarely kept before the later seventeenth century, and often scholars must rely on registers of graduates or even only lists of those who swore their oath before the rector. In either case, it is of course impossible to know what proportion of all students these represent. On the other hand, from the mid-sixteenth century, the success of the *collèges* (Jesuit for the most part) offered stiff competition to the faculties of arts, enrolment in which declined dramatically. This contraction of the university population simply reflected a shift in institutions, however, not a decline in upper-level studies, since all students in philosophy sections – even if their *collège* was not affiliated with a university – could legitimately be considered university students. Figures concerning French university faculties were seriously affected by reforms that changed the curriculum, unified courses of study and introduced new disciplines. This was the case with the reform of the study of law in the edict of 1679, which by instituting the study of civil law in Paris prompted an immediate rise in enrolment there. In this case as well, a conjunctural change does not mean there was any change in the proportion of the population undergoing schooling, but only that students transferred from one place to another. The rise in the number of jurisprudence students in Paris was, in point of fact, accompanied by a decline in both enrolment and bachelors' degrees granted by the faculty of jurisprudence of Poitiers and in the number of law graduates in Caen.

In spite of lacunae in the documentation and changes in institutions, there are a few long-term series of figures that allow us to sketch university enrolment in France (only from the early seventeenth century, however, and only for graduates). Let us take the faculties of Poitiers and Caen between 1600 and 1789 as an example. In Poitiers, an all-time high in the number of bachelors' degrees was reached between 1600 and 1619, with an average of 96.5 graduates yearly in the first decade of the century and 96.3 graduates in the second. In Caen, the 1630s marked a first peak with a yearly average of 103.8 graduates. After this first high point, bachelors' degrees in Poitiers show a regular decline, reaching between 50 and 60 graduates per year in the period 1620–99, and between 40 and 50 for the 1760s. In Caen, the curve is more gradual, with a maximum for all disciplines between 1670 and 1679 (105.3 graduates on an annual average) but also with a clear drop in the number of graduates from

1680 to 1759 (between 70 and 90 as an annual average by decades). In both cases, the three decades immediately preceding the French Revolution show a new rise in graduates to over 60 per year in Poitiers and over 100 per year in Caen during the 1770s.[38]

If these two examples can be taken as typical, the number of degrees granted by French universities (in jurisprudence at least) reached its maximum in the first half of the seventeenth century, then underwent a slight decline in the first thirty years of the eighteenth century, to undergo a clear but brief revival on the eve of the Revolution. Comments on this general outline must be made with extreme prudence since it concerns graduates and not entering students. Nevertheless, it seems to agree with the evolution of university enrolment in other European countries, since in France as elsewhere the universities produced more graduates in the seventeenth century than in the following century. There is one difference, however: the period 1760–90 shows a more vigorous upswing in France than in Castille or England.

II It is still impossible to measure the market in social positions desired or obtained by graduates of French universities. Precise studies to show the number of posts and benefices (and fluctuations in that number) are simply lacking. The one thing of which we can be certain is that an imbalance set in at the end of the eighteenth century between the number of graduates in jurisprudence (which rose in a thirty-year period) and the number of positions open to them, in particular as lawyers. In Toulouse the list of lawyers swelled (from 87 *avocats* attached to the Parlement in 1740, to 215 in 1789) and newcomers made up a larger part of the total number (an average of 7.5 persons per year between 1764 and 1789 as against 3.8 persons annually during the first half of the eighteenth century). The corps was also younger: more than one-half of the laywers in Toulouse were less than forty years of age in 1789. This means that a good many lawyers lacked clients and never had occasion to plead a case. This was true for 160 out of 300 lawyers newly enrolled between 1760 and 1790, or more than one-half of the bar.[39] In Besançon and in the Franche-Comté as a whole, a similar situation existed. More numerous – too numerous – and of more modest social origin, lawyers lacked cases and could neither accede to parlement, where the positions were monopolized by well-established families, nor buy a charge as secretary of the king, which included a patent of nobility and bore a price beyond their means.[40] Frustrated in their aspirations to rise in society, deprived of a clientele, rejected by the nobility, the lawyers of the end of the *ancien régime* were not happy with their lot. It is hardly surprising that they stood up against the officials of the sovereign courts, to which they were attached by tradition, and launched themselves whole-heartedly into the Revolution.

III Many texts in the seventeenth and eighteenth centuries attest to the ideological preference for social immobility that underlay denunciations of the over-production of university graduates. Two examples of this may suffice. The first is taken from a pamphlet published in 1615, at a time when the session of the Estates General invited criticism of existing institutions or calls for their reform, but also at a time when the sheer size and the increase in the number of jurisprudence students had become perceptible. In the *Image de la France représentée à Messieurs des Etats*, the anonymous author (probably the Jesuit, Pelletier) decried the harmful effects of this rush to juridical studies:

> It is quite observable that a change in [social] condition ruins and destroys the best and oldest families, as when a man who was a good and wealthy merchant gives in to the vanity of the century and wants to have his son study to make a man of the robe of him. That being done, everything in the father's house seems repugnant to his son, now an office-holder. He must have a dwelling with a formal entry for carriages and no trace of the shop sign or shop anywhere. He must nourish himself, be dressed, and be equipped in a totally different style. And the best is that since he comes to marriage as a son of Justice, he must make a match with nothing of working folk about it, indeed, that brings lustre and brilliance. Adieu common folk. There goes my official, son of a good Merchant allied to Nobility; there he goes to be married to a high placed Damoiselle, who he takes not so much for the means as for the [social] support. By marrying her, if his office is of the best and most costly, he will soon make her a damed Dame, as if his mule and his cassock had made him into a Knight of the Order. . . . The child to be born of the marriage of our *officier* will complete the picture since, disdaining the profession of his father, he will embrace the nobility of his mother, who will not have failed to raise him as a gentleman and with good courage. God knows whether our man will have struck a good bargain on the stuffs of his shop, or whether the other will not profit even more from the Library, the long robe, and the square hat. [The result] is precisely this little city knight who, his sword at his side, followed by pages and lackeys, spends more and games away more in an hour or in one pass of the dice than his forefathers had acquired in long years.[41]

Rising in society took three generations and was aided by two mechanisms, the study of law, which aided the transfer from the shop to the judge's chambers, and marriage, which sealed an alliance with the nobility that provided entry into the Second Estate.

The author of the *Image de la France* shows us this evolution by evoking the life-style and the symbolic attributes of each social level: for commerce, the shop, the family group, the connections with *le peuple mécanique*; for the magistracy, the house with a *porte cochère*, the library, the long robe and the squared hat; for the nobility, the sword and domestic retainers. For Pelletier, this social promotion was doubly dangerous. It led to aristocratic wastefulness and brought the ruin of bourgeois fortunes and it turned normal ways of living upside-down by making the son scorn his father. The text speaks of a society in which educational capital is easily converted into social capital, and in which a certain flexibility in 'estates' and 'orders' permitted upward mobility into the nobility, transmitted by wives, guaranteed and attested by life-style alone. Whether this is a faithful reflection of reality or not is, in the final analysis, less important than its reflection of a shared belief in a representation that placed the motif of a surplus of graduates within the context of a programme for social regulation aiming at clear frontiers between 'qualities' and stabilizing every family in its 'estate'. Stopping the flow of law students was undeniably one means of translating this ideal into reality.

A century later, a scene reported in his *Mémoires* by Valentin Jamerey Duval, although its formulation differs, attests to the durability of the ideology of social immobility. In 1716 the young Jamerey Duval, who was staying with the hermits of Saint Anne, chanced to meet the Duke of Lorraine and his court. Surprised by his taste for maps and for history, the courtiers discussed him as an astonishing case:

> I understood that I was the subject of their conversation and that the duke said that it was a pity to leave me in the obscurity of my situation, and that if someone were to rescue me to send me to the university of Pont-à-Mousson there was all likelihood that I would make good progress in studies. Then, turning to me, he smiled and said to me that geography was a science both agreeable and interesting and that I did well to apply myself to it. I was charmed with an approval so apt to encourage me, but most of the guests were not so favourable. One among them, whom I would name with resentment if he were still living, gave me to understand that since Providence had chosen to have me born into a working profession, it was to have me show my talents for manual labour, and not for me to amuse myself in academic speculations that were none of my affair. He added, in extremely elegant terms and a very sweet tone of voice, that if I persisted in countering the will of God by wanting to learn more than belonged to my estate, it was much to be feared that one day I would be found occupying a cell in the hospital for the deranged. . . . The noble

courtiers found my taste for studies most strange. Some approved it, others rejected it. At the end, however, the majority of the votes went against me, and it was decided that the idea of instructing me in matters so far above my condition was entirely out of place, and that in all likelihood it had entered my head thanks to some passing moonbeam. [42]

An unchanging distribution of social status is here tied to a divine will that gives everyone a proper place. Each 'condition' had its 'exterior', its 'way of thinking', and its level of learning. By taking on studies that clashed with his 'estate'. Jamerey Duval was both rebelling against God's law and risking madness. At a time when social status was strictly codified, the limits between social 'estates' rigidly marked and recruitment of the dominant groups from their own number posited as an absolute law, education was thought by many to be an attribute of status that ought to consolidate visible differences of 'quality' and profession. Agricultural labour did not admit of 'academic speculations', or the necessary harmony between the hierarchy of status and the hierarchy of learning would be upset. It should be noted, however, that the Duke differed from the general opinion, perhaps discerning in Jamerey Duval the exception that confirmed a social rule that he probably shared.

We need, then, to continue to gather texts that express the social ideology of traditional society, not in order to set them up as direct reflections of true social situations or to claim that they constitute homogeneous serial data, but to determine, in each individual instance, the conditions that may help us understand why they were produced and how.

IV It seems to me, to sum up, that it is by no means wasted effort to reconstruct the essential motifs that provided the scaffolding for traditional representations of the social world, nor is an attempt to do so vitiated by the affirmed primacy of socio-economic studies. Such representations were neither automatically produced reflections of society nor chance speculations, and they had a complex relationship with real social states. They lent existence to groups that were never constituted as such. [43] They were the source of strategies that favoured or resisted mechanisms for rising or falling on the social scale and were perceived as primordial and true. They underlay polemical discourses that were often translated into policy. All in all, representations of the social world, which are not limited to a taxonomy of orders, classes, or groups, but also offer a grasp of the mechanisms that modify the limits of those groups or control the balance among them, are just as 'real' a reality as the one studied in social analysis, since they constitute and shape that reality. [44] This is what assures representations a central place in a history of traditional societies.

NOTES

This text was first published in *Annales ESC*, 37 (1982), pp. 389–400. It came out of a collective study carried out at the Ecole des Hautes Etudes en Sciences Sociales on student populations in Europe between the sixteenth and the eighteenth centuries. It has thus also appeared in the volume summarizing that investigation, *Les Universités européennes du XVIe au XVIIIe siècle: Histoire sociale des populations étudiantes*, Dominique Julia, Jacques Revel, and Roger Chartier ed. (Éditions de l'École des Hautes Études en Sciences Sociales, Paris, 1986), vol. 1, pp. 245–60.

1   Mark H. Curtis, 'The Alienated Intellectuals of Early Stuart England', *Past and Present*, 23 (1962), pp. 25–43.

2   Pierre Bourdieu, *La Distinction. Critique sociale du jugement* (Editions de Minuit, Paris, 1979), p. 149 [*Distinction: A Social Critique of the Judgement of Taste*, tr. Richard Nice (Cambridge, MA., Harvard University Press, 1984), p. 133].

3   Bourdieu, *La Distinction*, pp. 145–85 (Nice tr., pp. 135–68).

4   For a critical survey of these studies, see Roger Chartier and Jacques Revel, 'Université et société dans l'Europe moderne: position des problèmes', *Revue d'histoire moderne et contemporaine*, 1978, pp. 353–74, reprinted in *L'Histoire des universités. Problèmes et méthodes* (Zesyty Naukowo Universytetu Jagiellonskiego DLXVII, Warsaw and Krakow, 1980), pp. 27–49.

5   Richard L. Kagan, *Students and Society in Early Modern Spain* (Johns Hopkins University Press, Baltimore and London, 1974), pp. 196–200, figs 7 and 8.

6   Lawrence Stone, 'The Size and Composition of the Oxford Student Body 1580–1910', in Lawrence Stone, ed., *The University in Society* (2 vols, Princeton University Press, Princeton, 1974), vol. 1, pp. 3–110, graph 1, p. 6 and tables 1A and 1B, pp. 91–2.

7   These percentages are calculated on the basis of the figures given in Lawrence Stone, 'The Size and Composition', p. 91 for Oxford; p. 92 for Cambridge; p. 103 for age distribution of the population at large, and in Lawrence Stone, 'The Educational Revolution in England 1560–1640', *Past and Present*, 28 (1964), pp. 41–80; p. 54 for entering students in the Inns of Court.

8   Willem Frijhoff, 'Surplus ou déficit? Hypothèses sur le nombre réel des étudiants en Allemagne à l'époque moderne (1576–1815)', *Francia*, 7 (1979), pp. 173–218.

9   Ibid., table 3, p. 205 and fig. 4, p. 206.

10   Ibid., table 5, p. 212.

11   Willem Frijhoff, *La Société néerlandaise et ses gradués, 1575–1814. Une recherche sérielle sur le statut des intellectuels à partir des registres universitaires* (Holland University Press, Amsterdam, 1981), appendix 4, p. 383.

12   Ibid., table 47, p. 209.

13   Kagan, *Students and Society*, table 3, p. 209.

14   Ibid., table 4, p. 93.

15   Frijhoff, *La Société néerlandaise*, graph 12, p. 255.

16   David Cressy, *Literacy and the Social Order: Reading and Writing in Tudor and Stuart England* (Cambridge University Press, Cambridge, 1980), p. 168.

17   Margaret Spufford, 'The Schooling of the Peasantry in Cambridgeshire, 1575–1700', *Agricultural History Review*, 8, supplement (1970), pp. 112–47.

18   S. M. Wide and J. A. Morriss, 'The Episcopal Licensing of Schoolmasters in the Diocese of London, 1627–1685', *The Guildhall Miscellany*, 11, 9 (1967), pp. 392–406.

19   Marchamont Nedham, *A Discourse Concerning Schools and Schoolmasters*, (1662), p. 9.

20   P. K. Orpen, 'Schoolmastering as a Profession in the Seventeenth Century: The Career Patterns of the Grammar Schoolmasters', *History of Education*, 6, 3 (1977), pp. 183–94, table 1, p. 185, and table 3, p. 190.

21   Bourdieu, *La Distinction*, pp. 157–9 (Nice tr., pp. 142–3).

22   Mateo Alemán, *Guzmán de Alfarache*, ed. Samuel Gili y Gaya (5 vols, Espasa-Calpe, Madrid, 1962–67) [*Le Gueux, ou la vie de Guzmán d'Alfarache*, in *Romans picaresques espagnols*, tr. M. Molho and J. F. Reille (Gallimard, Bibliothèque de la Pléiade, Paris, 1968), p. 655].

23   Alemán, *Le Gueux*, p. 677.

24   See Michael Molho, 'Introduction à la pensée picaresque', in *Romans picaresques espagnols*, pp. xl–lxxxvii.

25   A collection of such texts is available in François de Dainville, 'Collège et fréquentation scolaire au XVIIe siècle', *Population*, (1957); reprinted in his *L'Éducation des Jésuites (XVIe–XVIIIe siècles)*, ed. Marie-Madeleine Compère (Editions de Minuit, Paris, 1978), pp. 119–49, in particular pp. 126–34.

26   Cited in Dainville, *L'Éducation des Jésuites*, p. 134.

27   Ibid., p. 133.

28   On the thesis of the over-production of intellectuals in German lands, see the excellent summary in Frijhoff, 'Surplus ou déficit?' pp. 173–81.

29   Roger Chartier, Marie-Madeleine Compère and Dominique Julia, *L'Éducation en France du XVIe au XVIIIe siècle* (S.E.D.E.S. Paris, 1976), pp. 37–41.

30   Lenore O'Boyle, 'The Problem of an Excess of Educated men in Western Europe, 1800–1850', *Journal of Modern History*, 4 (1970), pp. 471–95.

31 On this statistical analysis, see the critical summary in Dominique
    Julia and Paul Pressly, 'La Population scolaire en 1798. Les
    extravagances statistiques du Ministre Villemain', *Annales ESC*, 30
    (1975), pp. 1516–61.
32 Cited in Maurice Crubellier, *Histoire culturelle de la France XIXe–XXe
    siècle* (Colin, Paris, 1971), pp. 105–6.
33 Robert Darnton, 'The High Enlightenment and the Low-life of
    Literature in Pre-revolutionary France', *Past and Present*, 51 (1971),
    pp. 81–115.
34 Carlo Ginzburg, 'High and Low: The Theme of Forbidden Knowledge
    in the Sixteenth and Seventeenth Centuries', *Past and Present*, 73
    (1976), pp. 28–41.
35 Cited in Ginzburg 'High and Low', p. 40.
36 Immanuel Kant, 'Réponse à la question: Qu'est-ce que les Lumières?',
    in his *Philosophie de l'histoire (opuscules)*, ed. and tr. Stéphane Piobetta
    (Denoël, Paris, 1965), pp. 48–9 [Immanuel Kant, *Foundations of the
    Metaphysics of Morals and What is Enlightenment?*, tr. Lewis W. Beck
    (Bobbs-Merrill, Indianapolis, Indiana, c.1959, 1975), p. 87].
37 See Martin J. Lowry, *The World of Aldus Manutius. Business and
    Scholarship in Renaissance Venice* (Cornell University Press, Ithaca,
    NY., 1979), p. 31.
38 These figures have been taken from the study carried out at the Ecole
    des Hautes Etudes en Sciences Sociales that will appear in *Les
    Universités européennes du XVIe au XVIIIe siècle: Histoire sociale des
    populations étudiantes*, ed. Dominique Julia, Jacques Revel (Éditions de
    l'École des Hautes Études en Sciences Sociales, Paris), vol 2: *France*
    (forthcoming).
39 Lenard R. Berlanstein, *The Barristers of Toulouse in the Eighteenth Century
    (1740–1793)* (Johns Hopkins University Press, Baltimore, 1975),
    pp. 12–14.
40 Maurice Gresset, 'L'État d'esprit des avocats comtois à la veille de la
    Révolution', *Actes du 102e Congrès National des Sociétés Savantes* (Limoges,
    1977), Section d'Histoire Moderne et Contemporaine, vol. 1:
    Contribution à l'histoire des mentalités de 1610 à nos jours (Paris, 1979), pp.
    85–93.
41 Cited in Denis Richet, 'La Polémique politique en France de 1612 à
    1615', in Roger Chartier and Denis Richet, eds, *Représentation et vouloir
    politiques: Autour des Etats Généraux de 1614* (Ecole des Hautes Etudes en
    Sciences Sociales, Paris, 1981), pp. 243–4.
42 Valentin Jamerey Duval, *Mémoires. Enfance et éducation d'un paysan au
    XVIIIe siècle*, ed. and preface Jean-Marie Goulemot (Sycomore, Paris,
    1981), pp. 243–4.
43 See Luc Boltanski, *Les Cadres, la formation d'un groupe social* (Editions de
    Minuit, Paris, 1982).
44 See Pierre Bourdieu, 'L'Identité et la représentation. Eléments pour
    une réflexion critique sur l'idée de région', *Actes de la recherche en sciences
    sociales*, 35 (1980), pp. 63–72. On another level, see also Roger

Chartier, *Figure della furfanteria. Marginalità e cultura popolare in Francia tra Cinque e Seicento* (Instituto della Enciclopedia Italiana, Rome, 1982), Introduction, pp. 13–20.

7

FIGURES OF THE 'OTHER'

Peasant Reading in the Age of the Enlightenment

From the book to reading: passing this threshold is not as easy as it may seem, particularly for anyone setting out to determine the reading habits of an anonymous multitude who neglected to confess what they read. This is the case with the people of country areas in France during the eighteenth century. To be sure, one or two took pen in hand to tell their life story, and in the process recalled their first encounter with books. Louis Simon, a muslin-weaver in the Maine region, for instance, began in 1809, five years after the death of a beloved wife, to write 'the principal events [that have] happened during the course of my life'. Remembering his youth, he noted that he had satisfied his taste for reading with the help of the parish priest, who lent him books from his library, and perhaps with that of a retired pedlar in the village.

> Thus I spent my time in the pleasure of playing [musical] instruments and reading all the books I could procure on all the ancient histories, on wars, geography, saints' lives, the Old and New Testaments, and other books sacred and profane. I also very much liked songs and hymns.[1]

Such witnesses, however, were few and laconic. A more loquacious writer, such as Valentin Jamerey Duval, was far removed from his peasant childhood when he wrote, and as he recounted his conquest of culture, it was the man of the Enlightenment who spoke, judged and reflected, not the shepherd of yester-year. Evidence of the sort thus needs to be interpreted first as a presentation of oneself subject to the enormous social and cultural distance from one's origins brought by an exceptional career.[2] Even if such life stories contain traits that are valid for all the self-taught, they tell us little about common uses of print and ordinary ways of reading. Autobiographies, then – few in number, laconic and produced by unusual circumstances – are insufficient to reconstruct peasant reading habits in the eighteenth century. This lends all the greater value to another sort of document, the reports sent to the Abbé Grégoire in response to his questions 'regarding the patois and the customs of country people'. Indeed, Grégoire, *curé* (parish priest) of Embermesnil and Deputy to the National Assembly, sent out a questionnaire on 13 August 1790 containing three questions that seem to hold promise for a history of popular reading:

35 Have [the parish priests and their curates] an assortment of books for lending to their parishioners?
36 Have country people a taste for reading?
37 What sorts of books are more commonly found in their homes?

Thus we have three precise questions concerning the presence of books in rural areas and on the preferred reading of the men and women who lived there.

These questions refer to works in French, since books written in patois were to be noted in response to questions 21 to 25, in particular to question 23:

23 Have you works in patois, printed or manuscript, ancient or modern, such as [books on] customary law, public acts, chronicles, prayers, sermons, asceticism, hymnals, songbooks, almanacs, poetry, traditions, etc.?

Grégoire's survey thus appears to be the earliest inquiry into cultural practices (reading practices, at any event) among the French, and it seems an unhoped-for inventory of the eighteenth-century rural library in the early stages of the Revolution. Scrutiny of the responses somewhat tempers enthusiasm, however. The responses are few in number: there are only forty-three reports extant, preserved in the Bibliothèque de la Société de Port-Royal and in the Bibliothèque Nationale in Paris.[3] Furthermore, the answers often do not cover all the forty-three questions posed by Grégoire. They leave out certain of them (in particular, for eleven responses, the questions that interest us here), they give one answer to several questions, or the respondents write freely without following the order of questions in the questionnaire.

Above all, the respondents were not the rural readers themselves, but men who stood somewhat apart from peasant culture. For one thing, their social position strongly differentiated them from rural folk. To gather information for his investigation Grégoire called on several networks of respondents. With some he enjoyed relations of erudite friendship, others were among his colleagues in the National Assembly and still others responded for the Societies of Friends of the Constitution affiliated with the Jacobin Club. Those who responded (between August 1790 and January 1792, for the most part between November 1790 and February 1791) had several important traits in common. They were city-dwellers and they were 'clerics' connected with the Church, the administration, the judicial system, or the liberal professions – all the 'robes' of the *ancien régime*. They were enlightened bourgeois; citizens of the 'Republic of Letters'. This first and objective detachment from the country and its inhabitants was accompanied by a second distinction of their own making that lay at the very heart of their descriptions. The investigators created a gap between themselves and the peasants – that 'other' whom the questionnaire set out to discover – which permitted a clear separation within the rural community between city notables in the position of observers and the rural world, the somewhat uncouth object of their observation. What Grégoire's respondents offered was not the result of 'field research' guided by ethnographic principles, but a complex blend of knowledge and acquaintance, of traditional stereotypes and the images in vogue, of things seen and texts read. We need to keep this in mind as we listen to their responses.

AN APPETITE FOR READING

'Have country people a taste for reading?' The question, formulated in the new vocabulary of the century, elicited contradictory responses. For some respondents this was too high an ambition for people who do not know how to read: 'They are still, for the most part, delivered over to the deepest ignorance. Not knowing how to read, they could not possibly have a taste for reading' (Friends of the Constitution of Agen, 27 February 1791); 'Country people have no taste for reading because they scarcely know how to read' (anonymous response, Mâcon and Bresse regions); 'Three-fourths of country people not knowing how to read, it would be useless to have books to lend them' (Jean-Baptiste de Cherval, 22 September 1790). Some even consider the question itself senseless. Lequinio says as much with the aid of his Latin learning: 'Country people have no taste for reading, *ignoti nulla cupido*.' Others, like the Friends of the Constitution of Mont-de-Marsan answered simply, 'Eh! How could they have?'

Several responses, to the contrary, insisted that although peasants had long been unable to read, the Revolution had awakened their appetite for reading. Abbé Rochejean, for example, responding for Salins and the surrounding region, says:

> Everywhere the people are beginning to read; this impulse needs to be maintained. In the most ignorant classes of society, one can find men worthy of instruction who ask only to learn. I know that the people is quite apathetic, but I know that it is less so from day to day, and that it contains enough men avid for instruction to make the taste universal sooner or later. [15 March 1791]

Canon Hennebert in the Artois concurred: 'I remark that since the Revolution, they have taken up a certain taste for writings that are relative to it' (26 November 1790). Events led some to change their judgement completely. Abbé Andriès, professor at the Collège de Bergues, had responded sarcastically to question 36, mocking the 'stupid vanity' of Flemish country folk who bragged of knowing everything without ever reading anything. They 'never find books in their region well enough written to engage them or make them enjoy reading, so they never open one'. He adds a comment to his response, however: 'The following note, comic though it is, was also true six months ago. Now the country people are fired with enthusiasm for reading. They know the constitution better than our city people who scorn the decrees.' Thus the Revolution totally reversed long-standing situations and unveiled the full force of aspirations hastily thought to be foreign to the peasant population.

Unfortunately, this new perspective encountered two as-yet unsurmounted obstacles. First, books circulated poorly in country areas: 'The people would undoubtedly have a taste for reading, and if there were books, they would devote many moments to it that they cannot devote to their profitable work,' wrote Abbé Fonvielhe, *curé constitutionnel* in the Dordogne (20 January 1791). A proof *a contrario* was offered by Bernadau, a lawyer in Bordeaux: 'I have remarked that when a peasant has a book at his disposal on a holiday, he prefers reading it to the tavern, although its use is quite familiar to him on days of rest' (21 January 1791). A second hindrance to a desire to read lay in the lack of primary teachers, which made literacy difficult. 'Country people like reading very much, and if they do not have their children taught, it is because they have no schoolmasters' (Bernardet, parish priest of Mazille in the diocese of Mâcon, 28 December 1790). Jean-Baptiste de Cherval adds, 'The ease with which one can read, the desire to acquire learning, the profit that one draws from his reading is ordinarily what gives a taste for reading, and as soon as country folk are able to enjoy these advantages, I have no doubt that they will love reading just as much as better governed men [*les hommes policés*].' Lorain, the Mayor of Saint-Claude, summarizes this notion haughtily: 'Instruction is necessary to a thirst for instruction' (14 November 1790).

The people, as seen by Grégoire's respondents, was thus awakened to self-awareness by the new direction in politics. Love of reading and avidity for instruction were indeed part of people's nature, but these qualities had been stifled by the cultural subjection in which the people had been held. The Friends of the Constitution of Auch proclaimed: 'It is insistently said that the country people have a taste for reading in their souls, and that they desire nothing more than to learn.' The first duty of the Revolution was thus to make country folk conscious of their own aspirations. Could it count on the Church for help in this endeavour? Many clerics were among the respondents to the questionnaire, and once again opinions were mixed. Some respondents portray the *curés* as dead set against peasant reading. For one thing, the parish priests had every intention of preserving their role as obligatory mediators between the faithful and the Bible. Abbé Aubry, himself a parish priest, wrote of the Ardennes: 'The priests and their curates . . . lend no books to their parishioners, who are prohibited from reading the Holy Writ. Thus there are few country people who have a taste for reading.' Others feared that the spread of reading might introduce confusion into social hierarchy or subvert male dominance. The lawyer Bernadau reported that he himself had met with hostility of this sort when he had attempted to introduce reading into the village school and to distribute to the better pupils useful works on the 'government of families'. He reports: 'The parish priest claimed that to inspire in children a taste for reading was tantamount to attempting to give them a superiority over their compatriots contrary to Christian modesty, and that reading girls were wicked women.' This entered perfectly into the imagery typical of the time, which showed the cleric, attached to traditional ideas and an adversary of education for the people as a source of disorder, combating the man of the Enlightenment, devoted to progress, domestic and public.

Although clerics might scorn education for the people, the Church nevertheless remained the only institution that incited the people to read. The ex-Capuchin François Chabot of Saint-Geniès testifies to this in negative terms: 'The laziness of the priests and the curates extends to all the parishioners: they only read while they are on the [school] benches – that is, until their first communion' (4–8 September 1790). Similarly, Lorain states of Saint-Claude peasants: 'A small number of them read in the Hours and that is all. Exceptions are extremely rare.' This contradiction is based on the ambiguous position of the parish priests in the discourse of Grégoire's respondents. On the one hand, the priests' own lacks are often obvious and they themselves were poor readers. The Friends of the Constitution of Perpignan report, 'Few, very few of them have books'; Abbé Fonvielhe adds, 'The people thus read very little and the *curés* (except for the news) now generally read as little as they.' The system of benefices was held responsible for this state of affairs, as it obliged the *curés* to too meagre a life and bound them to it with little hope of bettering their lot. Morel, *procureur* in Lyon, reports, 'How could it be possible for *curés à simple portion congrue* [without title to the benefice they occupy] to procure an assortment of books to lend to their parishioners?' (2 November 1790). The Friends of the Constitution of Auch state:

> If they had had all the knowledge of the Sorbonne in their heads, this would have led them neither to an abbey, nor to a high position in their chapter, nor to a better parish assignment. Moreover, the title of *curé* was an exclusion from any sort of rank, especially on the part of the court.

On another level, however, the *curés* played an essential role in a much-needed acculturation of the people. The very terms in which question 35 was formulated suggest this in its implicit reference to the lending library that Grégoire himself established before the Revolution in his parish of Embermesnil (perhaps imitating in country style a practice of the Jansenist *curés* of Paris). Some of his respondents understood the reference: 'An assortment of books that *MM. les curés* ought to have [on hand] to lend to their parishioners is an idea worthy of being conceived and executed by the author of these questions' (Abbé Rochejean); 'This question could only come from a philosopher who so loved humanity that he himself has already put into practice a custom or fashion that he would like to see established throughout the Empire' (Friends of the Constitution of Auch). In these early stages of the Revolution, a reformed and regenerated clergy was thus the patriotic educator charged with communicating instruction, diffusing Enlightenment and revealing its potential to the people. Along with the new civil authorities, it was to bring to light a desire to read that was buried in the people's very souls. In May 1794, when Grégoire read before the Convention his report on the results of his investigation 'on the necessity and the means of annihilating patois and making use of the French language universal', times had changed, leaving little room for book-lending parish priests.[4]

THE RURAL LIBRARY

'What sorts of books are most commonly found in their homes?' Question 37 on Grégoire's questionnaire invited his respondents to sketch the libraries of their country compatriots. Respond they did, but not as a historian hoping for precise and objective data might wish. Often they were content to cite a title or two or to give very general indications. Above all, their choice clearly had the function of illustrating and giving credence to their own representation of the peasant population's cultural dispositions or psychological properties. These experienced observers did not invent, to be sure, and the books they mention doubtless were to be found in peasant houses, but they select, they generalize and perhaps they omit so as to convey a sense of rurality (or at least of their image of it) by the titles they list. A systematic categorization of 'sorts of books' cited in one response after another and grouped into thirteen categories (nine of which are religious and four secular) does not constitute an inventory in the notarial fashion. Rather it offers a type and an ideal of the peasant library, drawn up at the point at which experience and imagery intersect, which indicates a certain acquaintance with the countryside through visits and travel along with some commonly shared archetypes of rusticity.

In this general picture, the book owned by peasants was religious in the overwhelming majority. Of the responses that mention specific books, all but three (those of the Friends of the Constitution of Mont-de-Marsan and of Perpignan and that of Canon Hennebert) indicate the presence of works of piety or church books. The Bible is cited, but often in the form of abridgements or adaptations: 'Nevertheless, one finds in some houses the Royaumont abridgement of the Old Testament, the Gospels, and the *Imitation of J[esus] C[hrist]*, but this is very rare' (Friends of the Constitution of Angers); 'They much like stories of the Lives of the Saints and the Bible' (Abbé Bouillotte, Bourgogne). The contrasting ways of Protestants and Catholics are clearly underscored by some respondents. Colaud de la Salcette in the *département* of Drôme, for instance, states: 'The parish priests have few books, and the peasants have little liking for reading. The Calvinists, who are numerous, are very careful to procure the Bible' (18 February 1792). Books of Hours are cited more often than Bibles or abridgements in French. 'Country people who know how to read read only in their Hours', states the elder Morel of Lyons. Grégoire's respondents of the end of the eighteenth

century thus corroborate an age-long familiarity with the Book of
Hours, which, two centuries earlier, was the most widely distributed
of all books.[5] The new literature of the Catholic Reformation
diminished its importance among the better educated or the more
pious, but it remained a popular work and a work of many uses,
since it offered both the text of the liturgy and extracts from the
Bible. For the enlightened patriots who wrote to Grégoire, however,
the Hours were not really a book, and reading them was not really
reading. The Friends of the Constitution of Auch said as much in
their own fashion in a brief portrait of the peasant who could read
but could not quite be called a reader:

> The young man going to school with the priest, who made him read
> once a month or more, although every day his poor parents deprived
> themselves of the small services that their child might have rendered
> them – this young man, we say, no sooner arrives at the possession of
> the *Hours* of the diocese than he had them constantly in his pocket at
> work and in his hands in moments of rest. He read his life long, and
> died without ever knowing how to read.

Knowing how to read was something other than merely being able to
decipher a single book; it was mobilizing, for utility or for pleasure,
the multiple riches of written culture.

Old texts appear in the repertory of devotional books drawn up by
Grégoire's respondents, the *Imitation of Jesus Christ*, for example
(cited by the Friends of the Constitution of Agen and Carcassonne),
but newer titles crop up as well, above all, works produced by the
Catholic Reformation and which had found a place in the catalogue
of the printers – in Troyes in particular – who printed books for wide
distribution. Bernadau mentions 'the Seven Tempests, an ascetic
work of a pitiable sort' (in reality, *Les Sept trompettes spirituelles pour
réveiller les pécheurs* of Barthélémy Solutive – Bartolomeo Cambi da
Saluzzo, the Recollect Franciscan), and François Chabot mentions
Le Chemin du ciel ou la voie que doivent tenir les enfants pour arriver au Ciel
and the *Pensez-y bien, ou réflexion sur les quatre fins dernières de l'Homme.*
(The first two of these titles had been republished several times in
the course of the century by the Troyes printers.) These works, as
well as liturgical works such as breviaries, *paroissiens* (parish prayer
books) and collections of hymns and prayers, appeared in rural areas
for two reasons. First, they reflected diocesan policy (in certain
places at least) for the distribution of books to schools and to
families. Thus in the diocese of Saint-Claude, according to the
lawyer Joly, 'The late bishop had many books distributed in the
parishes.' Second, during the last twenty years of the old monarchy,

a new rule of simple permissions to publish instituted in 1777 permitted free reprinting of all titles for which the *privilège* had expired, which considerably increased the number of religious books in circulation. The total number of copies of such works rose to 1,363,700 between 1778 and 1789 (or 63 per cent of all books published under the new authorization). Three sorts of religious works dominate the list at the end of the century: works of liturgy and practice (45 per cent of copies), Books of Hours (20 per cent of copies), books of piety inspired by the Catholic Reformation (which included the *Chemin du ciel* and the *Pensez-y bien*).[6] Thus we can believe Grégoire's respondents, who were noting accurately a new proportional distribution within the book market on the eve of the Revolution.

Next in order after books of piety, responses mention books of the *Bibliothèque bleue* (though the series appears only in five responses). The term is given in the singular (Bernadau notes the presence of 'a few works of the *Bibliothèque bleue*') and in the plural (Abbé Aubry, *curé* of Bellevaux in the Ardennes, states that 'the books that one usually finds in their homes are the Lives of Saints, prayer books, and the *Bibliothèques bleues*', perhaps referring to the different cities in which these works were printed). The list of titles that are cited by name is short: *L'Histoire des quatre fils Aymon* is given by the Friends of the Constitution of Mont-de-Marsan and of Carcassonne, the *Histoire de la vie, grandes voleries et subtilités de Guilleri* by the latter alone, the *Histoire de la vie et du procès du fameux Dominique Cartouche* and the *Histoire de Louis Mandrin* are listed by Canon Hennebert. Thus the reports give one chivalric romance (a standard of the *Bibliothèque bleue*) and eighteenth-century titles that assured the popular success of the new and ambiguous figure of the 'noble bandit'.[7] For Grégoire's respondents, these tales belonged to the same category. They give them varying names: the Montois call them 'fairy tales, [tales] of magicians, Bluebeard'; Hennebert notes 'the ancient tales of Mother Goose'; de Mirbeck from Lorraine lists them as 'blue tales'. In all instances, these are references to written texts, to books like those of the *Bibliothèque bleue* repertory, not allusions to the oral traditions of country people, of which our city observers seem unaware. Their reports offer two pieces of useful information. On the one hand, they attest that the name *Bibliothèque bleue* excluded religious books, even when the latter were printed in the same formats and by the same printers (thus confirming the distinction in Troyes catalogues, which reserved the name for 'recreational books commonly called *Bibliothèque bleue*'). On the other hand, these reports make it clear that this sort of story, no longer published uniquely by printers in Champagne or Rouen, enjoyed wide distribution within the entire kingdom, including the south.[8]

Eight responses show almanacs among the peasants' books. Three stop at this generic expression, except to specify 'one of those poor almanacs' (Abbé Fonvielhe). Five other reports are more precise. Bernadau cites the *Almanach des Dieux* (perhaps the *Dieu soit béni ou Almanach fidèle*), the Friends of the Constitution of Perpignan list the almanacs of Liège, of Larrivay (in reality, of Larrivey from Troyes) and the *Messager boîteux*. Frédéric-Ignace de Mirbeck mentions the *Almanach de Bâle* for Lorraine (that is, the same *Messager boîteux*), and Abbé Andriès, speaking for the districts of Bergues and Hazebrouck, gives Flemish almanacs 'that are distributed in our parts, but which come from abroad, at two *sols* apiece', adding, 'The country people are avid to excess for them because of the weather forecasts that they always contain.' It is worthy of note that almanacs printed abroad outnumbered those of the older Troyes stock, and that the same titles circulated from the northern to the southern limits of the kingdom, even if they came from Switzerland or the Austrian Netherlands.

The picture we get of the rural library from this portrayal could hardly be more negative. It shows a world of superstitious beliefs, trivial fables and long-standing prejudices. Complete responses to question 37 confirm this impression. The response of the Friends of the Constitution of Perpignan, from which we have only quoted extracts thus far, reads: '*Les Quatre Fils d'Aymon*, books of sorcery, ([an] opinion highly accredited in our parts among the people of the town and the country areas, which attests their profound ignorance); fairy tales, [tales] about magicians, Bluebeard, etc.' Fiction from the *Bibliothèque bleue*, tales, books of magic: this was precisely the reading-matter that Grégoire denounced in his report to the Convention when he stigmatized 'the puerile tales of the *Bibliothèque bleue*, old wives' [tales] and [tales] of [the witches'] Sabbath', which provided the entire basis for peasant conversations. To counter these books, 'which can dull the senses,' Lorain stated, enlightened men should impose works that teach and educate. Lorain continues, 'I have proposed the new work of Berquin [the *Bibliothèque des villages*] to several rural mayors, who showed little interest in it.' I have already mentioned the efforts of Bernadau to have the *Science du Bonhomme Richard* adopted as a school text and to have a work entitled *Avis au peuple sur sa santé* and a *Manuel du cultivateur* distributed to worthy boys, while the best-behaved girls were to get a New Testament and the *Avis aux bonnes ménagères*. In 1794 Grégoire backed a similar policy, on a national scale, however, when he proposed the preparation and distribution 'of patriotic pamphlets which will contain simple and extremely clear notions, which a man of slow conception and obtuse ideas could grasp' (on meteorology, for example, or elementary physics, politics, or the arts). He also recommended 'good journals' specifically for public reading: 'One sees with interests the sellerwomen at the market [and] the workers in the workplace chipping in to buy them, and taking turns reading them together.'[9]

THE USES OF READING

Grégoire's respondents disdain the ordinary reading-matter of country people because, far from instructing, aiding, informing, or awakening them, such reading kept prejudice and superstition alive. Still, some respondents perceived a difference among rural readers: peasants and notables did not read the same books. This recognized difference could introduce contradictory values, however, and for some respondents the dangerous reading-matter of the rural elites threatened the corruption of tillers of the soil. Joly in Saint-Claude speaks from personal experience:

> The office of judge, which I have exercised for quite some time, has given me opportunities for sojourns in the country [thus he was probably a seigneurial judge]. I saw their books in the moments that interrupted my occupations there [and] I have often seen works of piety. Acquaintance with certain famous authors who sullied and disgraced their pens toward the end of their careers [probably Voltaire and Rousseau] had spread [in the country areas] pamphlets dangerous for mores and for religion, which have introduced and fed confusion and anarchy in Geneva. I found these books in the shop of a merchant who was seduced [by them].

Canon Hennebert offers an image contrary to this picture of a virtuous and religious people threatened by libertine writings. He notes the presence of legitimate literature only among the wealthier countrypeople ('The honest farmers read [books of] voyages, the novels of the Abbé Prévost, and others of that sort'), whereas the less fortunate remained devoted to 'rough-hewn rhapsodies, obscene books, ancient fabulous legends, the old tales of Mother Goose, the lives of Cartouche, of Mandrin, etc.' How could one avoid replacing corruption by ignorance with corruption by knowledge? How could the book be made a source of examples to be imitated, not new depravations? Grégoire's later report suggests an answer: enlightened men or the state itself should select between useful and patriotic works and those that were less so and should take charge of their distribution.

Some of the men who responded to the survey did not limit themselves to a dry notation of one 'species of book' or another in peasant homes, going on to report further on their circulation, their reading and their use. Above all, these reports attest the existence of distribution by pedlars. 'Those of the country people of this district who know how to read are truly fond of reading, and for lack of anything else, read the *Almanach des Dieux*, the *Bibiothèque bleue* and other frivolities that the pedlars carry [*voiturent*] throughout country areas every year' (Bernadau). What is reflected here is the pedlar with a horse and cart – *colporteur voiturier* or the *marchand forain* – with a fairly large sales territory and a well-furnished stock of books.[10] None of Grégoire's respondents mentions the more modest commerce of the *porte-balle* or the *mercier* who peddled books carried in a box on his back or slung around his neck, which may have been more customary in urban areas than rural. The pedlars were not alone in introducing peasants to books. They were joined by others purveying other sorts of merchandise:

> Up to a certain age, one finds in their hands only the books spoken of above [books of devotion lent or given by the parish priests]. More advanced [in age], they keep to a number of *feuilles* [news-sheets] or *brochures* [pamphlets] that voyagers or tradespeople introduce into their villages and which often are extremely dangerous for mores and even more so for public tranquillity. (Friends of the Constitution of Ambérieu, 16 December 1790)

Once again we see the opposition that the lawyer Joly set up between the peasant and the merchant, the native and the outsider, natural piety and virtue in rural areas and the corruption that came from elsewhere – from the city. It is difficult to say exactly what literature the patriotic society in Bresse had in mind. Perhaps it was referring to pornographic novels printed outside France in foreign print-shops; perhaps to the obscene lampoons cited by Morel in his response (the *Lettres bougrement patriotiques du véritable père du Chêne*, the *Trou du cul du père du Chêne*, or the *Mouchoir des aristocrates*). In any event, their remarks lend an interesting nuance to the accepted picture of peasants reading only Books of Hours, the almanac, or the chap-books of the *Bibliothèque bleue*. In certain places at least, forbidden or polemical current books reached country areas – the same 'pamphlets sullied by lubricity or convulsive imprecations that exalt the passions rather than enlightening the reason' that Grégoire was to castigate four years later.

Grégoire's friends say little about actual reading practices. Two characteristics caught the attention of some of them, however. First, the peasant way of reading was not their own: 'They have a mania for going back over these miserable [books] twenty times, and when they talk with you about them (which they do eagerly), they recite their little books word for word, so to speak.' For Bernadau, a learned lawyer who wrote on many topics, this sort of repeated rereading of the same almanac or the same 'blue' book that led to knowing familiar texts almost by heart and was easily transformed into recitation, was part of the strangeness of peasants, on a par with superstitious beliefs or ignorance of morality. Second, peasant reading was characteristically communal and familial. It was listening to the written word spoken aloud rather than individual silent reading. Bernadau says: 'The peasants' books are always in sorry condition, even though carefully shelved. They transmit them in inheritance. During the long winter evenings, someone reads for half an hour to all the assembled household some saint's life or a chapter from the Bible.' Joly states, 'Country people do not lack a taste for reading, but they give a just preference to works of their estate. In the winter principally, they read or have their children read, in the family, ascetic books.' The two descriptions picture the same scene, the winter *veillée*, when the entire household would gather around to hear the father or a child read some religious book aloud. Thus, responses to Grégoire's survey seem to support two of the characteristics by which historians have defined traditional peasant reading: the habit of reading aloud in evening gatherings as the most prevalent means for the diffusion of printed works in societies in which large numbers of illiterates can only experience books by hearing them;[11] and the practice of 'intensive' reading distinguished by frequent rereadings of a highly restricted number of books, by memorization of their texts and a high level of recall, and by the respect attached to the book as a rare and precious object that is always to some degree considered as sacred.[12]

A doubt remains, nonetheless. Few respondents give witness to these peasant usages. In fact, for details we have to rely on only one among them, Pierre Bernadau, the Bordeaux lawyer. As it happens, his last letter to Grégoire, dated 21 January 1791, introduces a suspicious note:

> The books that I have most usually found among the peasants are Hours, a Hymnal, a Life of the Saints, among the more substantial farmers, who read several pages from them to their workers after supper. I remember in that connection several verses from a work on country life which competed seven years ago with the eclogue of *Ruth*

of M. Florian. Evening readings among the peasants were well
described in it, as they are with no less energy in the *Life of my Father*
of M. Restif.

Reading aloud after the evening meal in the bosom of the family
thus belongs to a repertory of representations common to bucolic
poetry, the autobiographic fable[13] and even to painting or prints (the
Peasant Reading to his Children submitted by Greuze to the Salon in
1755, which served as frontispiece to the second volume of the first
edition of Restif de la Bretonne's *Vie de mon père*, published in 1778).
Imagery of the sort had a dual function. It presented rural society as
patriarchal, fraternal and communitarian, in contrast to the corrupt
and 'out-of-joint' society of the big cities. It also depicted in this
intent deciphering and vigilant hearing ('I cannot remember
without being deeply touched with what attention this reading was
listened to,' Restif wrote) the total absorption of these individuals in
what they were doing, an involvement given as the total opposite of
the frivolity of the times.[14]

A PORTRAIT OF RURAL LIFE

For Bernadau and Joly, the motif of reading during the *veillée* was a
necessary component of their representation – or at least of one representation – of the peasant world. Indeed, this picture of total and
natural simplicity, recalling in its way a lost transparency that
should be rediscovered everywhere, stands in strong contradiction to
the picture of rural areas as formidable bastions of ignorance and
prejudice, missionary territory for enlightened men and educator
philosophes. Bernadau juxtaposes the two visions as if they belonged
to different registers or as if he had simply assembled the major
stereotypes which, for city elites, contained the uncertain truth of
rural society, both as a model or a scandal. Thus the description of
pious family reading after nightfall cannot pass for ethnographic
observation, but offers a scene that conforms with one of the
dominant *topoï* on peasant culture. Bernadau may indeed have seen
which books were 'carefully shelved' in peasant houses, but the
evidence he offers on the *veillées* (and that of the lawyer Joly, who
pleads for the innocence of village customs) is inadequate to prove
the frequency of reading within the peasant household. This is all
the more true since neither ecclesiastical condemnations in the
seventeenth and eighteenth centuries nor nineteenth-century research in folklore attest clearly to this practice. When these sources

mention the *veillée*, it is always as an occasion for work in common, for games and for dancing, for tales and songs, for exchanging news and gossip, and hardly ever as an occasion for community reading out loud (see appendix 1). The motif parallels family Bible reading among Protestants (whereas the Bible itself is rarely noted among the books cited in Grégoire's investigation). It is a better indication of the nostalgia or the expectations of literate people of the end of the eighteenth century than it is of peasant practices.

Can the same be said of all the notations contained in the responses to Grégoire's inquiry? Are they too of little 'objective' value for a history of peasant reading? Perhaps not. Indeed, although all the respondents arrange their observations so as to bring out an ideal configuration, positive or negative (or positive *and* negative) of the rural personality, and although they propose, consistently but unconsciously, traits that fit with the portrait that they intended to trace, nevertheless, their demonstration had to confront the reality – neither totally familiar to them nor totally foreign – of this rurality that seemed so uncouth but existed so near at hand. What they tell us is thus a heterogeneous combination, in unequal and varying proportions according to the respondent, of things seen, on-the-spot observations as judge, parish priest, or traveller, and of things read, literary reminiscences and clichés currently in vogue. Separating the first-hand from the second-hand is beside the point, since they form a coherent system of perception that lent the force of reality to the rural scene thus understood. What we need to do instead is to grasp each factual indication within the 'why' of its statement and put it into relation with what can be known by other means about the circulation and the use of printed matter in the rural world of the eighteenth century. If we do this, the testimony assembled by Grégoire teaches us how literature provincials represented peasant reading, for themselves or for others. It also shows us what were some of the popular uses of printed materials within this same representation, which has its own laws and its motifs and which translated, truncated and transformed reality.

The sharpest note in their description is perhaps the still somewhat vague awareness that the Revolution was in the process of upsetting deep-seated cultural habits. Events had set off a desire for reading and for information by means of print, that made the traditional rural library obsolete. Some thought of this change in terms of a simple transfer in which traditional practices took on new texts: 'Since the Revolution, the peasants have substituted for these readings that of the papers of the times, which they buy when their oldness makes them available at a lower price. The young have also substituted patriotic songs for hymns' (Bernadau, December 1790 or January 1791). In reality, though, the rapid advance of an ephemeral pamphlet literature, a mobile and nervous literature of value only as it related to current politics, rendered obsolete all of a traditional manner of reading connected to repetition of the same formulas from equally repetitious books (Books of Hours, almanacs, the fiction of the *Bibliothèque bleue*). This was the reason for the temporal ambiguity of many of the responses to Grégoire, which describe in the present tense a peasant culture that was already declining and which put the new enthusiasms of rural readers who were no longer the same as the readers imagined by the Enlightenment into the outworn framework of traditional reading.

APPENDIX 1   READING AT THE *VEILLÉE*: REALITY OR MYTH?

Did the peasant *veillée* in the eighteenth century constitute a privileged occasion for reading aloud popular booklets, in particular those of the *Bibliothèque bleue*? Contrary to the accepted opinion, I think not, both because the evidence cited fails to convince me, and because other, quite contrary evidence can be offered.

1 It is clear, first, that synodal statutes and episcopal ordinances that condemned the *veillées* do not mention reading – aloud or silent, collective or solitary – among the dangers or the activities of such gatherings. For example, the episcopal ordinances for the diocese of Châlons-sur-Marne of 1693 cited by Robert Mandrou (*De la Culture populaire*, p. 2) denounces the presence of young men at the *veillées* at which women and girls worked together to 'play and dance', but not to read.

2 When written texts were introduced into women's *veillées* in the beginning of the eighteenth century, it was on the initiative of priests, often of Jansenist leanings, in the interest of transforming traditional practices (in which reading had no part) and winning over the faithful. During his hearing before the diocesan court of the *officialité* in Vence in 1790, Jean-Baptiste Deguigues, *curé* of Tourrettes, stood accused on two counts: by witnesses, for his participation in assemblies at which people 'sang, laughed, and amused themselves as people usually do when they make love'; and by his bishop, for having distributed at such gatherings 'prayers and offices' that His Eminence had not authorized. In fact, the depositions note that Deguigues came to these assemblies 'with a book under his arm' and that he made 'readings from several books' there (see Marie-Hélène Froeschlé-Chopard and Marcel Bernos, 'Deguigues, prêtre janséniste du diocèse de Vence en 1709, ou l'échec de l'intermédiare', in *Les Intermédiares culturels*, Actes du Colloque du Centre Méridional d'Histoire Sociale, des Mentalités et des Cultures, 1978 (University of Provence, Aix-en-Provence, distributed by Champion, Paris, 1981), pp. 59–70; *idem*, 'Entre

Peuple et hiérarchie: L'échec d'une pastorale', *Dix-huitième Siècle*, 12 (1980), pp. 271–92).

3 The *mémoire* of 1744 on the *écreignes* in Champagne ('houses hollowed out underground and covered with bedding straw where the girls go to have their *veillée*'), cited by Robert Mandrou (*De la Culture populaire*, pp. 21–2), the ethnographic validity of which remains to be established, does not mention reading among the activities of the assembled women. The women are wholly occupied with their work in common, with conversations and confidences, with stories told and songs sung – in short, with activities pertaining to oral culture and in no way founded on the presence of the written word, printed or manuscript, read by one participant to the others.

4 In the diocese of Annecy in the nineteenth century, when parish priests describe the *veillée* in response to a questionnaire sent to them by their bishop, Mgr Rendu (31 out of 122 parishes responding, or one out of four), the activities are those mentioned and, in some cases, censured, in the seventeenth and eighteenth centuries: working in common (spinning, cutting hemp, cracking walnuts, cutting wood), conversing in ways qualified as 'dirty and maligning', playing card games and dancing. Only three *curés* allude to reading, one to say that the reading of 'bad books' was not found in the *veillées* of his parish (Châtel), the two others to indicate that 'sometimes' or 'rarely' the catechism was read at evening meetings among their parishioners (Duingt and Saint-Nicolas-la-Chapelle) – see Roger Devos and Charles Joisten (eds), *Moeurs et coutumes de la Savoie du Nord au 19e siècle. L'enquête de Mgr Rendu, mémoires et documents*, (Académie Salésienne, Annecy and Grenoble, 1978; 1987), pp. 293, 181, 261.

Although it is certain that the *veillée* was in fact a practice of village sociability (perhaps less universal in France than was thought, however), it seems most doubtful that it was customarily a place for reading.

APPENDIX 2   THE RURAL LIBRARY ACCORDING TO GRÉGOIRE'S RESPONDENTS

1 Table 7.1 is based only on the responses that mentioned at least one 'kind of book' in response to question 37 of the questionnaire. They are numbered in conformity with the list given in Michel de Certeau, Dominique Julia and Jacques Revel, *Une Politique de la langue. La Révolution française et les patois: L'enquête de Grégoire* (Gallimard, Paris, 1975), pp. 175–8.

2 The works thus mentioned by genre or by title can be grouped in the following categories [corresponding to the vertical columns on table 7.1]:

1 Bibles, abridgements of the Bible and stories from the Bible
2 Books of Hours
3 Catechisms
4 Collections of hymns
5 Collections of Noëls
6 Psalms
7 Books of prayer, breviaries, parish prayer books

TABLE 7.1   *The rural library according to Grégoire's respondents*

	Correspondent	Region covered by the response	1	2	3	4	5	6	7	8	9	10	11	12	13	
1	Bernadau	District of Bordeaux		■			■				■			■		1
4	Abbé Fonvielhe	Province of Périgord				■							■			4
5	Friends of the Constitution of Mont-de-Marsan	Gascony					■					■			■	5
6	Friends of the Constitution of Auch	Département of Gers		■	■	■										6
8	Abbé Barère	Département of Upper Pyrénées								■	■					8
9	Friends of the Constitution of Agen	Département of Lot-et-Garonne		■						■	■					9
12	Chabot	Département of l'Aveyron									■					12
13	Friends of the Constitution of Perpignan	District of Perpignan			■						■			■		13
14	Friends of the Constitution of Carcassonne	District of Carcassonne		■							■			■		14
16	Abbé Rolland	Provence							■		■			■		16
17	Colaud de la Salcette	Département of Drôme		■												17
18	Morel the elder	Province of the Lyonnais			■											18
19	Friends of the Constitution of Ambérieu	Département of the Ain			■					■						19
20	Anonymous	Mâconnais, Dombes and Bresse								■						20
21	Abbé Bouillotte	Burgundy		■					■							21

	23	24	25	28	29	30	31	32	34	35	36	37	40	43
23 Cherval — Bresse									■					
24 Lorain the younger — District of Saint-Claude									■					■
25 Joly — Bailliage of Saint-Claude									■					
28 De Mirbeck — Province of Lorraine				■					■					
29 Friends of the Constitution of Commercy — Lorraine										■				
30 Grünwald and Brother Lefebvre — Duchy of Bouillon							■		■	■				
31 Abbé Aubry — Duchy of Bouillon						■				■				
32 Abbé Andriès — Districts of Bergues and Hazebrouck				■										
34 Canon Hennebert — Artois										■				
35 Abbé Asselin — Districts of Château-Thierry and Soissons									■					
36 Riou — Dioceses of Léon and Tréguier												■		
37 Lequinio — Morbihan, Finistère and Côtes-du-Nord										■				
40 Abbé Perreau — Lower Poitou														
43 Abbé Poupard — Province of Berry														

NOTES

This text, published in *Dix-huitième siècle*, 18 (1986), pp. 45–64, originated in a paper given in my seminar at the Ecole des Hautes Etudes en Sciences Sociales. I wish to thank all those who gave criticisms and suggestions at that time, in particular Lise Andriès, Robert Darnton, Jean Hébrard, Dominique Julia and Jacques Revel.

1   Anne Fillon, *Louis Simon, étaminier 1741–1820 dans son village du Haut-Maine au siècle des lumières*, (2 vols, Centre Universitaire d'Éducation Permanente, Le Mans, 1984) (Dissertation de troisième cycle, Université du Maine, 1982).

2   Valentin Jamerey Duval, *Mémoires. Enfance et éducation d'un paysan au XVIIIe siècle*, ed. and preface Jean-Marie Goulemot (Sycomore, Paris, 1981); Jean Hébrard, 'L'Autodidaxie exemplaire: Comment Valentin Jamerey-Duval apprit-il à lire?', in Roger Chartier, ed., *Pratiques de la lecture* (Rivages, Paris, 1985), 23–60.

3   Twenty-nine responses have been published in Augustin Louis Gazier, *Lettres à Grégoire sur les patois de France* (A. Durand et Pedone-Lauriel, Paris, 1880); three in Michel de Certeau, Dominique Julia and Jacques Revel, *Une Politique de la langue. La Révolution française et les patois* (Gallimard, Paris, 1975); and eleven are unpublished, of which ten are in the collection of the Bibliothèque Nationale (MSS N.a.fr., 2798) and the eleventh in the collection of the Société de Port-Royal (MS *Révolution* 222). (My thanks to Dominique Julia for providing me with the text of these unpublished letters.) The responses to questions 35, 36, and 37 of Grégoire's questionnaire have been used briefly in Noë Richter, 'Prélude à la bibliothèque populaire. La lecture du peuple au siècle des lumières', *Bulletin des Bibliothèques de France*, 24, 6 (1979), pp. 285–97.

4   The text of this report is published in Certeau, Julia and Revel, *Une Politique de la langue*, pp. 300–17.

5   See Albert Labarre, *Le Livre dans le vie amiénoise du seizième siècle. L'enseignement des inventaires après décès 1503–1576* (B.-Nauwelaerts, Paris, 1976), 164–77.

6   Julien Brancolini and Marie-Thérèse Bouyssy, 'La Vie provinciale du livre à la fin de l'Ancien Régime', in *Livre et société dans la France du XVIIIe siècle*, (2 vols, Mouton, Paris and The Hague), vol. 1 (1965), vol. 2 (1970); see vol. 2, pp. 3–37.

7   See Roger Chartier, ed., *Figures de la gueuserie* (Montalba, Paris, 1982), pp. 83–96; Hans Jurgen Lüsebrink, *Histoires curieuses et véritables de Cartouche et de Mandrin* (Montalba, Paris, 1984), pp. 21–45.

8   Roger Chartier, 'Livres bleus et lectures populaires', in Henri-Jean Martin and Roger Chartier, eds, *Histoire de l'édition française* (4 vols, Promodis, Paris, 1983–), vol. 2 (1984): *Le Livre triomphant, 1660–1830*, pp. 606–12 ['The *Bibliothèque bleue* and Popular Reading', in his *The Cultural Uses of Print in Early Modern France*, tr. Lydia G. Cochrane (Princeton University Press, Princeton, 1987)].

9   See Françoise Parent, 'De nouvelles pratiques de lecture', in *Histoire de l'Édition Française*, vol. 2, pp. 606–12.

10 Anne Sauvy, ' "Noël Gille, dit La Pistole", marchand forain libraire roulant par la France?' *Bulletin des Bibliothèques de France* 12, 5 (May 1967), pp. 177–90.

11 Robert Mandrou, *De la culture populaire aux XVIIe et XVIIIe siècles. La Bibliothèque bleue de Troyes* (Stock, Paris, 1975), pp. 20–22.

12 Rolf Engelsing, 'Die Perioden der Lesergeschichte in der Neuzeit', *Archiv für Geschichte des Buchwesens*, 10, 3 and 4 (1969), pp. 945–1002.

13 Georges Benrékassa, 'Le typique et le fabuleux: Histoire et Roman dans "La Vie de mon père"', *Revue des sciences humaines*, 172 (1978), pp. 31–56.

14 Michael Fried, *Absorption and Theatricality: Painting and Beholder in the Age of Diderot* (University of California Press, Berkeley and Los Angeles, 1980).

8

THE TWO FRANCES
The History of a Geographical Idea

Once again, geographical considerations loom large in historical study. In traditional teaching, the space/time duality was closely linked, with hardly any distinction being made between the survey of places and events. On the triumph of the historical preoccupation with states and nations, conceived as abstract, administrative and homogeneous entities, this duality became somewhat looser: it was first of all the seas, primarily the Mediterranean, and then the lands, great and small, that reawakened in historians a taste for open-air history, for understanding the countryside, and thence the significance of spatial groupings. Historical research has availed itself of these geohistorical advances, which in themselves are no longer new; and, with its awareness of work in the neighbouring fields of economics and geography, it now sees the problems of the use and organization of geographical space as being among its central concerns. These new interests are clearly revealed in the professional vocabulary: demographic and nutritional basins, urban axes and networks and cultural spheres, have become essential notions both for the framing of new questions and the forging of new conceptual tools. In urban history, economic geography and the quantitative history of culture, there have been increasing efforts to reconstruct the various ways in which geographical disparities and contrasts come about. Such enquiries are, nevertheless, still in their early stages and any theoretical model that might give us a clear picture of the disparities revealed by the evidence so far collected is still tentative. This is doubtless the reason why people have looked to older geographical ideas for help; Giovanni Botero, Le Maître, and Johann Heinrich von Thünen (to mention only three of the names resurrected by Jean-Claude Perrot) have accordingly been examined for their interpretations of the interwoven relationships within a geographical community.

THE INVENTION OF A DIVISION

The following should be read in this context: it is intended as a survey of past opinion on spatial divisions. The chosen ground is that which has preoccupied French historiography for at least twenty years, i.e., the radical opposition that seems to exist between the two Frances separated by an imaginary line running from Saint-Malo to Geneva. Reference to such a line has in fact become a convenient way of distinguishing the major contrasts that differentiate the two countries that meet here. Everything appears different on either side of this diagonal territorial divide: agricultural landscape and technology, density of communications and manufacturing, the height of the inhabitants and their aptitude in the acquisition of writing skills. Persistently added to, this catalogue of French contrasts enables us to recognize the opposition between northern and southern France as a long-standing phenomenon, discernible as early as the end of the seventeenth century, and still frequently evident.[1] The collection and interrelating of new or refined indicators still have to be accomplished for our better understanding of this fundamental division of the country.[2]

Our concern here, however, is of another order. We shall be trying to give a conspectus of the various ways in which France was visualized in the past, and to understand how the differential geography of the country was conceived at various times. The assembled corpus, which no doubt has gaps, has been analysed with two objectives. First, there is the question of elucidating our national heritage: the issue of the two Frances is certainly not the invention of the recent past, or of historians. We must therefore establish its genealogy in order to grasp more clearly the ideological interests that favoured its emergence, and which it carried along in its wake. For, as the second point, the study of geographical representations seems useful for our understanding of the links between the blossoming of the social sciences and the political and economic debates that pervaded the social elites from Louis XV to Louis-Philippe. Seeing how and why it was that the concept of a divided France became prevalent makes us better able to understand the goals and nature of progress itself: hence the option of a retrospective approach. This would first of all highlight the period of the *monarchie censitaire,* which saw the multiform victory of the idea of the two Frances. Our attention would then shift to the second half of the eighteenth century, where we would remark upon the various texts in which this consciousness of an established partition of the kingdom came to the fore: thus we might understand why the idea should then remain confined within such narrow limits.

The history of the different Frances begins in 1822, buried among the pages of a work by the prolix Italian geographer Adriano Balbi. In volume II of his *Essai statistique sur le Royaume de Portugal et d'Algarve,* he devotes an exposition to institutions for public education under the French monarchy. In this he inserts, without comment, a table showing the number of pupils in royal and municipal *collèges,* the boarding-schools and the primary schools for each educational district. The total number of students in each district, including those in the various university *facultés,* is given in relation to the population in 1821.[3] Twenty years before Villemain[4] we have the publication of Balbi's new statistical material, the value of which was to be recognized, for example, by Guerry in 1832: 'The first documents published on the state of public education are to be found in this work of the Venetian geographical scholar.'[5] Published indeed, but not exploited. In fact it was the Danish geographer Conrad Malte-Brun who, settling in France during the Empire, first used Balbi's figures in a discussion of the divisions within France, in his book review in the *Journal des Débats.*[6]

Such a step was made possible by the distribution of the educational data into two broad homogeneous groupings. Relating the number of schoolboys at the various educational levels to that of the male population, Malte-Brun noted that: 'If we divide France into two parts, one including the north and east, and the other including the south and west (excluding Paris, if so desired), we obtain two completely different results.' In the first grouping, comprising twelve *académies* (administrative educational districts), there were 123 schoolboys to every 1,000 men, while in the second, which was thirteen districts strong, the rate was 49 per 1,000. Hence the basic conclusion that: 'Public education in the south and west of France thus compares to that in the north and east in the order of 1 to 2½.' The article did not draw any clear frontier between these two Frances, so unequally educated, since Malte-Brun, using the framework of the *académies* was led to place the districts of Orléans, Lyons and Grenoble within the north and east groupings whereas they were equally oriented towards the south. But he did lay down the essential procedure, which was to divide provincial or regional inequalities into two parts. The established fact of the differences was not dissipated among myriad minute contrasts, but could be read as a clearly discernible pattern, open to reason.

As a footnote to this new basic division he introduced, Malte-Brun touched upon several questions that were to provide food for further thought. First of all, he situated France on the European map: 'We would never have imagined that several parts of southern and western France were on a level with the most educationally deprived countries of Europe, while in the same respect the north of France was on a footing with the most civilised lands in the world.' The dividing-line which clove Europe thus passed through the kingdom. This might henceforth be considered as a microcosm within which could be found, on a reduced scale, the same contrasts visible across the whole continent. Secondly, via a phrase on the subject of Austria, he returned to the link established by the Enlightenment between the progress of education and the fall in crime: 'In quite recent administrative reports, we have had the satisfaction of seeing the crime rate diminish in proportion to the increase in the number of primary schools.' This claim, which was later to become a bone of contention, was not taken as decisive by Malte-Brun. What was important for him was rather the relationship between education and the 'administration'. The effective exercise of power ultimately presupposes the homogeneity of the social body over which it rules, whereas the figures revealed that France was not at all uniform, and that immense cultural gaps separated its provinces. Politics had to take these variations into account; they were not random, but could be shown by careful analysis to have a coherent pattern.

The internal boundary of this divided France, identified by Malte-Brun, was first traced by Baron Charles Dupin in 1826. Having marked on a map the number of inhabitants necessary in each *département* to produce one primary school pupil, he thus addressed his audience at the *Conservatoire des Arts et Métiers*:

> Observe, from Geneva all the way to Saint-Malo, a clear, dark line separating the north and south of France. To the north there are only thirty-two *départements* with a total of thirteen million inhabitants; to the south fifty-four *départements* with eighteen million inhabitants. The thirteen million inhabitants of the North send 740,846 young people to school; the eighteen million inhabitants of the South send 375,931 pupils to school. It thus follows that for every million inhabitants the North of France sends 56,988 children to school, and the South 20,885. Primary education is therefore three times more widespread in the North than in the South.[7]

The inventor of a line which, under Maggiolo's name, was destined for an illustrious future,[8] Dupin was also the author of the formula which saw the north as 'enlightened France',[9] and, subsequently, the south as 'benighted France'. This text, perhaps less original than was believed, prompts two complementary remarks. Firstly, it shifts the debate on popular education from the political to the economic sphere. For Malte-Brun, the value of primary education, taken as an 'instrument of civilization', in effect basically depended upon the authority of power: 'To be able to read, march in line, and fire straight with a rifle are equally dangerous or equally useful talents in a monarchy or democracy, according to how well governments can direct popular opinion.' For Dupin, the development of popular education had a completely different significance, since it constituted the very condition for universal progress, economic and intellectual.

'Enlightened France' was actually the wealthier, as witnessed by land-taxes and *patentes*, and was the most fertile in talent, as demonstrated by patents, prizes awarded by Paris colleges, entrants to *Polytechnique,* and members of the *Académie des Sciences.* The figures which Dupin placed on either side of the decisive line agreed sufficiently well to show the benefits of popular education, posited as the decisive factor in explaining the unequal development of the kingdom.

Systematizing the contrasts between north and south, Dupin in the above-mentioned address, proposed what amounted to a new geographical interpretation: one that was to be somewhat forgotten in the *Forces productives et commerciales.* The south and west of France were not really a single entity at all: thirteen of its *départements,* in the Rhône, Languedoc and Pyrenean areas constituted its 'most industrious and affluent part', because there popular education was 'the least backward'.[10] This statement implicitly designated Brittany, the Loire valley and the centre of France as the least economically and culturally developed, wedged between the more enlightened parts of the country. This division, which contrasted an eastern France, stretching down from the Channel across to the Mediterranean, to an Atlantic France, penetrating far into the interior, was to meet with less success than the one dividing north and south. Nevertheless, Stendhal was acquainted with it long before Edward Fox:[11] 'A Minister of the Interior who wanted to do his job thoroughly, instead of intriguing with the King and in the Chambers like M. Guizot, ought to ask for a loan of two million a year to bring up to the educational level of the rest of France the inhabitants of that unlucky triangle that lies between Bordeaux, Bayonne and Valence.'[12] But the attention that Charles Dupin was shortly to focus upon the economic inequalities was to obliterate this subtler geography in favour of the dualistic interpretation.

THE NORTH AS A MODEL

Book 6 of Dupin's *Forces productives et commerciales de la France*, published in 1827, was devoted to a 'Comparison of the north and south of France with the whole of France'. In this, he approached the differentiation within the kingdom in terms of a developmental model.[13] Taking the statistics published by Jean Antoine Claude Chaptal in 1819, or those of the administrative authorities (for indirect taxation and from the departments of forests and mines), he distributed them between the two regional groupings established in the educational sphere, and incorporated them in the framework proposed in his address a year earlier. In doing this, Dupin brought up a new question: that of the overall spatial organization of the national economy. The imperial administrators, who used statistics furnished by the prefects,[14] had a different geographical conception, based on two representations: one which took into account the infinite diversity of reality, and the other which clung to the idea of national unity. In Peuchet's works, the synthesis of prefectural statistics took the form of a series of juxtaposed departmental or regional descriptions; but the data collected were never aggregated so as to reveal large contrasts on the imperial scale.[15] Chaptal's work, on the contrary, was dominated by a unitary vision. Even if his tables were presented by *département*, his favourite descriptive terms were 'everywhere' and 'nowhere', which attest to a monolithic conception of the area of France.[16] Between the perception of differences dispersed at the local and departmental level and of the unity of the country, transferred from the political to the economic sphere, there is no room for an intermediary level of interpretation;[17] and it is here that we are better able to gauge the innovative contribution of the 'arithmeticians' of the Restoration.

Working on the basis of the value of agricultural and industrial products, per caput income, and public revenue, Dupin concluded upon the unquestionable superiority of northern France: the Saint-Malo (or Cherbourg)–Geneva line did indeed divide two distinct economic universes. Reading between the lines of such a claim, we can see the outlines of an explanation that operates on three levels. In the first place, one can point to natural assets. Thus, at the beginning of Book 7, which deals with internal traffic, we find a stress on northern France's provision with natural water resources, and therefore canals. But this cannot be the heart of the matter, since the south has other compensations, being endowed with a climate that permits types of agriculture not possible in the north.[18]

Other reasons must therefore be advanced for the inequalities of development: one of them – history – is indeed suggested. Taking the problem of peasant incomes, Dupin wrote:

> Agricultural workers' wages in the south of France are sufficient, at a pinch, for survival as long as they remain healthy and strong; but as soon as they become ill, infirm, or old, they are without resources and cannot survive with their families without recourse to the charity of individuals, to the poorhouse, etc. *Throughout the kingdom, such was the deplorable condition of the peasants before the revolution.*[19]

This reasoning is informed by a historical schema, which proceeds from the observation of a disparity to the actual differentiating process. It is as though history stopped at the Saint-Malo–Geneva line, and as though the absence of development in the south came to be seen as an inferior development in contrast to the progress of northern France. The key to such a progression was a cultural one: not only was primary education more widespread in northern France, but academic competition was keener there also. For every 100 pupils admitted to the royal colleges, there were 15,980 primary schoolchildren in the north, but only 6,931 in the south:

> Those individuals picked out of the ordinary class to go on to the higher-level schools are therefore selected from among a far greater number of competitors in the north than in the south. This, in my opinion, is the reason for the superiority of the northern French in letters, the sciences, and the arts.[20]

And one might add, without doing any injustice to Dupin, in all those activities and ways of earning one's living that depend 'upon the learning of the population rather than upon the fertility of the soil'.

This academic forerunner of Darwinism constitutes Dupin's basic explanation of northern France's lead, which he proposed be imitated by his 'compatriots in the South'. This is the burden of the two volumes of the *Forces productives et commerciales:* to provide those who have been forgotten by, or who are oblivious to, progress, with the description of a France that might serve as a guide. Thus the book opens with the solemn exhortation: 'Compatriots of the South, it is to you that I dedicate this description of northern France. For your open-minded emulation, and thoughtful imitation, I present the model of a part of the kingdom.'[21] Hence the survey, in the form of an imaginary trip round the thirty-two *départements* situated on the more fortunate side of the internal frontier. Their pre-eminence was revealed above all by their greater industrial strength, which determined the inequality of the conditions of exchange between the two Frances:

> There is a considerable trade between the north and south of France. The south sends large quantities of wine, spirits, oils, livestock, wool, silks, and silkware, etc. In return it receives iron wrought into a thousand forms, the work of goldsmiths, jewellers, and cabinet-makers, woollens of every description, spun and woven cottons, books, engravings, and many works of art. We can see that the south of France sends mainly agricultural products to the north, whereas the north on the other hand, sends mainly manufactured products to the south. These products, such as woollens, are even in part produced from southern raw materials.[22]

Here, Dupin was outlining a possible analysis of French inequalities in terms of the geography of underdevelopment, all of whose corollaries he was unable to deduce since he did not posit the structural imbalance of north–south trade as constituting, but simply as symptomatic of, the disparity. As far as he was concerned, the important thing was not the manner in which the north exploited the south, but the example set by the former, whose progress could be imputed to its proximity to neighbouring industrial nations. Northern France was 'favoured above all by the proximity of highly advanced industrial nations with excellent institutions, such as the British, the Swiss, and the Dutch'. Southern France, on the other hand, only had for neighbours 'those nations of Spain and Portugal, Sardinia and Africa, which for so long have been backward and degraded through bad laws and bad governments'.[23] In Dupin the theme of the two Frances became the vehicle for a fervent plea, uniting the exaltation of industry with the celebration of parliamentary institutions. The model of development lay in the north, in England and Scotland, where a new and optimum balance had been found between the agricultural and industrial populations. By following this example northern France would progress still further, and the south would set history in motion again and make up lost time. Thanks to the shift of the surplus agricultural population into industry and the spread of popular education, the Saint-Malo–Geneva line would disappear, and the whole of France, with no internal division, would savour the delights of English prosperity.

STATISTICS AND POLITICS

To the paired contrasts of enlightened France/benighted France and prosperous France/impoverished France, there was added another which shook the geography of values. The publication in 1827 of the first *Compte général de l'administration de la justice criminelle* introduced new statistical material and at the same time heightened the debate about the various 'influences' capable of explaining criminal acts. [24] The statistical information that it contained was popularized rapidly, as can be seen from its presence in a sheet published by Balbi in 1828 under the title *La Monarchie Française comparée aux principaux Etats du Monde*. [25] It was used above all as the foundation of the 'moral statistics' which the Academy of Sciences was to place in 1833 'in the highest rank of the various branches of general statistics'. It is in this context that we must view the research of the lawyer André Michel Guerry, who was the first to recognize a geography of criminality. [26] To aggregate the data for each *département* contained in the *Compte général*, Guerry made his own subdivisions, stating their impartiality:

> We shall therefore divide France into five natural regions: the north, south, east, west, and centre, each one combining seventeen contiguous *départements*. This is not an arbitrary division, nor does it tend to favour any system, since it is totally geometrical and the boundary of each region is determined by that of the other four. [27]

Guerry's procedure is interesting on two counts: for a start, his apologia is meant to reconcile nature and geometry, thus legitimizing an entirely theoretical subdivision of the area of France by a reference to a permanent datum, natural regions. Here we see again Dupin's concern to identify his two Frances with those which 'our ancestors distinguished as the lands of the *langue d'oïl* and the *langue d'oc*', [28] and doubtless also the tensions attendant upon the division of the country into *départements* in 1790. Whether for tracing out area boundaries or marking out units on a map, such a voluntaristic way of redefining space is in need of supporting evidence drawn from nature or history. In addition, by partitioning France into five, Guerry was immediately breaking up the Saint-Malo–Geneva line, and with it its whole accompanying value system.

In fact, the geography of criminal acts drawn up according to the *Compte général* for the years 1825–30 did not obey a single law, but varied according to the crime. In the case of crimes against people we find the south at the top of the list, the east second, the north third and the west and centre last. With crimes against property the order is different, with the west and centre still last and the east second, but the south and north occupying reversed positions, the latter being here the most crime-prone region. Such a distribution might give rise to optimism, since 'The parts of the kingdom guilty of most crimes against the person record only very few against property';[29] but it did pose the essential question of the relationship between ignorance and crime. To support his argument, Guerry referred to new educational indicators. The figures for school-attendance, which formed the basis for Malte-Brun's and Dupin's reasoning, were not enough. We should rather look at the percent-ages of army conscripts with reading and writing skills, available since 1827. The geography suggested by these was of a France divided into three: the north and east, where nearly three-quarters of the young men were literate; the west and centre, where the maxi-mum ignorance was to be encountered; and finally the south, which fell between the two. Reviving the ternary interpretation of the geography of France outlined by Dupin in 1826, Guerry used it to refute the long-assumed link between crime and ignorance: the edu-cated north was the most felonious with regard to property, and the violent south was not the most ignorant. This showed, therefore, that: 'The *départements* in which there is the greatest ignorance are not, as is stated every day, those in which most crimes against the person are committed. We need make no mention here of crimes against property, since these take place mainly in *départements* with the most education.'[30]

This demonstration by Guerry seems exemplary: not because he advances any new ideas, but because of the way he proceeds. Casting doubt upon the positive correlation between educational progress and the decline of criminality is not, in fact, peculiar to him. Among others, Benoiston de Chateauneuf put it thus in 1827:

> If we observe the religious lands, we find them to be no less crime-prone than the others, while those ruled by ignorance often transgress less than those enlightened by learning. It has been long recognized that in Berry, Poitou, the Auvergne, and Savoy, lands unenlightened by the academies and the sciences, justice rarely had a criminal to punish; whereas thefts and murders were common among the Spanish, an extremely religious people, and equally so among the English, an extremely educated nation.[31]

But this pronouncement on its own was not sufficient to stop the interminable merry-go-round of arguments that nothing could sub-stantiate. This is why Guerry considered that his claim required the support of a statistical and geographical analysis capable of giving it the force of fact. The detour via geographical reasoning, whence the subdivision of the country, was a necessary element in a device aimed at testing public opinion and popular beliefs. The face of France thus became the scene of an experimentation which led Guerry to two conclusions, the one explicit: i.e., that school is not sufficient to prevent the 'demoralization' of nations, and the other implicit, locating the morality of France in its most culturally backward area. Thus unobtrusively began the requital of the disinherited and illiterate France.

This was to be more glaring and polemical on another level: that of pauperism. With Bigot de Morogues[32] or Villeneuve-Bargemont[33] the implications of the divided France became instrumental in a political struggle, turned against the theses of Baron Dupin. If they accepted the Saint-Malo–Geneva line, it was in order to subvert its significance. In Bigot de Morogues, it marked a frontier of happiness and morality, the advantage lying entirely with the fifty-four southern *départements*, in which the offenders judged in intermediate-level courts (*en correctionnelle*) were less numerous, crimes against property less frequent, and suicides rarer. As he put it so neatly: 'Those who speculate and reckon along with our great industrialists of the north often throw themselves in the river; those who laugh and dance with our village girls of the south take good care not to fall in.'[34] To this evidence, which extolled southern sociability, Villeneuve-Bargemont added another decisive claim, to do with the distribution of poverty. According to his information and calculations, one finds one pauper to every nine inhabitants in the north, but only one to every twenty-one inhabitants in the south; and if one looks carefully at the percentages of those invalided out of the services either through infirmity or deformity, it becomes clear that: 'The physical condition and the state of health of the working classes in the south is incomparably better than that of the same classes in the north.'[35] Thus the two Frances exchanged positions on the scale of values, since industrial development implied the physical, material and moral distress of the greatest number.

This lesson was valid for Europe as well as France. A surprising, gradated map of pauperism actually revealed the following rank-order: one pauper to every six inhabitants in England, one to every seven in the Netherlands, one to every ten in Switzerland, one to every twenty in Germany, one to every twenty-five in Austria, Denmark, France, Italy, Portugal and Sweden, one to every thirty in Prussia, one to every forty in Turkey, and finally one to every hundred in Russia. There was a simple logic to this distribution:

'The number of the poor is seen to grow everywhere by reason of the growth and congregation of the working population, the predominance of manufacturing industry over agricultural, the application of English doctrines of civilization and political economy, and the abandonment of the principles of religion and charity.'[36] By thus placing hell in England and heaven in Russia, Villeneuve-Bargemont avowed his ideology, Christian, aristocratic and agrarian; and he pointed out the enemy, which was a combination of Protestantism, philosophy and industry. Ranked in the middle of the scale of European pauperism, France was traversed by the 'front' separating the two political economies; the English and the Christian. Where the former already prevailed, i.e., in the north and east of the country, industry had already imposed its own train of miseries: 'The industrial and agricultural system practised in that part of France ceaselessly tends on one hand to increase the manufacturing population, and on the other to lower wage-rates, to concentrate capital and the profits of industry, and to bring together all the poverty-creating elements.'[37] This iron law had to be broken, by looking to the example set by southern France, with its balance of charity and agriculture, and by tirelessly attacking the opinions of those who, like Dupin, would like to force 'the bitter fruits of modern materialistic civilization' upon the whole nation. The Saint-Malo–Geneva line had to be erased but only by repulsing the changes coming down from the north.

Although sometimes naïvely reactionary, Villeneuve-Bargemont's work is of interest to us for two reasons. On one hand, it bears witness to the way in which the issue of the two Frances was capable of being turned into ammunition for the political battle under the July Monarchy. The choice of statistical indicators, their interrelationship and the value attributed to one France or the other were not arrived at by chance, but were simply the expression of opposite schemes and programmes. References culled from history were complemented or replaced by the contradictory lessons of social events; and confrontations over past issues gave way to battles of numbers and maps. It was the impact of the distribution on the map of the newly acquired statistical data which gave a new face to politics: the ideological discussions having their origins in the Revolution were for a while set aside. In addition the *Economie politique chrétienne*, more than any other work, placed France squarely on the European map. In Dupin, or later on in d'Angeville, the area of France remained closed in upon itself. There were doubtless administrative reasons for this, since the statistics used would have tallied badly with those available from outside the kingdom. But the essential factor lay perhaps elsewhere: it is really only by thinking in terms of a closed unit that variations can be discerned and located. The internal divisions of the kingdom implied a previous operation: that of detaching it from the whole of which it forms part. It took all the ideological Manichaeism of a Villeneuve-Bargemont to place France within a cultural space that transcends it, and which explains so much about it.

Adolphe d'Angeville's better-known *Essai sur la statistique de la population française*, published in 1836,[38] forms a sequel to this first survey. From several viewpoints it may be regarded as a culmination, primarily on account of the unusually broad scope of the statistical material. Eight tables of figures in effect comprise ninety-seven different indicators, thirty-three concerning 'moral statistics', twenty-seven the data for physical and cultural anthropology, seventeen the economy and sixteen demography. Such abundance allowed d'Angeville to increase the number of cross-tabulations and to attempt 'every manner of combination' so as to test previously established relationships between social phenomena, such as, for example, between education and criminality (p. 69), industry and pauperism (p. 80), industry and criminality (pp. 102–3), or to validate new ones, such as between the spirit of Catholicism and morality (p. 104), or education and nutrition (p. 116). The *Essai sur la statistique de la population française* was the result of fifteen years' work and statistical argument. It introduced no innovation, either in methods of quantification or in its reliance upon correlations, but it did carry them to a level never attained by previous arithmeticians.

We do, on the other hand, find in his work a juxtaposition of the various scales according to which the area of France was perceived. The basic grid is provided by a 'study of France by *départements*', in the form of a series of separate sections each presented identically and classified in alphabetical order. This dispenses both with the pretence of a journey, as maintained by Dupin, and the regional groupings sometimes present in works of the Empire period. Among the multitude of indicators, sixteen are shown on maps to reveal the 'agglomerations' that permit the partition of France into several large groupings. Even more importantly, the maps and statistics show a major rift, reminiscent of Dupin and his division of the country:

> The more one studies human statistics, the more one finds this division to be rational in terms of facts relating to the population. One might even be tempted to believe that two populations have just run into one another on the line linking the port of Saint-Malo with the city of Geneva.[39]

D'Angeville makes only two slight corrections to Dupin's two Frances: he slips the Loiret into northern France and the Ain into the south; and in geographical language inherited from Buache he explains the basic division which places the 'basins' of the Rhine, the Seine and the Saône on one side, and those of the Rhône, the Garonne and the Loire on the other side. D'Angeville thus integrated different geographical approaches to the concrete reality of France, and in doing so he laid claim to and systematized the heritage of his time.

It was when he came to pronounce judgement as to which was the better France that he found himself in a quandary. In his view, the parallel dividing north and south worked clearly to the advantage of neither of the two protagonists. The maps of the *départements* were sufficient to show the differences between the indicators: height and nutrition were better in the north, but the life-span was longer in the south and the constitution of the inhabitants more robust; in the north, education was more widespread but crime more common, there was greater wealth but less morality. The final diagnosis could only record the interplay of contradictions in a factual discourse that was no longer of polemical value.[40] With d'Angeville, geographical thinking lost its pedagogical and polemical force, insofar as it became less obsessed by the reference to a model, be it of English manufacturing or traditional agriculture. Although he was an agricultural innovator, this political conservative nevertheless pleaded the cause of industry: 'Were France to adopt the industrial system, then those central regions at present so backward and sluggish would gain a certain prosperity; the country would become more homogeneous.' All the same, he knew the price, and after 1834 the risks, of industrialization. As opposed to Dupin, he wanted to restrain the pace:

> Let us hope that we will not confuse the orderly and desirable industrial development of our provinces and minor towns with the industrial centralization which concentrates vast numbers of the proletariat into a few cities, and vast amounts of capital into a few hands; this is one supposed English virtue that we certainly have no wish to emulate.[41]

'A theoretician of development' d'Angeville certainly was; but forewarned by the complex lesson of the two Frances, he dreamed of a dispersed development.

THE SPATIAL ECONOMY OF THE PHYSIOCRATS

Thus, within the fifteen years between 1822–36 there emerged an issue that dominated, and formed the focal point of, a whole series of political and scientific debates. We could let the matter rest with d'Angeville, the last and outstanding example of the period preceding the *Statistique Générale de la France*. It is tempting, however, to go further upstream and review the geographical conceptions of France that were advanced in the eighteenth century. Our enquiry, incomplete of necessity, took us first to the political physiocrats and arithmeticians who, in a variety of ways, presented a holistic geographical conception of the kingdom. Among the first, the guiding principle was theoretical, based upon the distinction made by François Quesnay in his two articles in the *Encyclopédie*. The first was formulated in the article on 'Fermiers': 'The fields are generally cultivated by farmers with horses, or by share-croppers with oxen',[42] and the second is defined in the article on 'Grains': 'We have already examined the state of agriculture in France, and the two kinds of cultivation in use, large-scale cultivation, or that which uses horses, and small-scale cultivation, based upon oxen.'[43] These two economic categories, abstract by definition, and the result of a theoretical framework in which technology and agricultural methods were related, became the favourite analytical tools of the physiocratic school. Witness the work of Charles de Butré in which the opposition of large-scale to small-scale farming is made explicit:

> In France there are two types of farming: the large-scale which is practised by the rich *fermiers* with horses, and the small-scale, which is practised by the share-croppers who only use oxen. These two types of cultivation are very different in their use of the land, their costs, and their produce.[44]

But for the physiocrats, these two categories, which were used as basic concepts of economic thought, could equally well be translated into geographical terms. Applied to the territory of the kingdom, they made it possible to locate the essential agricultural contrasts geographically. In Quesnay, as in de Butré, this amounted to tracing the boundaries of the area of large-scale farming, so as to show the pitifully small size of this area and to recommend rational emulation of this sort of farming. In the words of Quesnay: 'Large-scale farming is presently confined to about six million *arpents* of land, mainly comprising the provinces of Normandy, Beauce, the Ile-de-France, Picardy, French Flanders, Hainaut and a few others.'[45] De Butré revised the count, adding Artois and part of Champagne, but including only a part of Normandy.[46] Six million *arpents* out of the 30 m. actually cultivated left immense tracts to small-scale farming: 'Almost all the inland provinces have lapsed into small-scale farming.'[47] Thus the France of the physiocrats was also dualistic; but the inequalities between the two parts were even greater than they were to be in Dupin, so much so that this geographical division conjured up a past in which it had had a different aspect and a history of decline. To recognize the shrinking of the areas under large-scale cultivation is at the same time to admit the degraded state of agriculture in the country.

Within this primary theoretical and geographical division there were others permitting a more sophisticated analysis and distribution. For de Butré, in fact, there were three categories of large-scale farming, ordered according to the relationship between annual investment and net return: the affluent, in which investment yields 100 per cent in terms of net return; the average, in which it yields no more than 66 per cent; and finally the poor, in which only a modest return is possible. Here again, the theoretically defined economic categories can be mapped out territorially: the logic of their distribution being a function of their proximity to the city. Affluent large-scale farming, for example, 'is hardly ever practised except in those provinces which are a short distance from the capital or some other major city. This favours sales, and ensures the market price necessary to repay the cost of cultivation.'[48] The same division into three categories, and the same principle of distribution are also valid for small-scale farming. In this case, the categories are defined according to the amount of income from cultivatable soil. Small-scale farming of the first category provides: '1st costs, 2nd taxes, and 3rd a very small income for the owners'. In the second category: 'The soil itself yields no income, the harvest hardly covering costs and taxes; what income there is comes from pasturage, and amounts to rather less than the interest on the capital cost of the livestock.' Finally, in small-scale farming of the third category: 'The soil does not even repay costs and taxes, the major part of which has to be taken out of the income from pasturage.'[49] These three categories spread out around the towns in a series of concentric circles. The first category 'is to be found only around the provincial capitals and major cities in areas of small-scale farming'; the second appears 'beyond the outskirts of provincial capitals and major cities in the areas of small-scale farming, far away from the banks of any river' while the third is confined 'to the provincial backwoods which are far from the capital'.[50]

This work thus provides the fundamentals of a 'spatial' economy. To some extent it foreshadows that of Johann von Thünen,[51] while at the same time laying down a simple principle for mapping out an area: a principle owing nothing either to history or the picturesque. We may note with some interest the statement that it is the cities, and in particular the provincial capitals, which act as polarizing forces upon geographical distribution. The basic division between large and small-scale farming is itself dependent upon the location of the capital, the pre-eminent city. The power of the urban presence is such that it pushes natural factors into second place, and itself shapes the landscape of the hinterland: 'Compared to the provinces under large-scale farming, those outside the orbit of the capital put one in mind of some other world, of another climate in a new world.'[52] Although subsequently overlooked in divisions that tended to ignore them, here the cities are accorded their full significance as focal points of the interlocking and intersecting regions that comprised the kingdom. The physiocratic interpretation was to leave its mark, even when stripped of all the complexities with which de Butré had invested it. We may note that the only overall division of France alluded to by Chaptal, who thought in monolithic terms, was precisely the one taken from Quesnay.[53]

THE LOGIC OF THE DEMOGRAPHERS

Matters are less clear when we turn to the eighteenth-century demographers, since the principles of geographical analysis varied from one to another, depending upon which factor each posited as the determinant in the study of population. For Moheau, the key to demographic behaviour, expressed in terms of densities, was to be found in the various types of economic activities. For this reason he proposed a scale of agricultural occupations, arranged according to the extent to which they stimulated population growth. At the top were the coastal areas: 'Because here the population finds an easily obtainable food in the form of fish, and a firm guarantee of employment in the commercial demand for labour.' Next came the wine-growing areas; then, 'far behind', the areas of wheat, followed by those of pasturage and finally those of forest and heathland.[54] But, in view of the overlapping of products, this theoretical scale of densities loses its usefulness: for the vine is never omnipresent, and wheat never totally absent. This makes impossible any clear and obvious territorial division of the kingdom on the basis of agricultural activity. Moheau was thus the victim of his initial premise, and never succeeded in constructing a geographical division of the kingdom that would permit the classification of demographic data. This is an interesting example, therefore, of a strong theoretical distinction that was of doubtful validity in terms of its grasp of the actual geographical reality.

Among other political arithmeticians, however, we do find workable systems of classification organizing statistical data and structuring thinking. It was Des Pommelles who divided France into five roughly parallel bands, based upon degree of latitude.[55] This reveals the obvious influence of the aerist theories which identified the type of air, its warmth and humidity, as the essential factor in the explanation of human behaviour. The neo-hippocratism of eighteenth-century medicine emphasized geographical location, and thus produced totally geometrical divisions of the country. Messance himself went back to three bands, slanting diagonally across the kingdom and dividing it into north, central and southern regions. Despite appearances, aerism was not the only basis for this division. It was also justified by a complex combination of natural, demographic and economic factors:

> Justice demands that all taxation be proportionately adjusted between the provinces according to their respective resources in terms of population, output, industry, commerce, and location. And reason demands that provinces be compared with their neighbours, since they tend to have so much in common with one another; the analogy is enlightening and permits the comparison to be gradually extended, shedding light from one extremity to the other.[56]

This says everything: both the ineradicably fiscal roots of political arithmetic, and the possibility of defining, in terms of the information gathered and of reasoning, geographical units suitable for analysis.

For all these demographers, all population data revealed a simple logic; i.e., the univocal and regular evolution from north to south. Thus it was in the case of density; as Messance asked: 'Why is northern France more populous than the south, and why is the south even more sparsely populated than the centre?'[57] And Des Pommelles wrote: 'It will be seen that the population per square league diminishes progressively by two for every two degrees from north to south.'[58] For Des Pommelles, the search for the cause of this diminution provided an opportunity to refine the aerist theory. With regard to the north, he referred to 'the nature of the land, which is less broken up by mountains and which, being more fertile, makes better provision for the subsistence of the inhabitants'. Messance found a different reason:

> It is because there is a greater number of towns in northern France than in the other parts, and until someone shows that northern France owes its larger population to some other cause, the large number of towns existing there, which provides a large number of consumers, may be regarded as one of the principal causes, even if not the only one. This being the case, it would be the towns which populate the countryside, contrary to what has been said.[59]

Demographic variations thus lent fuel to one of the major debates of the century. Furthermore, the identification of a polarity between north and south as regards density provided an opportunity to refute the thesis of the depopulating and parasitic town.

If density decreased from north to south, fertility, on the other hand, increased, as was underlined by both Moheau and Des Pommelles. The latter found in this a corroboration, if there was any need for one, of the aerist theories: the proportion of births to marriages

> increases progressively from north to south, except in those provinces where the large area of wood and pasture makes the air very humid (i.e., La Rochelle, Poitiers, etc.). It seems to me that one can thence conclude that when low morals, or any other ethical factors, do not stand in nature's way, then marriages are more fertile in warm lands with dry air and high ground, than in those which are low, marshy, and where the air is heavy.[60]

Ten years earlier Moheau had adopted a similar explanatory scheme, but with some qualifications concerning dietary habits: 'The type of diet has no less influence and effect; people who drink wine and consume astringent foodstuffs or spirituous liquor have a talent for multiplying.'[61] In the absence of some simple statistical index such as the ratio of births to marriages, mortality is more difficult to deal with: hence the shift towards statements about life expectancy. Here again, the quality of the air is the determining factor: 'In the north, where the lack of warmth fosters a more sluggish development of the individual, the period of growth, maturation, and decline must be longer.'[62] Nevertheless, this initial statement must be modified in the light of topographical details: 'It appears that the areas in which man can look forward to the longest days are those among the hills and mountains. Those in which life is shortest are the marshy areas. The plains and valleys may prolong the days of their inhabitants according to their orientation.'[63]

For the eighteenth-century arithmeticians, the division of France into homogeneous geographical units became a source of problems. All or most of them worked within a system of thought which dominated their way of reasoning irrespective of its object. Aerist medical theory provided a prime cause since, as Moheau wrote: 'The sovereign law of climate acts upon all that grows and breathes.' Above all, their France was a climatic one, and the criteria of classification were based on latitude and altitude, which together determined the properties of the air. Such a principle held good at every level; it took regional contrasts into account, and at the same time permitted the division of the kingdom into several large units. But once this partition had been effected, dividing France into three or five, the original certainty faltered somewhat. It was not easy to dispose entirely of those elements which, even if they did to some extent depend upon climate, might act independently upon demographic behaviour: hence the role conceded to economic activities, cultural habits and moral attitudes. The pre-eminence accorded to the qualities of the air dominated geographical understanding, which almost always worked in terms of a shift from north to south, rather than outright opposition. But other designs appeared on the canvas which no longer owed anything to the tyranny of climate. Thus we find in Messance the opposition between an urbanized France and one which was hardly so at all, and between a completely agricultural central France and a peripheral one to the north, west and south, where 'the main factories and commerce' were located.[64] These contradictory visions were expressions, in terms of geographical configurations, of a dilemma lying at the very heart of the epistemology of traditional demography.

The place of France on the map of Europe was signalled less by population statistics than by the data of physical anthropology, subsequently overlooked until d'Angeville. First Moheau, and then Abbé Jean-Joseph Expilly, dealt with the height of inhabitants, establishing that in France they were shorter than in other countries such as Germany and Switzerland. To understand this phenomenon involves going back into history: 'It is my opinion that in France where the ancient inhabitants, as witnessed by the Romans themselves, were notable for their marked height and strength, the race may have degenerated because subsistence became more difficult for the mass of the people.'[65] But the height of the French is better explained by that north/south law that governs all aspects of the population, than by some process of shrinkage, and it immediately puts the kingdom in a European perspective:

In France, as well as in the more southern countries such as Spain, Portugal, and the states of Morocco, Algeria, Tunis, and Tripoli etc, one does find men who are extremely sturdy, tall, and strong, but they are less numerous than in northern countries such as Switzerland and Germany.[66]

The same principle, on the other hand, accounts for the contrasts observed within the kingdom:

France itself varies according to province; and it has been generally observed that those in the north produce men of greater height than those in the south. An examination of police reports on deserters, including their description, show that those from Flanders or Picardy have a marked height advantage over those from Provence.[67]

This steady decline in men's heights, from north to south, did not prevent the feeling that France, as a whole, belonged to southern Europe. Expilly, in passing, admitted as much when he wrote: 'France cannot boast of the height of its inhabitants . . . which is the same as in the *other* southern countries'; and Moheau likewise, speaking of the greater fertility of the southern provinces, remarked that here the kingdom had the edge 'vis-à-vis the North of Europe'. The theme of a France that was divided because it was torn between two Europes had not yet appeared, since this supposed the recognition of a linear rift across the nation. As far as eighteenth-century demographers were concerned, and perhaps others too, France was part of the southern community of nations: this feeling of membership remains to be analysed in terms of political allegiances, economic relations and shared culture.

THE PREFERENCE FOR REGIONALISM

The physiocrats and political arithmeticians were thus able to conceive the geography of France as a unified entity; and this allowed them to identify units more or less reconcilable with their respective schemes: extending large-scale farming, or increasing the population. This kind of geographical interpretation hardly ever appeared outside their circle, and we must now try to understand this absence by looking at several other contemporary bodies of text.

If we turn to the geographers of the second half of the eighteenth century, one fact seems clear; and that was the pre-eminence given to the regional monograph, most commonly under the heading of 'natural history'.[68] The list of titles reflects a bias towards the

provinces of the south, no doubt on account of their fuller comple-
ment of academic institutions, and perhaps also because there was
already an active pre-romantic disposition there towards mountain-
ous landscapes. The internal structure of these 'natural histories'
reveals the tension between the administrative aspect (since data
were still often presented in the context of *bailliage*, the *sénéchaussée*,
the diocese, or the *généralité*), and the geographical, in that the most
innovative borrowed from Buache's theory of river basins for the
division used in their surveys. This type of regionalist approach
spawned its own theoretical justifications. First there was stated the
necessary priority of local study: 'We can only hope to see a
complete and general survey of France after a close survey of the
provinces, executed on the spot by local scholars.'[69] Secondly, works
of this genre served utility rather than simple curiosity:

> Any natural history of a province that set its sights simply on
> documenting its fossils, describing its mountains, climate, and
> produce, would do no more than satisfy the curiosity. One which, on
> the other hand, related the various parts together, attempted to draw
> conclusions bearing upon mankind, and where possible related these
> to public utility, would be far more valuable.[70]

Covering the areas of varying size, the regional survey was the most
urgent and sensible undertaking because it made the relationship
between phenomena apparent, and also had an ecological orientation. The geography of the *Philosophes* as far as it confined itself to
the kingdom, made this into a major genre (soon to be based upon
new work in provincial cartography), pushing into second place
those general surveys of the kingdom that perpetuated the rather
fading traditions of Jean Aymar Piganiol de la Force. But the
corollary of this preference was the obvious impossibility of conceiving, readily at least, the totality of the kingdom, and consequently of conceiving its overall spatial organization.

A similar assertion of regionalism is to be found in the collective
studies undertaken by the provincial academies.[71] One out of every
two of these undertook a local history of either its city or province;
and some, such as Bordeaux, Clermont and Auxerre, drew up
schemes for documenting their region's riches and resources. The
horizons of one's own local region appealed for obvious emotional
reasons, but also because it provided a frame of reference for a
possible observation. Even before the provincial academicians, the
Benedictines had conceived a similar idea, and had outlined a
plan for a series of regional histories, covering the whole kingdom.
These finally survived in manuscript form, save for the one on the

Languedoc.[72] In these 'natural and literary histories', the region once again showed itself to be the most manageable area; it was convenient for exhaustive study, and for the useful and rational classification of data collected. Thus, in their own manner, the provincial academies expressed that discovery of the provinces which marks the second half of the eighteenth century, another expression of which is to be found in the various literary forms (plays, novels and essays) which contrasted the world of the capital and the universe of the provinces.[73] Though overlooked by the cartographical statisticians of the *monarchie censitaire*, this tension sometimes reappeared, as in Guerry's geography of suicide: 'Generally speaking, from no matter which point in France one begins, the number of suicides grows steadily as one advances towards the capital.'[74] In this reminder of the baneful influence of the bloated city can be heard the echo of an old idea: that Paris and the provinces also constitute two Frances, whose contrasts might well be examined. This was perhaps the opposition most familiar to men of the eighteenth century.[75]

Since the provinces did not constitute a single entity, they had to be dealt with in either historically or naturally determined areas, if they were to be understood. The medical topographies were a good illustration of this approach. These, as is well known, emerged in three stages: first in 1768 through the initiatives of Lépecq de la Cloture, who organized a network of correspondents from a base in Rouen; then in August 1776, with the decree of the *Conseil* creating the *Société Royale de Médecine* and instituting a national enquiry into epidemics and epizootic diseases; and finally with the October 1778 session of the *Société Royale*, which drew up a plan for a physico-medical survey of the kingdom, based on an increasing number of regional monographs.[76] This gave birth to a whole movement, inspired by the local or provincial, and which reached its zenith in the nineteenth century. The immense mass of material remains to be studied, but some idea of the scope of such surveys can be gleaned from the example of Normandy: this comprises towns, with or without surrounding countryside, district and *département*.[77] In 1778 the *Société Royale de Médecine* had pronounced in favour of the 'canton' or province. Throughout the medical topographies one may discern a regional consciousness which voluntarily confined itself within restricted areas, and which was unquestionably the principal obstacle in the eighteenth century to a macroscopic conception of the kingdom. The persistence into the following century of a picture of France that was neither bipartite nor tripartite, but shattered into myriad units, each with its own abiding uniqueness, shows that even if the theme of the two Frances did dominate the major debates, it

did not suppress people's continued attachment to their own native
regions.

This survey – incomplete though it is in its coverage of the
documentary evidence and confined to one century – raises an
essential question which is that of the relationship between statistical
and geographical conceptions and the exercise of power. Politicians
had, in fact, long appeared reconciled to the disparities that
chequered the kingdom: that 'aggregation of disunited peoples' was
something both accepted and, except by those obsessed by systems,
appreciated. In their contrast to the capital, the provinces formed a
whole, but a motley one, and towards the close of the eighteenth
century men applied themselves enthusiastically and with dedication
to the painstaking study of the history of those provinces and the
promise they held for the future. Moreover, in the final days of the
absolutism that had always had to compromise with this teeming
diversity, it was in regional and provincial consciousness that
schemes for reform were nurtured, and in which rebellions took
root. Revolutionary and imperial Jacobinism were to endeavour to
change this co-existence between centralizing power and a fragmented country. To what extent they were successful is not
important here, but it is clear that after this juncture we find a new
relationship between political power and the area over which it was
exercised. The spatial homogeneity of the nation became both desire
and designs, the condition and hallmark of good policy. It was not
surprising, therefore, to see people of distinction becoming arithmeticians under the *monarchie censitaire*; to them, the continuing
acceptance of these economic, cultural or moral disparities seemed
both deficient and dangerous, a condition to be overcome by
reducing to simple laws those variations which might be thought,
which indeed had been thought, to be contingent. Ideally, proposals
for a society should start upon even foundations, or at least with the
identification of any unevenness. Born of the nostalgic longing for
unity, the theme of the two Frances becomes the vehicle of opposed
futures, and its very incertitudes were the expression of a new
conception of the relationship between power and society.

For this reason, choosing it as our subject of study might also
prompt one or two remarks on the relationships between modern
historical discourse and these voices from the past. The continuing
construction of quantifiable economic and social indicators on the
basis of which historians then drew their own particular France on
the map of the Kingdom, the Empire, or the Republic, has had the
result of making previous ideas seem obsolete. All that is needed is to

validate or invalidate the intuitions of one's most lucid precursors among past sources. But in doing this we are, perhaps, forgetting two things. First, that it is not so easy to disentangle traditional issues from current problematics, and that we therefore need, parallel to one another, a methodical analysis of past conceptions and a critical appraisal of contemporary historical praxis. Secondly, the debates of the past are not simply dim signposts to the present, but must be interpreted as to their specific structure, organization and function. On the basis of this we shall be able to lay bare the successive contradictory ideological commitments that accompanied so apparently neutral a theme as that of the two Frances. It would also enable us to ask both constructive and useful questions about the validity, origins and position of our own historical discourse.

NOTES

This chapter is based on a paper presented at Fernand Braudel's seminar at the Maison des Sciences de l'Homme in 1977. It owes much to the help and scholarship of Catherine Duprat. It was published in English in a translation by Paul Rowland (edited here) in *Social Science Information*, 17, 4–5 (1978), pp. 525–54. It has also been published in French in *Cahiers d'histoire*, 1978, pp. 393–415.

1 For the combined interpretation of economic, demographic and anthropological indicators, see Emmanuel Le Roy Ladurie, 'Un Théoricien de développement: Adolphe d'Angeville', in introduction to the new edition of Adolphe d'Angeville, *Essai sur la statistique de la population française, considérée sous quelques-uns de ses rapports physiques et moraux* (Bourg-en-Bresse, 1836; reprint Mouton – De Gruyter, The Hague, 1970); reprinted in Emmanuel Le Roy Ladurie, *Le Territoire de l'historien* (2 vols, Gallimard, Paris, 1973), pp. 349–92.

2 Michel Demonet, Paul Dumont, Emmanuel Le Roy Ladurie, 'Anthropologie de la jeunesse masculine en France au niveau d'une cartographie cantonale (1819–1830)', *Annales ESC*, 31 (1976), pp. 700–55.

3 Adriano Balbi, *Essai statistique sur le royaume de Portugal et d'Algarve comparé aux autres Etats de l'Europe* (2 vols, Rey and Gravier, Paris, 1822), vol. 2, pp. 134–49. The table showing the number of pupils for each of the twenty-six educational districts is to be found on p. 146.

4 Dominique Julia and Paul Pressly, 'La Population scolaire en 1789. Les extravagances statistiques du Ministre Villemain', *Annales ESC*, 30 (1975), pp. 1516–61.

5 André Michel Guerry, 'Statistique comparée de l'état de l'instruction et du nombre de crimes', *Revue encyclopédique*, (August 1832).

6 Conrad Malte-Brun, review of Balbi's book in the *Journal des débats* (17 June, 4 July, 21 July, 1823). The statements quoted are from the third instalment of the review.

7 Charles Dupin, *Effets de l'enseignement populaire de la lecture, de l'écriture et de l'arithmétique, de la géométrie et la mécanique appliquées aux arts, sur les prospérités de la France*, address to the opening session of the *cours normal de géométrie et de la mécanique appliquées aux arts* on 30 November 1826 at the Conservatoire des Arts et Métiers, Paris, 1826, p. 27. The map presented on the occasion of this lecture was to be included in Charles Dupin, *Forces productives et commerciales de la France* (2 vols, Bachelier, Paris, 1827), plate 1 and has been republished in Marie-Madeleine Compère and Dominique Julia, *L'Éducation en France du XVIe au XVIIIe siècle* (S.E.D.E.S, Paris, 1975), p. 17.

8 In 1877, the *recteur* Louis Maggiolo embarked on a vast investigation of the literacy of the French between the seventeenth and the eighteenth centuries based on the proportion of signatures of married couples, men and women, in parish and then in civil registers for the four periods 1686–90, 1786–90, 1816–20 and 1872–6. The statistics that resulted from this survey, carried out by thousands of schoolteachers in all *départements*, were mapped by Michel Fleury and Pierre Valmary, 'Les Progrès de l'instruction élémentaire de Louis XIV à Napoléon III, d'après l'enquête de Louis Maggiolo 1877–1879', *Population*, 1957, pp. 71–92. On their maps there is a clearly discernible dividing-line from Saint-Malo to Geneva that separates a more literate France in the north from a less literate zone in the south. The term *ligne Maggiolo* has thus become a familiar reference in French historiography.

9 Dupin, *Effets*, p. 28.

10 Ibid., pp. 34–5.

11 Edward W. Fox, *History in Geographical Perspective: The Other France* (Norton, New York, 1972).

12 Stendhal, *La Vie de Henri Brulard*, first published unabridged by Henry Debraye, (2 vols, Champion, Paris, 1913), vol. 1, pp. 240–1 [*The Life of Henry Brulard*, tr. Jean Steward and B. C. J. G. Knight (University of Chicago Press, Chicago, pp. 167–8]. This text is quoted with comments in François Furet and Jacques Ozouf, 'Trois siècles de métissage culturel', *Annales ESC*, 32 (1977), pp. 500–1.

13 Dupin, *Forces*, vol. 2, pp. 249–80.

14 See Jean-Claude Perrot, 'L'Âge d'or de la statistique régionale (an IV–1804)', *Annales historiques de la Révolution Française*, (April–June 1976), pp. 215–76.

15 Jacques Peuchet, *Statistique élémentaire de la France*, (Gilbert, Paris, 1805); Pierre Grégoire Chanlaire, *Description topographique et statistique de la France* (2 vols, P. G. Chanlaire, Paris, 1810).

16 Jean Antoine Claude Chaptal, *De l'Industrie française* (2 vols, A.-A. Renouard, Paris, 1819). The following are two examples of the descriptive method employed: p. 153, 'Everything has been given over to

cultivation, and the harvests have multiplied tenfold. Examples of this kind are to be found *in every* part of France'; p. 154, '*Nowhere* are the animals sufficiently numerous, save in two or three provinces' (my emphasis).

17 On the tension between the particular and the uniform at the very heart of the departmental prefectural statistics, see Marie-Noëlle Bourguet, 'Race et folklore. L'image officielle de la France en 1800', *Annales ESC*, 31 (1976), pp. 802–23.

18 Dupin, *Forces*, vol. 2, p. 252.

19 Ibid., p. 263 (our emphasis).

20 Ibid., pp. 273–4.

21 Ibid., vol. 1, p. 1.

22 Ibid., vol. 2, p. 267.

23 Ibid., vol. 1, p. 1.

24 On this essential document, see Michelle Perrot, 'Délinquance et système pénitentiaire en France au XIXe siècle', *Annales ESC*, 30 (1975), p. 67–91.

25 The complete title of this sheet (in the typographical sense of the word), which was sold at six francs (eight francs mounted on canvas) reveals as much about the various statistical parts as it does about their public: *The French Monarchy Compared to the Principal States of the World, or an Essay on the Statistics of France Considered in their Geographical, Moral, and Political Implications, Showing in a Single Table the Maximum, Minimum, and Average Figures for its Population, Wealth, Industry, Commerce, Education, and the Morality of its Inhabitants, Compared to their Correlatives in Several Countries of the Old and New Worlds; for the Use of Statesmen, Administrators, Bankers, Merchants, Travellers, and Especially of Messieurs the Peers of France and of Messieurs the Deputies.*

26 André Michel Guerry, *Essai sur la statistique morale de la France* (Crochard, Paris, 1833). An extract from this work had been published in August 1832 in the *Revue encyclopédique*.

27 Guerry, *Essai*, p. 9.

28 Dupin, *Forces*, vol. 1, p. 1.

29 Guerry, *Essai*, p. 42.

30 Ibid., p. 47.

31 Benoiston de Chateauneuf, *De la Colonisation des condamnés* (Martinet, Paris, 1827), pp. 3–4.

32 Pierre Bigot de Morogues, *De la Misère des ouvriers et de la marche à suivre pour y remédier* (Huzard, Paris, 1832).

33 Alban de Villeneuve-Bargemont, *Economie politique chrétienne, ou recherches sur la nature et les causes du paupérisme en France et en Europe* (3 vols, Paulin, Paris, 1834).

34 Bigot de Morogues, *De la Misère*, p. 120.

35 Villeneuve-Bargemont, *Economie politique*, vol. 2, p. 46.

36 Ibid., p. 10.

37 Ibid., p. 23.

38   See note 1.
39   D'Angeville, *Essai sur la statistique*, pp. 15–16.
40   Ibid., pp. 125–6.
41   Ibid., p. 124.
42   François Quesnay, article, 'Fermiers (Econ. Polit.)' in the *Encyclopédie*, (January 1756), reprinted in *François Quesnay et la physiocratie*, (2 vols, I.N.E.D., Paris, 1958), vol. 2, p. 428.
43   François Quesnay, article, 'Grains' in the *Encyclopédie*, (November 1757), in *François Quesnay et la physiocratie*, vol. 2, p. 461.
44   Charles de Butré, 'Apologie de la science économique sur la distinction entre la grande et la petite culture contre les critiques de M. de F.', in his *Ephémérides du citoyen*, (Lacombe, Paris, 1769), vols 9, 10 and 11 (here see vol. 10, pp. 8–9). My thanks to Jean-Claude Perrot for bringing this text to my notice.
45   Quesnay, 'Grains', in *François Quesnay et la physiocratie*, vol. 2, p. 461.
46   De Butré, *Ephémérides*, vol. 10, pp. 80–1.
47   Guillaume-François Le Trosne, *La Liberté du commerce des grains, toujours utile et jamais nuisible* (Paris, 1765), pp. 28–9.
48   De Butré, *Ephémérides*, vol. 9, p. 21.
49   Ibid., vol. 10, pp. 133–4.
50   Ibid., p. 78, 88 and 119.
51   Jean-Claude Perrot, *Genèse d'une ville moderne. Caen au XVIIIe siècle* (2 vols, Mouton, Paris and The Hague, 1975), vol. 1, pp. 237–40.
52   De Butré, *Ephémérides*, vol. 10, pp. 80–1.
53   Chaptal, *De l'Industrie française*, p. 140.
54   Moheau, *Recherches et considérations sur la population de la France* (Moutard, Paris, 1778), pp. 67–9.
55   Chevalier Des Pommelles, *Tableau de la population de toutes les provinces de la France* (Paris, 1789), p. 55.
56   Messance, *Nouvelles recherches sur la population de la France* (Frères Périsse, Lyon, 1788), p. 43.
57   Ibid., p. 48.
58   Des Pommelles, *Tableau*, p. 56.
59   Messance, *Nouvelles recherches*, p. 87.
60   Des Pommelles, *Tableau*, p. 63.
61   Moheau, *Recherches*, p. 139.
62   Ibid., p. 191.
63   Ibid., p. 202.
64   Messance, *Nouvelles recherches*, p. 87.
65   Jean-Joseph Expilly, *Tableau de la population de la France* (Paris, 1780), p. 28.
66   Ibid.
67   Moheau, *Recherches*, p. 118.
68   This is based upon Numa Broc, *La Géographie des philosophes. Géographes et voyageurs français au XVIIIe siècle* (Editions Ophrys, Paris, 1975), pp. 406–19.

69   Edme Beguillet and Claude Courtépée, *Description générale et particulière du Duché de Bourgogne* (7 vols, Dijon, 1774–85), introduction quoted in Broc, *La Géographie des philosophes*, p. 415.

70   Michel Darluc, *Histoire naturelle de la Provence* (2 vols, J.-J. Niel, Avignon, 1782–86), p. vii, quoted in Broc, *La Géographie des philosophes*, p. 407.

71   Daniel Roche, *Le siècle des lumières en province. Académies et académiciens provinciaux (1680–1789)* (Mouton, Paris and The Hague, 1978), ch. 6.

72   My thanks to Jean Glénisson for having drawn my attention to this regional history project.

73   Perrot, *Genèse d'une ville moderne*, vol. 2, appendix 28, p. 1028, gives an introductory account of the literature on the Paris/provinces duality, listing twenty-one titles between 1737 and 1793.

74   Guerry, *Essai sur la statistique morale*, p. 65.

75   To cite one text among many (taken from Roche, *Le siècle des lumières*), a letter from Chalamond de la Visclède, permanent secretary of the Académie de Marseille, to the Académie Française 12 January 1726: 'You, Messieurs, have already ensured good taste at the heart of the kingdom; now it only remains to carry it to the frontiers.'

76   Jean-Pierre Peter, 'Une Enquête de la Société Royale de Médecine (1774–1794): Malades et maladies à la fin du XVIIIe siècle', *Annales ESC*, 22 (1967), pp. 711–51; Perrot, 'L'Age d'or de la statistique régionale', p. 222.

77   Perrot, *Genèse d'une ville moderne*, vol. 2, p. 892, note 168.

INDEX

thought, 23-8, 36; *see also*
knowledge
Thünen, Johann Heinrich von,
172, 188
time-spans, 3, 30, 59, 80-1
totality, 57, 58
Toynbee, Arnold, 53
Turkey, 182
Turnhout, 117

universals, 60
United Provinces, 130-1, 142
United States, 19, 37-8
universities, entrance requirements
for, 137; degrees, devaluation
of, 127-9, 133, 134; enrolment
in, 127, 129-31, 132-3, 137,
138, 141-3; graduates of, 127-9,
131, 134, 135-6; record keeping
on, 137; *see also* England;
Germany, German states; Spain

Vaissière, Pierre de, 75
Valladolid, 129-30, 132
Veblen, Thorstein, 76
veillée, la, 163-5, 166-7
Venturi, Franco, 33
Vernant, Jean-Pierre, 28-9
Veyne, Paul, 46-7, 60, 62

Villemain, Abel-François, 138, 174
Villeneuve-Bargemont, Jean Paul
Alban, vicomte de, 182-3
Vincent, Jacques, 99, 105
violence, 118; state monopoly of,
9, 81-3, 85
Voltaire (François Marie Arouet),
139, 161
voluntarism, 22
Vorstius, Conrad, 140
Vovelle, Michel, 96

Wallon, Henri, 28
Watteau, Antoine, 89
Weber, Max, 73, 75, 76
White, Hayden, 45-6
will, ruler's, 71, 72
witches, witchcraft, 98, 107-8;
see also sorcery
world turned upside-down, prints
of, 115-25; borrowings and
changes in, 118, 120-2, 123-4;
dates of, 117; lay-out of, 119;
themes in, 115-25 *passim*; uses
of, 122, 125
world vision, 32, 34
writers, discontented, 139

Zeitgeist, 23, 24, 81